Freud, Surgery,

and the

Surgeons

Freud, Surgery,
and the
Surgeons

Paul E. Stepansky

THE ANALYTIC PRESS

1999   Hillsdale, NJ   London

Published by The Analytic Press, Inc.
101 West Street, Hillsdale, NJ 07642

Typeset in Electra by Laserset, New York City

Library of Congress Cataloging-in-Publication Data

Stepansky, Paul E.
    Freud, surgery, and the surgeons / Paul E. Stepansky.
       p.   cm.
    Includes bibliographic references and index.
    ISBN 0-88163-289-9
    1. Psychoanalysis - Philosophy. 2. Psychoanalysis - History.
    3. Freud, Sigmund, 1856–1939 Views on surgery. 4. Surgery.
    5. Metaphor. I. Title
       [DNLM: 1. Freud, Sigmund, 1856–1939. 2. Psychoanalytic
    Therapy. 3. Surgery. 4. Metaphor.   WM 460.6 S8275f 1999]
    RC506.S733   1999
    616.89'17—dc21
    DNLM/DLC
    for Library of Congress   99-13483
                                                                   CIP

Printed in the United States of America
10 9 8 7 6 5 4 3 2 1

TO

My Mother
Selma Brill Stepansky
woman of valor

∞

My Father
William Stepansky
first among healers

∞

My Wife
Deane Rand Stepansky
carae immortali

Contents

Preface

∽

There is a gripping interlude in Oliver Sacks's *A Leg to Stand On* in which the injured neurologist, having undergone successful surgical repair of a severed tendon in his left leg— the product of an untoward encounter with a wild bull on a desolate mountain in Norway—awakes only to discover a leg so neurally, functionally, and existentially dead as to have effaced the very inner image or representation of the leg. The leg had become "a foreign, inconceivable *thing*, which I looked at, and touched, without any sense whatever of recognition or relation" (1984, p. 74). Profoundly unsettled by this "neuro-existential" pathology regarding what had once been *his* leg, Sacks looked to his doctor, his surgeon, for reassurance, as if surgical enlightenment about an alienated piece of body would enable him to reclaim peace of mind. Thus did Sacks anticipate his first postoperative contact with the surgeon:

> What sort of a man would Swan be? I knew he was a good surgeon, but it was not the surgeon but the person I would stand in relation to, or, rather, the man in whom, I hoped, the surgeon and the person would be wholly fused. . . . I ought not to demand too much of him, or overburden him with the intensity of my distress. If he was a sensitive man he would be instantly aware of the distress and dispel it, with the quiet voice of authority. What I could not do for myself in a hundred years, precisely because I was entangled in my own patienthood and could not stand outside it, what seemed to me insuperably difficult, he could cut across at a single stroke, with the scalpel of detachment, insight and authority [1984, p. 92].

But, alas, the surgeon revealed himself to be merely a surgeon. And the encounter yielded catharsis only as an occasion for Sacks's rage at the kind of colleague who "never listens to, never learns from, his patients. He dismisses them, he despises them, he regards them as nothing" (p. 105). Here is the passage in which Sacks recounts the postoperative exchange that gave rise to this reaction:

> "Well, Sacks," he said. "How does the leg seem today?"
> "It seems fine, Sir," I replied, "surgically speaking."
> "What do you mean — 'surgically speaking'?" he said.
> "Well, umm —" I looked at Sister, but her face was stony. "There's not much pain, and — er — there's no swelling of the foot."
> "Splendid," he said, obviously relieved. "No problems then, I take it?"
> "Well, just one." Swan looked severe, and I started to stammer. "It's . . . it's . . . I don't seem to be able to contract the quadriceps . . . and, er . . . the muscle doesn't seem to have any tone. And . . . and . . . I have difficulty locating the position of the leg."
> I had a feeling that Swan looked frightened for a moment, but it was so momentary, so fugitive, that I could not be sure.
> "Nonsense, Sacks," he said sharply and decisively. "There's nothing the matter. Nothing at all. Nothing to be worried about. Nothing at all!"
> "But . . ."
> He held up his hand, like a policeman halting traffic. "You're completely mistaken," he said with finality. "There's nothing wrong with the leg. You understand that, don't you?"
> With a brusque and, it seemed to me, irritable movement, he made for the door, his Juniors parting deferentially before him [pp. 104–105].

No less than lay persons, it would seem, physicians — including this most perspicacious of neurologists — have special attitudes toward, and special expectations of, surgeons, especially the surgeons who minister to them in their time of need. The painful disillusionment attendant to learning that surgeons can be all too human, and frequently all too surgical, is but the opposite side of the coin. It follows from the omniscience and technical mastery we are wont to impute to all surgeons, those special doctors who are able to penetrate to the very anatomical substrate of human suffering and whose promise of cure is the most radically uncompromising among all the medical specialists. It is for this reason, among others, that physicians in nonsurgical specialties look to their surgical brethren as exemplars of what doctoring is all about. Indeed, they are inclined to invoke surgery in proffering their own claims of knowledge, of procedural expertise, and of curative power.

Psychiatrists and psychoanalysts, whose healing ministrations address the mind rather than the body, have not been exempt from this understandable tendency. Far from it. If anything, the historically precarious standing of psychiatry and psychoanalysis as clinical disciplines—the ambiguous and hence problematic character of their claims to healing efficacy—has lent special resonance to the appeal of surgical models. This was certainly true for Freud, who in 1912 urged his colleagues "to model themselves during psychoanalytic treatment on the surgeon, who puts aside all his feelings, even his human sympathy, and concentrates his mental forces on the single aim of performing the operation as skillfully as possible" (p. 115). Five years later, in 1917, Julius von Wagner-Jauregg legitimated invasive somatic treatments in clinical psychiatry by demonstrating that inoculation with malaria parasites successfully counteracted the symptoms of general paresis (dementia paralytica), a previously incurable manifestation of late-term syphilis. The advent of radical somatic therapies in the late 1930s embodied the explicit, albeit short-lived triumph of a more pointedly surgical analogizing. Insulin coma therapy, for example, which achieved great popularity in the 1940s, was presented to the psychiatric community in the guise of "an operative procedure" (Kalinowsky and Hock, 1946, p. 10). The same can be said of electroshock therapy, whose still greater appeal was partly attributable to "the ease of handling the [electroshock] apparatus" among overburdened clinicians and hospital superintendents (Millet and Mosse, 1944, p. 226). With the development of lobotomy at this same historical moment, the psychiatric appropriation of surgery transcended the realm of metaphor altogether; it became quite literal.

In psychoanalysis, of course, surgery can never escape the realm of metaphor. But even here, as I argue throughout this work, the use of the surgical metaphor is not to be breezily dismissed as mere polemical mimicry by doctors of the mind. In point of fact, the choice of metaphor has been historically important and therapeutically consequential in a variety of ways. Perhaps one brief example will highlight this claim and give some flavor of the chapters to follow.

During the same historical period that witnessed the ascendance of shock treatment and lobotomy, the lure of surgery not only embraced analysts seeking anchorage for their therapeutic activity but also the critics of analysis who looked askance at analytic claims of healing efficacy. In 1939, in perhaps the first survey of the attitude of neurologists, psychiatrists, and psychologists toward psychoanalysis, the Boston psychiatrist Abraham Myerson elicited the following reply from a colleague, one Tracy Putnam, who lauded Freud for effecting tremendous advances in psychology and psychiatry:

> It seems to me that one can well compare psychoanalysis to neurological surgery. It has some brilliant successes to its credit, some gallant failures, some egregious mistakes and some charlatanism, but even the mistakes have contributed information, and it is inconceivable that we can ever do without it in the future [1930, pp. 631–632].

But Myerson himself remained much more skeptical, and not only about these allegedly "brilliant successes." He was specially chagrined with the analysts' failure to respond to their critics, and in this respect, like Putnam, he was quick to invoke a surgical analogy:

> The psychoanalysts have a very ingenious subterfuge for escaping criticism. So long as you have not been psycho-analyzed, you cannot judge the results of psychoanalysis. But I am not a surgeon and yet I can judge the results of surgery. I can tell when my patient has had a successful operation for brain tumor, even though I could not bore a hole straight in the skull [p. 638].

Why should the *surgical* model come so readily to mind in making the case for *and* against psychoanalysis? What is it about the surgical enterprise that has long animated those seeking to explain, to defend, or to debunk psychoanalysis?

This historical study, which charts the rise and fall of Freud's "surgical metaphor"—his description of the psychoanalysis as a surgical procedure, with the psychoanalyst cast in the role of a surgical operator—seeks to broaden our understanding of this metaphoric proclivity and its residual legacy. It is first and foremost a study in psychoanalytic history, since I am concerned with tracing the history of Sigmund Freud's own initial embrace and subsequent repudiation of the surgical metaphor. To this end, I have approached Freud's understanding of surgery and surgeons both historically and biographically. To wit, I have turned to the history of surgery in order to place the surgical metaphor in historical context and to illuminate its informing assumptions. Examination of Freud's own exposure to the "heroic surgery" and "heroic surgeons" of his time, which draws us into his fascinating relationships with Theodor Billroth, Carl Koller, Ernst Fleischl von Marxow, Josef Breuer, and especially Wilhelm Fliess, is the biographical sequel to this task.

In examining the abandonment of the surgical metaphor in the years following World War I, I have relied on the traditional tools of Freud scholarship, Freud's writings and voluminous correspondence. And I have rounded up the usual suspects— Karl Abraham, Sándor Ferenczi, and Ernest Jones—in fleshing out a narrative in which the shared experiences of the first generation of psychoanalysts, including professional and personal experiences of surgery, all contributed to the fate of medicosurgical analogizing in psychoanalysis and psychiatry. Needless to say, Freud's own surgical tribulations of the 1920s and 30s, which resulted in his lifelong dependency on surgeons, including one very special surgeon, Hans Pichler, figure prominently in the story I tell.

Since the effort to understand Freud's "surgical metaphor" opens to reflection on what surgery has meant throughout history and continues to mean in our own time, I am hopeful that this study will also be read as a modest contribution to the history of medicine. I realize I have only scratched the historical surface in pursuing such reflection, and only in a manner consistent with a primary interest in the history of psychiatry and psychoanalysis. In considering the aftermath of Freud's surgical metaphor, this study turns to a consideration of the relationships among psychiatry, psychoanalysis, and surgery in the era of shock treatment and lobotomy. And I conclude with a chapter of reflections on modern surgery in America that focuses on how surgeons of our own time have gradually worked their way toward a psychodynamic, even a nascent psychoanalytic, sensibility about the surgical calling. These reflections are preliminary to some concluding remarks on the major surgical advances of the past half century that culminate in the suggestion that medicosurgical analogizing based on the insights of modern surgery may still have something valuable to offer contemporary psychoanalysts and psychotherapists.

With this final claim, I appear to be swimming against the tide of "postmodernism," which, in the realm of psychoanalysis and psychoanalytically inspired psychotherapy, has tended to an understanding of the psychotherapeutic enterprise as an ongoing construction of meanings in which therapist and patient conjointly participate. This vision construes psychoanalysis as an intimate encounter of two people, neither of whom has privileged access to "truth" or "reality" and both of whose subjectivities shape an evolving therapeutic dialogue. It is self-evidently a vision far removed from the world of surgeons and surgery. In the face of this apparent sea change in what it means to "practice" psychoanalysis and psychotherapy, I make a modest counterclaim in defense of medicosurgical analogizing: that metaphoric inclusiveness per se is a good thing, and that analysts and other doctors of the mind are at epistemic risk if they shut off any of the metaphoric tributaries that flow into their sense of vocation and provide anchorage for their "doctoring" activities.

The psychoanalytic vocation may now be "postmodern" and therefore nonmedical in many significant ways (see Benjamin, 1997), but it is still actualized in, and sanctioned by, a culture that, in the realm of help-seeking and professional care-giving, continues to fall back on traditional assumptions about doctors and patients. A postmodern psychoanalyst or therapist who is licensed by the state to provide professional remedial services, who uses the appellation "doctor," who ushers "patients" from a waiting room to a consulting room, and who undertakes treatment on a fee for service basis—that psychoanalyst participates in a tradition of care-giving that is thoroughly medicosurgical, whether or not that psychoanalyst is himself or herself a physician. This is not an epistemological claim but a cultural reality.[1]

I am aware that in taking this position I am incorporating aspects of the "modernist" position, which is now widely viewed with suspicion. That is to say, I am assuming that in the domain of professional care-giving, authority and technical expertise are in principle compatible with the values of intimate encounter, despite elements of inevitable strain. Those critics who view the tension between "inspired healing" and "professional technique" (Benjamin, 1997) as the unique burden of psychoanalysis in particular and psychological therapy in general are inattentive to the manner in which this very tension gains expression in all manner of modern therapeutics, surgery included. Nor are analysts and therapists alone in the obligation

---

[1] This is not to deny the emergence of what the historian Edward Shorter (1985, pp. 211–240) has termed "the postmodern patient," whose alienation from medicine takes the form of a revolt against medical authority. But postmodernism, in this usage, suggests little more than cynicism about doctors in particular; it is not a questioning of conventional assumptions about the objective reality of disease and the possibility of expert treatment in general. Indeed, this type of cynicism, which accounts for the popularity of alternative healers outside the medical establishment, is a recurrent and well-documented phenomenon throughout medical history. It follows that postmodernism of this sort comfortably coexists with traditional expectations of diagnosis and treatment, whether in the realm of drug therapy, acupuncture, or holistic medicine. A postmodern sensibility may impel us to seek help in nontraditional ways but with the most conventional of expectations. Indeed, as Shorter observed, "The great paradox for patients today is that as they acquire a postmodern sensitivity to their bodies, their attitudes toward the medical profession are becoming once again *traditional* (p. 211, emphasis in the original).

to tolerate not-knowing and to reflect on the epistemic uncertainty that inheres in their therapeutic labors.[2]

In concluding with the call for a new attentiveness to the metaphorical possibilities inhering in modern surgery and immunology, I am pushing the outer edge of the modernist envelope considerably further than clinical writers customarily do. I hope and trust that contemporary therapists and analysts will share my sense that the "push" is historically broadening and heuristically valuable. At the very least, it enables us to glimpse the fascinating ways in which a truly modern modernism — in the guise of late-twentieth-century surgery — addresses a number of concerns that lay at the heart of the postmodern turn. It certainly is something to think about.

---

[2] See Benjamin (1997) for a thoughtful and nuanced discussion of the dilemmas inhering in the notion of a psychoanalytic vocation. I take issue with many of her assumptions but am appreciative of her scholarly grasp of the issues at stake. Among recent clinical writers, she is admirably sensitive to the dangers inhering in the radically postmodern embrace of an "ethos of healing" shorn of any claims to objective knowledge and professional technique: "As valuable as we have found the stance of tolerating not-knowing, and the reflection on uncertainty, it is unquestionably dangerous to move from that stance into an ideal of not-knowing. Such an ideal would be, I think, equivalent to returning to the arms of the old church" (p. 797). Of course, her socioeducational strategy for addressing this danger (the distribution of knowledge via "democratic relationships of learning" (pp. 797–798, 800) is a far cry from the medically "modernist" track I am pursuing in this study.

Acknowledgments

ご

As an independent scholar working in the wilds of suburban New Jersey, I have become, perforce, a child of the internet. I have relied on "Medline" to search the medical and psychiatric literature, and then called on the New York Academy of Medicine Library to provide me with copies of the articles that I needed. I have likewise relied on, and am grateful to, John Gach (of John Gach Books) and Matthew von Umwerth (of the A. A. Brill Library of the New York Psychoanalytic Institute) for providing me with psychoanalytic source material essential to this undertaking. My son Michael Stepansky, a student at Brandeis University, cheerfully obliged my photocopying requests and lugged home books from the Brandeis University Library that I could not obtain locally.

Two presentations deriving from this project were delivered to the Section on Psychiatric History of the Department of Psychiatry at Cornell Medical Center-New York Hospital, where they received appreciative and critically stimulating receptions. I am proud to be a member of this fine and inspiriting circle of academics and clinicians, and gratefully acknowledge their long-standing support of my work, both academic and editorial, over the past two decades. Special thanks go to two valued colleagues, Stephen A. Mitchell and Frank Summers, who read preliminary versions of the manuscript and shared their thoughts and reactions with me.

It is a pleasure to acknowledge my devoted colleagues at The Analytic Press—Eleanor Starke Kobrin, Joan Riegel, Nancy Liguori, Meredith Freedman, Rosa Nitzan, and Mary Martin— who have collectively provided an ideal "holding environment" for me over the years. Their supportive interest in my work and their innumerable acts of thoughtfulness and kindness—some small and some not so small—made it possible for me to incorporate this scholarly endeavor into a schedule overcrowded with editorial and administrative responsibilities. As both colleague and friend, John Kerr provided steadying support and helpful scholarly advice from the outset. As my editor and primary reader, he has given me the full benefit of his discerning editorial eye and luminous intelligence. I fully share in the feeling of gratitude and indebtedness of his many Analytic Press authors. This same feeling goes out to Lenni Kobrin, dear friend and invaluable helpmate, who copy edited the manuscript skillfully and empathically and then ushered it through the production process with that unique combination of good cheer, grace under pressure, and utter competence that has won her the praise of all who are privileged to work with her. Andrea Schettino, another valued colleague who has become a friend, brought her fine talent and impeccable judgment to bear in designing the dustcover.

Crucial support of my work has come from the home front. It is a pleasure to acknowledge, with gratitude and affection, Virginia and George Meyerson, who value the life of mind and have encouraged me in my scholarly peregrinations over the past quarter century. In pursuing this project, I have had before me the inspiring example of three remarkable brothers, David Stepansky, Robert Stepansky, and Alan Stepansky, each of whom exemplifies, in his particular life's work, the pursuit of excellence, the pride of commitment, and the imperative of compassion. My mother, Selma Brill Stepansky, the extraordinary woman who instilled these values in all of us, introduced me to the world of reading and writing and provided loving support and guidance as I proceeded to make this world my world. My sons, Michael Stepansky and Jonathan Stepansky, have provided their own much-valued measure of encouragement, and I thank them for their understanding acceptance of the countless evenings and weekends I have spent ensconced in my study. As to the contribution of my wife, Deane Rand Stepansky, my partner in all life's projects, I must contemplate poesy of a higher order, with words written for her alone. Here it must suffice to acknowledge that without her steadfast belief in my scholarly calling and her abiding love, I could not have undertaken this project.

For me, *Freud, Surgery, and the Surgeons* marks the changing nature of my own scholarly concerns. It is rooted in the world of Freud and psychoanalysis, which has occupied me in the past, but it engages psychoanalytic history through examination of a particular topic—Freud's surgical metaphor—that opens to the domains of medicine and surgery and poses fundamental questions about the techniques of care-giving and the temperament of the care-giver. It thus has personal significance as a transitional endeavor; it underscores where I have come from, intellectually speaking, while pointing to new interests and future projects framed more fully within the history and sociology of medicine. In returning to the medicosurgical roots of psychoanalysis, and, especially, in giving serious consideration to surgical metaphors of healing within psychoanalysis and psychiatry, this work reflects the profound influence of my father, William Stepansky, a physician whose all-embracing clinical sensibility and magnificent clinical gifts have enabled him to span the seemingly disjunctive worlds of surgery and psychotherapy and all that lies between them. What I have learned about Freud and psychoanalysis I have learned from books and study. But what I have learned about healers and healing, including the meaning of the inviolable lifelong commitment awakened by the true therapeutic calling and the manner in which the healing hand and healing word oftimes coalesce in the curative endeavor—these things I have learned from my father, my greatest teacher.

Paul E. Stepansky
Upper Montclair, New Jersey
16 November 1998

Introduction
"I Cannot Advise My Colleagues Too Urgently"
∽∽∽

I cannot advise my colleagues too urgently to model themselves during psychoanalytic treatment on the surgeon, who puts aside all his feelings, even his human sympathy, and concentrates his mental forces on the single aim of performing the operation as skillfully as possible. Under present-day conditions the feeling that is most dangerous to a psychoanalyst is the therapeutic ambition to achieve by this novel and much disputed method something that will produce a convincing effect upon other people. This will not only put him into a state of mind which is unfavorable for his work, but will make him helpless against certain resistances of the patient, whose recovery, as we know, primarily depends on the interplay of forces in him. The justification for requiring this emotional coldness in the analyst is that it creates the most advantageous conditions for both parties: for the doctor a desirable protection for his own emotional life and for the patient the largest amount of help that we can give him today. A surgeon of earlier times took as his motto the words: 'Je le pansai, Dieu le guérit.' The analyst should be content with something similar [Freud, 1912, p. 115].

The metaphor of the surgeon has been a part of psycho-analytic discourse from Freud's early papers on technique down to the revisionist writings of our own time. But the history of the surgical metaphor is a curious one. It has, over the decades, been a metaphor psychoanalysts "live by"[1] less in the sense of eliciting unequivocal endorsement than of serving as a touchstone for elaborating how exactly psychoanalysts ought to feel toward the patients they treat and what exactly their treatment consists of; psychoanalytic writers have long subsumed these interrelated issues under the headings of the "psychoanalytic attitude" and the "psychoanalytic method."

Consensus about the relation of the surgical metaphor to this attitude and this method seems to fall back on little more than historical acknowledgment of Freud's own use of the metaphor in the papers on technique he wrote between 1912 and 1915. Because Freud invoked and endorsed the metaphor in these papers—and because he never felt it necessary to retract the endorsement—psychoanalysts have, over the decades, been led to engage the analogy between surgical and psychoanalytic work, whether as an act of affirmation, qualification, or repudiation. Mostly, however, the surgical metaphor has been resorted to obliquely; awareness of the metaphor and its historical lineage functions as a type of tacit knowledge informing any number of discussions of the analyst's "neutrality" in the face of the patient's emotional neediness and emotional demands—the *Sturm und Drang* of the psychoanalytic treatment process.

In our own time, the surgical metaphor has surely been invoked more to be repudiated than affirmed or even qualified. Long embraced as a strategy for explaining and justifying the canons of classical psychoanalytic technique—to wit, the attitude of detachment and neutrality and even emotional coldness prerequisite to the employment of Freud's psychoanalytic method—the metaphor now figures in relational, interpersonal, self-psychological, and modern Freudian writings that seek to dethrone these selfsame canons in presenting a different vision of what psychoanalysis is and what exactly psychoanalysts do. Even when unmentioned, the metaphor under-

---

[1] See Lakoff and Johnson's classic *Metaphors We Live By* (1980) for a persuasive presentation of the strong, constitutive sense in which we all live by and through our various metaphors.

lies recent critiques of classical technique, where strategies of "postmodern" therapeutic engagement are juxtaposed with surgically classical analysis, an "aggressively interpretive approach" seeking to remove "diseased infantile thoughts" (Mitchell, 1993, p. 30).

More interestingly, if not paradoxically, the surgical metaphor enters into the articulation of newer alternatives to traditional psychoanalysis. Consider a recent book by the interpersonal psychoanalyst Jay Greenberg, *Oedipus and Beyond* (1991). In this impressive piece of post-Freudian theorizing, the surgical metaphor is given great play; it provides a justificatory strategy for both a "relational" motivational theory and a theory of technique that revolve around a model of two fundamental human "drives." Greenberg begins by offering an astute critique of the limitations of any dual-drive theory. Ultimately, however, despite the force of his own critique, Greenberg opts for just such a theory over and against multiple-drive and mixed-model frameworks. Why does he do so? It is because "the same constraints that limit dualistic frameworks also make them penetrating . . . The narrow [interpretive] instrument is also sharp; it penetrates beneath the surface" (pp. 127, 128). Now, the two drives that Greenberg believes to be fundamental to the human condition are, to be sure, quite different from the sexual and aggressive drives that were the centerpiece of later Freudian theory. But Greenberg's preference for *some* dual-drive theory as the best way to order clinical observations and interpretations is classically Freudian in its surgical preconception about what makes any theory pragmatically efficacious, about what, we may say, renders it interpretively *penetrating*. What goes unexamined, of course, is the assumption that sharp penetration "beneath the surface" is invariably therapeutic.

We do not need to turn to recent postmodern writings to locate a dialogue about the surgical metaphor that Freud invoked in 1912. Within the history of psychoanalysis, we discern a spectrum of opinions about the metaphor—about whether Freud actually meant what he wrote, and whether his analogy with the surgeon is compelling even within the framework of his own theory and method of treatment.

At one end of the spectrum, we locate analysts, generally identified with traditional or "classical" psychoanalysis, for whom the surgical metaphor resonated with the psychoanalytic attitude and psychoanalytic method. Such analysts, following Freud, appealed to the special requirement of psychoanalytic technique as a warrant for the analyst's surgical attributes.

For Otto Fenichel, writing in 1935, analytic technique was a special type of living art that, in accord with Freud's views, had to guard against two extremes: that of analyzing "according to a rational plan, by intellect alone" and that of analyzing by intuition alone, giving too much play to the irrational. In the effort to mediate between these two extremes, Fenichel held, "the frequently used comparison between analytic and surgical technique is here indeed in place; for analytic technique, too, one needs endowment and intuition, but these, without training, do not suffice in surgery either" (p. 335). Just as surgical technique was worthless in the absence of "a thorough command of topographical anatomy," so the gift of analytic intuition counted for naught in the absence of a thorough grounding in "the topographical anatomy of the psyche" (1936, p. 13). And the surgical metaphor obtained as well in contemplating the measured manner in which the analyst was to set about penetrating the patient's character resistance through necessarily, but not needlessly, aggressive interpretations. What if such interpretations severely wounded the patient's narcissism and thereby provoked a therapeutic crisis? "As analysts," Fenichel held, "we should in principle certainly not be afraid of 'crises' (the surgeon isn't afraid of blood either when he cuts); but that is no reason for inviting such 'crises' in every case" (1935, p. 339).

By the 1950s, analytic theorists tended to shy away from the surgical metaphor while still conveying an appreciation of the force of Freud's analogy. For the authors of classic works on psychoanalytic technique, the surgical metaphor receded to the background of awareness. When authors like Edward Glover (1955) and Ralph Greenson (1967) incorporated Freud's papers on technique into their discussions of the analytic attitude, they invariably landed on the "mirror simile"[2] and "rule of abstinence"[3] as conceptual points of departure. But these authors had read their Freud, and the surgical metaphor, while not explicitly engaged in their explication of technique, remained a shadowy background assumption, perhaps an aspect of what Victorian Hamilton (1996) has recently termed "the analyst's preconscious." Occasionally the background assumption leaps to textual foreground, and we encounter new and intriguing permutations of Freud's analogy. Consider the language in which Glover (1955) presents the newly trained analyst approaching his first case:

---

[2] In "Recommendations to Physicians Practicing Psychoanalysis" (1912), where Freud expatiated on the surgical metaphor, he also introduced the mirror simile as further illustration of the attitude requisite to the employment of the psychoanalytic method: "The doctor should be opaque to his patients and, like a mirror, should show them nothing but what is shown to him" (p. 118). The mirror simile, more than the surgical metaphor, addresses the analyst's need to forego an "intimate attitude" that would have a "suggestive influence" on the patient. It too has been a topic of decades-long dialogue among psychoanalysts, and it is often discussed independently of the surgical metaphor. See Greenson (1967, pp. 211–216, 271–275) for a typically qualified endorsement of the mirror simile that culminates in the verdict that the "rule of the mirror . . . possesses dangers for the establishment of the working alliance if it is carried to extremes" (p. 275).
[3] Freud set forth what is known as the "rule of abstinence" in his "Observations on Transference-Love" (1915), where he observed that "analytic technique requires of the physician that he should deny to the patient who is craving for love the satisfaction she demands. The treatment must be carried out in abstinence. By this I do not mean physical abstinence alone, nor yet the deprivation of everything that the patient desires, for perhaps no sick person could tolerate this. Instead, I shall state it as a fundamental principle that the patient's need and longing should be allowed to persist in her, in order that they may serve as forces impelling her to do work and to make changes, and that we must beware of appeasing those forces by means of surrogates" (pp. 164–165). Classical psychoanalysts (e.g., Fenichel, 1936, pp. 29–30) have generally construed this "rule" as directing them to abstain from providing their patients with transference gratification, e.g., from reciprocating the patient's feelings of friendship, love, and/or gratitude as they arise in the transference relationship mobilized by the psychoanalytic process.

I have the impression that many approach their first case with something of the trepidation which accompanies the young surgeon to his first abdominal operation, and, if I may pursue this comparison without prejudice, the rational elements in this attitude have much the same basis in both instances. The budding surgeon fortifies himself overnight by careful study of surgical anatomy, only to find that his anticipated difficulties do not materialize, whereas numerous unexpected bewilderments appear from nowhere. In the same way the analyst has gathered from his theoretical reading many so far uncharted apprehensions about complicated analytical situations; and when these do not appear to materialize immediately may on the rebound proceed cheerfully enough, until he is faced with such a perplexing situation as the heaping up of negative transference [p. 7].

And here is Greenson, a decade later, adducing language skills among the desirable personality traits contributing to successful analytic work:

The ability to use spoken language vividly and economically is a valuable asset to the analyst and is parallel to the importance of manual dexterity for the surgeon. The latter cannot replace clinical judgment or the knowledge of anatomy and pathology, but it makes it possible for a sound clinician to perform proficiently rather than clumsily. Deep psychoanalysis is always painful, but inexpertness makes for unnecessary and prolonged pain. In some cases it can mean the difference between success and failure [1967, p. 386].

In his text on technique of 1976, the analyst Charles Brenner does not cite the surgical metaphor, but his provisos about the "humanness" of the analyst as it may or may not gain expression in treatment hearken back to the metaphor in a compelling way. "Behaving naturally *as an analyst,*" Brenner writes, "is often a very different matter from behaving naturally as a friend, an adviser, a parent, or even as a good doctor in the ordinary meaning of the term" (p. 29, emphasis in original). And again: "Being 'natural,' or, for that matter, being therapeutic or compassionate as an analyst means something different from being a sociable, friendly, sympathetic 'good doctor' or 'good parent' " (pp. 33–34).[4] And Theodore Shapiro, writing in 1984 of the analyst's need for an attitude of neutrality, urged on his physician colleagues the recollection of dissecting cadavers in medical school as a prototype of how to overcome unwanted subjective involvement on behalf of achieving objective knowledge of the patient's unconscious: "The distressing feelings as we see its skin, its face, its fingers, is a common experience, but once we are at work on the organ systems below, we put aside the feelings about the surface. The task becomes more technical, more universal" (p. 277).

At the opposite end of the spectrum from theorists who endorse, whether explicitly or implicitly, the surgical meta-phor — a dwindling minority, be it noted, among contemporary analysts — are those theorists who proffer a minimalist reading of the surgical metaphor. They tell us, in effect, not to take the surgical metaphor too seriously, for Freud himself did not really mean what he appeared to be saying. Specifically, he did not mean that the analyst should *model* himself on the surgeon, but only that the analyst, in the employment of his method, should incorporate certain surgeonlike *safeguards* to guarantee the integrity of the psychoanalytic procedure. These safeguards are the operational aspects of neutrality and abstinence, concepts that Freud introduced "in order to protect both patient and analyst from the analyst's acting on his own passions" (Hamilton, 1996, p. 167). Stone (1961) and Schafer (1983) espoused this viewpoint at an interval of two decades, and Lohser and Newton (1996) have reiterated it in a recent book-length reappraisal of Freud's actual technique with his patients. Here the surgical metaphor invoked in the papers on technique is reduced to one particular technical guideline drawing the

---

[4] Forty years before Brenner, Lawrence Kubie articulated the same surgically grounded provisos more forcefully still: "Other physicians may play a pacifying, reassuring, comforting role toward their patients. The psychoanalyst, on the other hand, when he believes that he is dealing with a patient for whom it is possible to achieve a fundamental and lasting cure, must do just the opposite. He may be as tactful and judicious as possible in the administration of pain, but in the end he must be merciless in hounding the neurosis out of every false cover" (1936, pp. 140–141).

attention of analytic beginners to specific therapeutic contingencies and temptations. Of Freud's recommendation that the analyst proceed with "emotional coldness" and put aside all his feelings, "even his human sympathy," Lohser and Newton write:

> This is a reminder that at times analysts have to ignore their feelings of compassion and empathy. In other words, their kindness must ultimately be subordinated to the task of the analysis, which by its very nature involves suffering on the patient's part. Rather than constituting a prescription for an overall approach to treatment — a later interpretation of these passages in Freud's writings — his statements address particular procedural difficulties [p. 21].

In addition to sanctioning the analyst's obligation to inflict suffering on the patient, the surgical metaphor addresses other "procedural challenges," to wit, the analyst's need to harness his therapeutic ambitiousness (p. 190) and his need to cultivate "the desired professional demeanor in the face of a temptation like erotic transference" (p. 192).

A quarter century before Lohser and Newton, Stone had subsumed such technical challenges within a broader framework of comprehension. Via the surgical metaphor and "mirror" simile, he believed, Freud was broadly referring

> (1) to the essential long-term purpose of the analysis, i.e., to elucidate the patient's own unconscious mental life to him, as opposed to the revelation of the (personal) contents of the analyst's mind to him; and (2) to the operational fact that the latter procedure, in most instances, and in the long run, interferes with the essential purpose. There is no evidence that "coldness" or "lifelessness" were [sic] directly or indirectly adjured in this particular recommendation; it is of purely cognitive-communicative reference [1961, p. 27].

It followed for Stone that the surgical metaphor could not be revelatory of the analytic demeanor in general; it was not prescriptive of what he termed "a general personal attitude." Rather, it was "specifically applicable to the analyst's only scalpel, his interpretations, which may, indeed, at times be painful" (p. 26).

In the readings of Lohser and Newton and of Stone before them, the surgical metaphor is not merely shorn of its status as a guiding metaphor; as a *seeming* characterization of the analytic attitude in general, it becomes a misleading metaphor, since it "stands in contrast to the subjective and intuitive approach [Freud] generally suggested the analyst adopt" (Lohser and Newton, 1996, p. 21). Ellman, in a recent reprinting of, and commentary on, Freud's papers on technique, opts for this same minimizing strategy through the use of qualifying conjunctions that effectively neutralize the import of the surgical metaphor. "When Freud invokes the surgeon as a standard of neutrality," he contends, "he is using an interesting, impersonal metaphor. *Yet* he has also written about the sympathy and tact that the analyst should display. *Moreover*, we have his published account of how he provided the Ratman, Dr. Ernst Lanzer, with a meal when he felt that this patient might have to go hungry for some period of time" (1991, pp. 332–333, emphasis added).

Wedged between the appreciative and dismissive renderings of the surgical metaphor are various middle-ground positions that take the metaphor as a seriously intended characterization of the analytic attitude, albeit one that fails to encompass the intrapsychic consequences of the analytic process and the relational richness of the analytic situation. A sophisticated variant of the middle-ground position is found in the work of Heinrich Racker, a British Kleinian theorist whose astute appreciation of the interdigitating character of transference and countertransference has been influential among current relational and interpersonal theorists.

Racker took quite seriously Freud's admonition that the analyst's attitude toward his patient resembles that of a surgeon. "The fundamental importance of this objective attitude continues to be valued by everyone," he wrote in 1958. "But in addition," he continued, "many analysts now would use the perception of a feeling like the one of compassion, which is aroused by the patient, to understand the underlying transference process" (p. 26). Construed as a mandate for the analyst's passivity, the surgical metaphor, no less than the mirror simile, had been "emphasized and carried out one-sidedly, at the expense of other concepts" (p. 29). And what are these "other concepts" that soften the surgical attitude? Racker had in mind the broadened recognition and use of the analyst's countertransferential responsiveness to the patient. This technical requirement was wedded to an appreciation of the need for greater activity on the analyst's part on behalf of therapeutic goals. Such activity, which was tantamount to supportive engagement with the patient during the latter's halting struggle toward insight, could not be reconciled with the "internal attitude" of the surgeon. And, in point of fact, Racker wrote,

> the concept of the 'surgeon's' attitude lends itself to misunderstandings and may induce a repression of the countertransference and, moreover, a denial of the desire to understand and to lead the patient towards a great insight and a new way of feeling. Freud counseled the attitude of a 'surgeon' to protect the analyst and the patient from the disadvantages which the ambition to cure and an identification without reservations imply. But on the other hand, Freud assigned great importance to the active, fighting, and, I believe, even warm attitude. This does not only follow from his own attitude, which we know through his case histories, but also from some expressions in his theoretical writings on technique [1958, p. 30].

Racker's nuanced formulation probes the limitations of the surgical metaphor while still assigning it a constitutive role in the analytic attitude. Here the "internal attitude" of the surgeon interacts dialectically with the more contemporary call for an active analytic stance. Less nuanced than Racker but very much in the same vein is Karl Menninger, a paragon of pragmatic orthodoxy in American psychoanalysis through the 1950s. In his *Theory of Psychoanalytic Technique* of 1958, the very year Racker presented the paper on "Classical and Present Techniques in Psychoanalysis" quoted above, Menninger situated the surgical metaphor within a linear narrative of technical enlightenment, albeit one that did not posit specific turning points in this trajectory of analytic progress. The surgical metaphor, he wrote, "set an ideal which analysts, *for a time,* strove to achieve. *Later,* of course, it was realized that the analyst must not only be this surgeon, but he must also be the warm, human, friendly, helpful physician. He must be both" (p. 85, emphasis added).

Guy Thompson, in a recent book-length reappraisal of Freud's technique, offers a qualified endorsement of the surgical metaphor from precisely the opposite direction. That is, he understands the metaphor as a cautionary proviso about the analyst's limited ability to serve as the "warm, human, friendly, helpful physician." According to Thompson (1994), Freud's advice that analysts model themselves on the surgeon in his "Recommendations to Physicians Practicing Psychoanalysis" (1912) achieves its import from the remark about therapeutic ambition that follows it: "The feeling that is most dangerous to a psychoanalyst is the therapeutic ambition to achieve by this novel and much disputed method something that will produce a convincing effect upon other people" (p. 115). The surgical metaphor, Thompson believes, is Freud's remedy for the penchant of analysts to assume "an excessive proportion of the burden that properly belongs to one's patient who, after all, is a partner in the treatment."[5] In short, therapeutic ambition must be tempered by the limited healing resources of the patient on whom the analytic "operation" is to be performed. Thus,

> Like surgeons who must put their feelings aside and do their best to perform their task, analysts mustn't allow their feelings for their patients to obscure the limitations of their role. That doesn't mean they aren't involved in the treatment process.

---

[5] Compare Ellman's (1991) gloss on this same passage from "Recommendations to Physicians Practicing Psychoanalysis," which, in additive fashion, urges consideration of both Thompson's reading and the more dismissive rendering of Lohser and Newton: "This is a much-quoted passage of Freud's and is in a sense contradicted by other things that he has said and certainly by his recorded behavior with various patients. One can reconcile these contradictions by simply accepting that Freud at times was not totally consistent. One can also say that his powerful metaphor is used here to help the analyst with rescue fantasies that are frequently present as countertransference tendencies. Freud is attempting to counteract therapists' tendencies to do something dramatic and 'meaningful' to help the patient. Here, Freud seems to be reminding the analyst that the patient is not under one's command and that there are other factors beyond the analyst's powers that will determine the outcome of the analysis. While this type of dispassionate reserve may at times be desirable, it is nonetheless difficult to achieve" (p. 158n).

They are. Nor does it imply that they shouldn't have feelings. They do. But they must put them to the side and not assume that their zeal for success can in any way compensate for what may be lacking in their patient [1994, p. 150; cf. p. 171].

By conceptualizing the surgical metaphor as propaedeutic with respect to a single treatment contingency—the analyst's tendency to become therapeutically ambitious—Thompson can deny its salience in other explanatory contexts. Apart from the problematic of therapeutic ambition, that is, readers are enjoined—in the manner of Stone, Schafer, and Lohser and Newton—to distinguish between what Freud said and what he actually meant. Here is one example:

In the same vein, patients who want to be analyzed in order to cure one symptom but not others are wasting their time. Despite Freud's allusions to surgery and medicine he didn't believe that analysis could be used "surgically" in order to resolve an isolated problem. As with sexual impregnation, Freud believed that psychoanalysis sets forces in motion that, unlike science, can't be controlled or predicted [p. 163].

There are, no doubt, scores of other passing references to the surgical metaphor scattered throughout the psychoanalytic literature. It is not my purpose to offer a compendium of these remarks, nor do I believe a comprehensive review of citations of, or allusions to, the surgical metaphor would be a particularly profitable scholarly exercise. Suffice it to say that, if one reads deeply enough into the literature, one is readily persuaded that all commentators, from Freud's own circle of followers through the theorists of our own time, have incorporated the surgical metaphor into discussions of the psychoanalytic attitude, technique, and method on the basis of a single unexamined assumption: that Freud's understanding of surgeons and surgery, from which he elaborated the surgical metaphor, is somehow accurate and universal, an incontestable "given" in our own time as in Freud's.

It is precisely this unexamined assumption that provides the touchstone of this study. For as soon as we examine the idea of surgery that informs the metaphor, as soon as we deconstruct it in terms of both the history of surgery and the history of Freud's personal experience of surgeons and surgery, we see that the metaphor opens to a wealth of meaning about Freud and the evolution of his psychoanalytic method. Beneath the surgical metaphor that Freud invoked in 1912, that is, there is an intriguing bit of history to unravel—intriguing because it occupies an unexplored interstice between medical history and psychoanalytic history.

How shall we go about filling in this interstice? Our inquiry must be three-pronged. In locating the understanding of surgeons and surgery that informs Freud's surgical metaphor, we must make a brief excursion into the history of surgery, since we are intent on establishing the historical circumstances that gave rise to *Freud's* time-bound assumptions about surgeons and surgery. At the same time, we are led into the interrelated domains of Freud biography and psychoanalytic history, since we are intent on illuminating the assumptions underlying the surgical metaphor by considering Freud's lifelong relations with surgeons and surgery—relations, be it noted, that arose in both professional and personal contexts.

The origin and ground of the surgical metaphor, we shall see, are but part of the story. For the fact is that Freud invoked the metaphor in a chronologically compact series of writings, after which he withdrew from it in no uncertain terms. Why did Freud, in the years following World War I, abandon his surgical vision of the psychoanalytic procedure, especially given a variety of life circumstances that drew him to the surgeon's world? Examination of the personal and professional reasons that Freud distanced himself not only from the surgical metaphor but from medicosurgical analogies more broadly constitutes the second part of our inquiry. We conclude by considering the equivocal relationship of psychodynamic psychiatry to surgery, particularly in the United States, in the decades following Freud's death—this by way of aftermath to Freud's own retreat from the medicosurgical analogizing of his early years.

Before proceeding to these tasks, however, we must attend more systematically to the surgical metaphor itself. Analysts generally glean their sense of the metaphor from the oft-cited passage from Freud's "Recommendations to Physicians Practicing Psychoanalysis" (1912), where it is tied to his concern lest the analyst develop an overweening therapeutic ambition (e.g., Thompson, 1994, pp. 150, 171). But, in point of fact, Freud's use of the metaphor spans a decade and includes several discrete if interrelated meanings. Let us see what those meanings are.

PART I

THE METAPHOR ASCENDANT

"It May Make the Same Claims as Surgery"

∞

In writings between 1909 and 1917, and especially in the papers on technique written between 1912 and 1915, Freud used the surgical metaphor in three distinct if complementary senses:

Surgery as metaphor for the analyst's attitude of neutrality, detachment, and "emotional coldness." The passage from "Recommendations to Physicians Practicing Psychoanalysis" (1912) is the best-known example of this use of the surgical metaphor. Yet Freud's use of the metaphor has several collateral meanings that have nothing to do with his concern about the analyst's "therapeutic ambition" or even with the broader issue of analytic neutrality. He enjoins the analyst to think of himself "as a surgeon" with respect to the arrangements for, and expectations of, analytic treatment. In discussing fee arrangements at the beginning of treatment, for example, he advises colleagues "not to allow large sums of money to accumulate, but to ask for payment at fairly short regular intervals—monthly, perhaps." This, he adds, is "not the usual practice of nerve specialists or other physicians in our European society. But the psychoanalyst may put himself in the position of a surgeon, who is frank and expensive because he has at his disposal methods of treatment which can be of use" (1913, p. 131). Another collateral meaning is that the analyst, like the surgeon, is "practically healthy"; he undergoes a preparatory training analysis without being driven to it by "illness" in the manner of his prospective patients (1912, pp. 116–117).

Surgery as metaphor for the analyst's deep penetration of unconscious contents. This use of the metaphor supplements the foregoing. Not only must the analyst approach his work with surgical detachment, but the work itself is deemed analogous to a surgical intervention. In his final Introductory Lecture on "Analytic Therapy," Freud makes the point quite explicitly in differentiating the use of suggestion in analysis from its use in hypnosis:

> Hypnotic treatment seeks to cover up and gloss over something in mental life; analytic treatment seeks to expose and get rid of something. The former acts like a cosmetic, the latter like surgery. The former makes use of suggestion in order to forbid the symptoms; it strengthens the repressions, but, apart from that, leaves all the processes that have led to the formation of the symptoms unaltered. Analytic treatment makes its impact further back toward the roots, where the conflicts are which gave rise to the symptoms, and uses suggestion in order to alter the outcome of those conflicts [1917, pp.450–451].[1]

To be successful, the analytic operation, like surgery, must be pursued to successful completion. In his recommendations "On Beginning the Treatment" (1913), Freud reminds colleagues that the treatment contract is not binding and that an analysand may break off treatment whenever he likes. "But I do not hide it from him," Freud adds, "that if the treatment is

---

[1] This notion of analytic "surgery" as penetrating to the roots of unconscious conflict has obvious antecedents in Freud's preanalytic writings, particularly his applications of Josef Breuer's "cathartic method" in the *Studies on Hysteria* (Breuer and Freud, 1895). There the weight of Freud's chapter on "The Psychotherapy of Hysteria" was to compare repressed pathogenic material to a foreign body, with treatment "working like the removal of a foreign body from the living tissue" (p. 290). Here, though not in later analytic writings, Freud was quick to point out the manner in which the simile was limited, though his refinement of it was still cast in surgico-anatomical language: "A foreign body does not enter into any relation with the layers of tissue that surround it, although it modifies them and necessitates a reactive inflammation in them. Our pathogenic psychical group, on the other hand, does not admit of being cleanly extirpated form the ego. . . . In fact the pathogenic organization does not behave like a foreign body, but far more like an infiltrate. In this simile the resistance must be regarded as what is infiltrating" (p. 290).

stopped after only a small amount of work has been done it will not be successful and may easily, like an unfinished operation, leave him in an unsatisfactory state" (pp. 129–130).

An interesting, anticipatory gloss on the analytic operation had been introduced by Freud several years earlier, in the fifth and final Clark University lecture of 1909. It concerns the analyst's surgical prerogative to cause pain in the service of cure. Freud here introduced the surgical metaphor in the context of considering a particular form of resistance to psychoanalysis: the fear of bringing to consciousness repressed sexual instincts, lest they overwhelm the patient's "higher ethical trends" and rob him of "cultural acquisitions." "People notice," Freud continued, "that the patient has sore spots in his mind, but shrink from touching them for fear of increasing his sufferings" (1909, p. 52).

Freud ceded the force of the analogy, acknowledging that "it is no doubt kinder not to touch diseased spots if it can do nothing else but cause pain." But he construed analytically induced pain as analogous to surgical pain. It was a medical necessity, a necessary prelude to radical analytic cure:

> But, as we know, a surgeon does not refrain from examining and handling a focus of disease, if he is intending to take active measures which he believes will lead to a permanent cure. No one thinks of blaming him for the inevitable suffering caused by the examination or for the reactions to the operation, if only it gains its end and the patient achieves a lasting recovery as a result of the temporary worsening of his state. The case is similar with psychoanalysis. It may make the same claims as surgery: the increase in suffering which it causes the patient during treatment is incomparably less than what a surgeon causes, and is quite negligible in proportion to the severity of the underlying ailment [1909, pp. 52–53].

Consonant with the surgical nature of the analytic procedure and the surgical prerogative of the analytic operator is the visual imagery that Freud invoked in contemplating the deployment of the procedure. By way of endorsing the desirability of a training analysis for "everyone who wishes to learn analysis," for example, he observed that "the sacrifice involved in laying oneself open to another person without being driven to it by illness is amply rewarded" (1912, pp. 116–117). The development of transference love, to take another example, "is an unavoidable consequence of a medical situation, like the exposure of a patient's body or the imparting of a vital secret" (1915, p. 169).

Surgery as metaphor for the preconditions of successful analytic treatment. This use of the metaphor pertains neither to the procedure nor to the analyst's attitude during the procedure. Rather, it has to do with the "external conditions" that must be satisfied if analytic intervention is to succeed. Thus, it invokes the notion of an analytic field as analogous to a surgical field. In this use of the surgical metaphor, Freud was thinking not of internal resistance to exposure of mental sore spots, but of "external resistances which arise from the patient's circumstances" and may, in the manner of a contaminated surgical field, sabotage treatment:

> Psychoanalytic treatment may be compared with a surgical operation and may similarly claim to be carried out under arrangements that will be the most favorable for its success. You know the precautionary measures adopted by a surgeon: a suitable room, good lighting, assistants, exclusion of the patient's relatives, and so on. Ask yourselves now how many of these operations would turn out successfully if they had to take place in the presence of all the members of the patient's family, who would stick their noses into the field of the operation and exclaim aloud at every incision [1917, p. 459].

The preconditions of successful analytic treatment likewise implicated the authority of the analyst-surgeon who undertook the "psychical operation." In fact, it was the authority of the analyst that ensured compliance with the external conditions that made possible analytic success. As early as "The Future Prospects of Psychoanalytic Therapy" (1910), Freud invoked the increased authority of the analyst as one factor promising a "substantial improvement" in the "therapeutic prospects" of analysis in the future. He contrasted increasing recognition of the analyst's claim to medical authority with the unhappy state of affairs when he alone represented psychoanalysis. During these early years, the forces of cultural and medical authority, with their "enormous weight of suggestion," were arrayed against Freud's newborn science: "All our therapeutic successes have been achieved in the face of this suggestion: it is surprising that any successes at all could be gained in such circumstances" (p. 146). Here is the language with which Freud underscored the inability of the analyst to operate psychically in the absence of the specifically surgical authority appropriate to his role:

> Nor was it really pleasant to carry out a psychical operation while the colleagues whose duty it should have been to assist took particular pleasure in spitting into the field of operation, and while at the first signs of blood or restlessness in the patient his relatives began threatening the operating surgeon. An operation is surely entitled to produce reactions; in surgery we became accustomed to that long ago [1910, p. 146].

What do recent commentators offer in the effort to make historical sense of the tone, tenor, and substance of Freud's various strictures in the papers on technique, including his use of the surgical metaphor? In general, they have been content to explore these strictures as technical responses to the struggles with transference and countertransference love that preoccupied him during this time. I refer to what Gabbard and Lester (1995) term the "sexual boundary transgressions" by colleagues in which Freud was deeply involved, as analytic father confessor, mediator, and peacemaker. Viewed thusly, Freud's metaphor of the surgeon has an overcompensatory significance: it is a thinly veiled judgment of the harmfulness of Jung's embroilment with Sabina Spielrein (Kerr, 1993), of Ferenczi's infatuations with Elma and Gisela Pálos, and of Ernest Jones's sexual impulsiveness with various patients, which led to Freud's analysis of Jones's common-law wife, Loe Kann, in an ill-fated effort to save Jones's marriage. Freud's emphasis on analytic objectivity and abstinence, including the surgical metaphor, so this line of reasoning goes, represents an effort to learn from the "boundaryless behavior" of his disciples (Barron and Hoffer, 1994; Gabbard and Lester, 1995) and thereby prevent new followers from straying from the fold, whether theoretically or in their manner of professional conduct (Lichtenberg, 1994).

This is a plausible line of explanation, but it drastically foreshortens inquiry into what is, I propose, a historical question. Much is to be gained by locating Freud's understanding of surgery in the here-and-now of his life history. We shall see that Freud's response to the boundary violations of his disciples was to invoke an image of the analyst as a special type of surgeon, a surgeon of the mind, and that this image, has intriguing biographical roots. But these biographical roots, in turn, occupy a certain historical ground, for Freud arrived at his understanding of surgery at a precise juncture in surgical history. The surgical metaphor both reflects and participates in this history. Let us survey this ground prior to exploring these biographical roots.

"Let Us Do Battle With Knife"
❧

T he delineation of surgery as a branch of knowledge conveyed in technical writing occurred in Europe from the twelfth to the fifteenth centuries. This development was part of the social and economic growth that led to the emergence of new crafts and the guild movement in general. But its more specific anlagen were the translations—first into Latin and, in the fourteenth and fifteenth centuries, into vernacular languages—of ancient Greek and Islamic surgical treatises by Arabic medical encyclopedists like Rhases, Haly Abbas, Albucasis, and Avicenna. Literate surgeons, those who read and wrote Latin, followed their medical colleagues in turning to Aristotelian logic and natural philosophy, and they used Aristotelian terminology to set forth their expertise. Yet, in reality, medieval medical and surgical practice overlapped to the point that a clear boundary between professions or crafts cannot be drawn (Siraisi, 1990, p. 175). But this much can be said: medieval and Renaissance surgery was anathema to the metaphor of deep penetration. To be sure, surgery involved the knife, used principally in phlebotomy—the minor procedure of bloodletting routinely performed by all medici of the time. But it also encompassed, as more characteristic activities, the suturing of wounds and the setting of fractures and dislocations, so that the body of early surgical knowledge was a rich assortment of techniques for treating broken limbs, sprains, dislocations, burns, scalds, cuts, bites, and bruises. Bonesetting, bandaging, suturing, and bloodletting, not deep cutting, were the tools of the trade and the surgeon's professional raison d'être (pp. 154–155, 174–175). Whereas Renaissance physicians practiced internal medicine, Renaissance surgeons ministered to external conditions; only military surgeons, faced with dying patients on the battlefield, attempted internal operations with any regularity (Park, 1985, pp. 62, 62n).

One of the best-known episodes in medieval surgery had nothing whatsoever to do with the knife; it was the controversy over the cleaning and dressing of wounds—a major topic in all surgical texts (Siraisi, 1990, p. 169). Proponents of keeping wounds open so that they could heal by secondary intention, from the bottom up via suppuration (the "laudable pus"[1] of later centuries), ranged against proponents of cleaning and closing the wound, so that it could heal by primary intention, from the top down (pp. 169–170). For the authors of surgical and medical treatises alike, actual surgical intervention was one of the three therapeutic resources of medicine, which were always to be employed in succession: diet, followed by medication, and only then surgery, the measure of last resort (p. 174).

These dicta of medieval and Renaissance practice apply to the early modern period as well. Even when the surgeon's lancet came into play, it continued to function at the surface rather than the interior; it assumed a subordinate role in a medical epistemology that revolved around the restoration of inner motion of flow ("flux") by intervention directed at outer flow. In the world of eighteenth-century German medicine, for example, where inner flux and outer flux were mirror images of each other, surgeons administered medical remedies that aimed at luring an inner flux outside, lest it be driven back inside the body to congeal and harden. For women patients whose fear was "not the discomfort of an evacuation, but the perception of the inner space as a space of induration and stoppage" (Duden, 1991, p. 132), the healing process entailed

---

[1] " . . . the dirtiest, messiest, most pernicious, and most persistent mistake in the history of surgery," exclaimed the pathologist and historian Guido Majno in 1975, on discovering the first known statement of the doctrine of "laudable pus" in the Ebers papyrus of ancient Egypt. For Majno, "Trying to heal a wound by making it throw more pus is about as reasonable as getting more children to stop pregnancies. Yet rivers of pus flowed for another 3,500 years, and the dreadful doctrine of good and laudable pus, *pus bonum et laudabile*, has only recently faded out" (p. 102).

"supporting the external flow of impure, dirty, pustular matter until the body had been sufficiently cleansed" (p. 133).

It followed that the lancet operated at the surface, where, via bleeding, the lancing of abscesses, and the creation of fontanels (artificial wounds kept open by a hair ick, a seton) an oozing flux could be restored and inner stagnation averted (1991, pp. 134–139). Here the surgeon was not the master of reparative penetration; rather, his domain was the more gentle "drawing off" of overabundant fluids, which, if not lulled to the surface, would result in inner decay.

An even more extreme variant of this epistemology is found in the surgical writings of John Hunter, the British surgeon of the late eighteenth century whose subordination of surgical intervention to principles of pathophysiology earned him the title of "father of scientific surgery." Hunter's conception of pathophysiology revolved around his belief in the self-righting propensities of the body, teleological propensities that directed the surgeon to harmonize his healing art with the inherent curative power of nature (Jacyna, 1992, p. 141). This vision led Hunter to diminish the surgeon's role altogether, even to the point of radical passivity in the face of major wounds. In the case of a man who had "three Balls shot thro his Body," for example, the surgeon's charge was merely to behold the therapeutic character of inflammatory processes—to let nature take its remedial course. Via the adhesions formed by the "natural surgeon," Hunter believed, "whatever cavities the balls had entered, there the surrounding parts had adhered, so that the passage of the ball was by this means become a complete canal." There was no warrant here for penetration into the interior, nor even for the gentle facilitation of outer flow, since no foreign body could enter the body "but must be conducted to the external surface of the body, either through the wounds, or from an abscess forming for itself, which would work its own exit somewhere" (quoted in Jacyna, 1992, p. 147). Small wonder that Hunter, in his surgical lectures, spoke of operations—"this last part of surgery"—as measures of last resort. They could be justified only when noninvasive variants of the healing art proved unavailing. As such, operations represented "a tacit acknowledgment of the insufficiency of surgery. It is like an armed savage who attempts to get that by force which a civilized man would get by stratagem" (quoted in Temkin, 1951, p. 491).

The premodern concern with surgery at the surface, with surgery as perpetrator, or simply as guarantor, of the external wound that restores internal balance, shades into the modern concern with surgery as the science of wound management. During the final decades of the eighteenth century, the rapprochement of medicine and surgery was well under way, especially in the military medical schools of France and Prussia (Bonner, 1995, pp. 54–58). As continental and British surgeons spent increasing time learning materia medica and noninvasive strategies of clinical management, so their operative intentionality was further subordinated to practical therapeutics.[2] Given that medicine and surgery were drawn together under the aegis of military medical training programs,[3] it is unsurprising that wound management became the surgeon's defining preoccupation in the nineteenth and twentieth centuries.

The point is briefly made: the surgical calling over the past two centuries has centered less on the efficacy of the penetrating knife than on the surgeon's healing ministrations to the wound. And it is in the surgery of war, revolving around the management of gunshot and shrapnel wounds, and battlefield amputations, that this preoccupation emerges most clearly. Beginning with the Napoleonic Wars, extending through the Crimean War, the American Civil War, and the Franco-Prussian War, and ending with the two World Wars of our own century, war has been the crucible of surgical progress. It is in the context of war that surgeons gained decisive knowledge about the role of anesthesia and nursing (Napoleonic Wars), antiseptic and

---

[2] The "immensely popular teaching" of John Hunter, which made surgical intervention subordinate to principles of anatomy and pathophysiology, was influential in this development (Bonner, 1995, p. 57).

[3] "By the very nature of military service, distinctions on the battlefield between surgical and medical therapies were blurred and often nonexistent. 'The military surgeons of all countries,' writes one modern student, 'made a vital contribution to the coming together of both healing professions in the course of the eighteenth century'" (Bonner, 1995, p. 56). On the rapprochement of surgery and medicine in the eighteenth century, see also Temkin (1951).

open wound management (the American Civil War), blood transfusions and the failure of Listerism with respect to cellulitic wound infections (World War I), and, finally, the effectiveness of chemotherapeutic and antibiotic measures in dealing with infections (World War II). And yet, until the 1930s, the modern surgical calling, enlarged by the insights of war, had little to commend it over and against the premodern surgeon's role as the drainer of external flux. As the Wangensteens have written, "The role of the surgeon before sulfanilamide was essentially that of pus evacuator" (1978, p. 516).

Following the discovery of the anesthetizing properties of nitrous oxide, ether, and chloroform in the 1840s, surgeons themselves envisioned an era of deep and painless surgical penetration as a godsend to suffering humanity. Yet, in the Crimean War of 1854, the first wide-scale use of chloroform in wartime surgery resulted in catastrophic death rates. "This is the first war in which operations have been performed under chloroform. And never before have so many men died of wound fever. Just open your eyes, man."[4] Thus speaks the British surgeon McGregor to the wide-eyed narrator[5] of Jürgen Thorwald's *The Century of the Surgeon* (1956, p. 176). He continues: "There's something to the charge: ever since we have been operating under chloroform and have been able to cut deep and do a thorough job, wound fever has been on the increase. Chloroform would not be the first innovation that has resulted in more agony than it alleviated" (p. 177).

Some four decades would pass between the discovery of anesthesia and the common acceptance of Lister's antiseptic

---

[4] Likewise the American surgeon James Gregory Mumford: "At the time of Lister's going to Edinburgh the frightful mortality of troops in the Crimean War was exercising men. Soldiers were being killed in battle by tens and hundreds, but they were dying of surgical diseases by thousands" (1908, p. 103).

[5] Thorwald's companion volumes *The Century of the Surgeon* (1956) and *The Triumph of Surgery* (1957), which epitomize the triumphalist vision of surgery in the nineteenth century, are cast as third-person narratives, with each successive episode in surgical progress viewed through the eyes of an imaginary young physician whose career brings him into contact with the great surgeons and groundbreaking operations of his time.

methods.[6] During this time, roughly from 1845 to 1885, the surgeon's progressive recourse to deep penetration conveyed the likelihood of wound infection and death no less than the promise of radical cure.[7] By the late 1850s, European and American surgeons, freed from the moral and psychological burden of routinely inflicting excruciating pain on their patients, espoused a new liberality in their pursuit of deep penetration. Despite the routine occurrence of severe and often fatal septic disease—the so-called "hospital diseases"[8]—in the aftermath of surgery, mid-century surgeons not only operated on a larger proportion of cases but also devised new operations for diseased joints and the repair of hernia, palate and lip abnormalities, and vaginal fistula.

And they often penetrated in the absence of pathology, simply because penetration had finally become a surgical possibility. The naked glorification of penetration is clearest—and most sinister—in the realm of nineteenth-century gynecology. The first four decades of the century contain scattered accounts from

---

[6] Within the literature on Listerism in the nineteenth century, A. J. Youngson's (1979, pp. 157–211) excellent review of the fight for antisepsis in Britain deserves special mention.

[7] I phrase this claim in a way that allows for the controversy among American historians as to whether the advent of anesthesia actually *increased* the death rate from surgery. Throughout the nineteenth century, the consensus among physicians was that anesthesia did indeed increase the surgical death rate; Rothstein (1972, pp. 251–252), among others, has endorsed this claim. Pernick (1985, pp. 217ff.), however, in a review of the scant available data, suggests that the evidence supporting a causal relationship between the development of anesthesia and a higher surgical infection rate is "very thin" (p. 218). He proposes, on the basis of equally thin evidence, an alternative explanation for an increased surgical death rate in the 1840s and 50s: following the development of general anesthesia, surgeons' willingness to operate on high-risk cases associated with industrial accidents "probably led to more deaths following *surgery* but fewer deaths overall. . . . It was the industrial revolution, and the growing ability of surgeons to operate on previously hopeless cases, not increased careless or unnecessary surgery, that accounted for the rise in surgical deaths following 1846" (p. 220).

[8] Mid-nineteenth century surgeons spoke of four varieties of sepsis or "hospital disease": erysipelas (an acute streptococcal cellulitis involving the skin), pyemia and septicemia (both terms denoting bacterial infection of the blood stream), and hospital gangrene. Prior to the 1860s or 70s, these infectious diseases were not clearly distinguished from one another (Youngson, 1979, p. 33).

the United States, Italy, and England of surgical removal of ovarian cysts undertaken as a lifesaving operation. With the advent of general anesthesia at mid-century, however, this type of surgery became common and, as such, a prototype of abdominal surgery in general (Dally, 1991, p. 135; Shorter, 1992, pp. 74–75). It was fueled by the peculiar linkage between gynecology and psychiatry that gained ground in the second half of the century: the belief that pelvic lesions of all types— via a "reflex irritation" that ran up the spinal column and on to the brain—were responsibile for all manner of mental disturbance, indeed for insanity (Shorter, 1992, pp. 69ff.). Paradoxically, as surgical removal of ovaries became common, its lifesaving rationale was countered by its life-threatening reality. In Britain, for example, professional and public acceptance of the surgical removal of ovaries dates from the early 1840s, but the staggeringly high preanesthesia mortality rates (tabulated as being as high as 44.5%) did not fall until the 1870s and 1880s (Moscucci, 1990, pp. 137, 152–156).

We would expect such mortality rates to induce operative restraint. But this was not the case. European surgeons were not content to penetrate the abdominal cavity to remove cystic ovaries; by the 1870s, the procedure, dubbed "ovariotomy," had evolved into the surgical removal of normal ovaries, dubbed "Battey's operation"[9] or "oophorectomy." The latter procedure

---

[9] The removal of healthy ovaries was first performed by 1872 by two surgeons operating on different continents: Alfred Hegar, a professor of gynecology at the University of Freiburg, and Robert Battey, of Rome, Georgia. A skilled battlefield surgeon for the South during the American Civil War and a founding member of the Georgia Gynecological Society, Battey performed his first ovariotomy in 1869 and subsequently developed a rationale for the removal of apparently normal ovaries that were still, so he believed, associated with symptoms that could be relieved by producing an artificial menopause. "At first these 'other symptoms' for which ovaries were removed were gynecological, for example 'excessive' menstrual bleeding, but surgeons soon extended the operation to women who were 'insane,' hysterical, unhappy, difficult for their husbands to control, for example those who were unfaithful to their husbands or disliked running a household" (Dally, 1991, pp. 147–148). Cf. Shorter (1992, pp. 69ff.), who comprehends the latter development within the history of nineteenth-century reflex theory; to wit, he suggests that the surgical removal of healthy ovaries was the logical surgical extension of local vaginal procedures resorted to earlier in the century "in the name of curing reflex neurosis and insanity" (pp. 73–74).

lacked any anatomical warrant; it was strictly and simply a method of behavioral control. By artificially inducing menopause, that is, surgeons undertook to control masturbation, "nymphomania," depression, hysteria, and a host of other "symptoms" of social dysfunction (Dally, 1991, pp. 137, 146ff.). Within a decade of Battey's initial removal of healthy ovaries in 1872, the indications for oophorectomy had become so all-inclusive as to give rise to a new diagnostic entity — ovariomania — as a way of justifying mutilating operations for a panoply of symptoms "whose severity decreased as the indications for the operation became ever vaguer" (Dally, 1991, p. 151). By the 1890s, a number of North American asylums took this all-inclusiveness one step further: they retained staff gynecologists to "Battey-ize" female inpatients as a matter of course (Shorter, 1992, pp. 79–81).

Nor did the surgeons' operative frenzy begin and end with the removal of healthy ovaries. Surgical removal of the superficial portion of the clitoris, clitoridectomy, was common in England until 1867, when it was superseded by a "boom" for cauterizing and applying caustics to the clitoris (Shorter, 1992, pp. 85–86). The 1870s and 1880s also witnessed the development of abdominal surgery for a host of spurious "displacements," especially "malposition" of the womb. An entire category of gynecological disorders was fabricated out of normal variations in human anatomy, with pride of place given to the belief that a backward-facing or "retroverted" uterus was an abnormality that made women ill and called for immediate surgical correction; this notion remained conventional wisdom among gynecologists throughout the century (Dally, 1991, pp. 142–44).

Whether we look to the indications for surgery or the outcome of surgery, then, we cannot view the second half of the nineteenth century as providing a univocal endorsement of the healing efficacy of surgical penetration. Rather, we witness a period in which surgical advance, the leading guard of "the golden age of surgery," is accompanied by descent into "the dark ages of operative furor" (Fluhmann, 1955). This element of essential paradox is greatest in the 1870s, when the gulf between operative technique, sustained by the recent advent of Listerian antisepsis, and medical science was at its greatest. When the French-Swiss neuropathologist Paul Dubois reminisced in 1905 about the "astonishing discoveries" of Pasteur and Lister three decades earlier, he sought to capture the glaring disjunction between surgery and medicine in language that was circumspect and even jocular. He recalled how in the 1870s the younger generation "was carried away by the powerful rush of ideas, and more than one old physician regretted that he was no longer on the school benches and could not be associated in this magnificent work." Yet, Dubois continued, the excitement attendant to antisepsis led to "exaggerations," and, among the specialties prone to exaggerate the immediate consequences of the new discovery,

> surgery took the first place; it hesitated at nothing. Operations that had formerly been considered dangerous became possible, and one could hear the public exclaim: Surgery has taken immense strides, but medicine is at a standstill; it is today exactly where it was in the time of Hippocrates. The watchword seemed to be: No sickness without visible lesions; behold your enemy, the microbe. Let us do battle with knife, cautery, and antiseptics! Since that day surgeons have had for their brothers in internal medicine a patronizing smile mingled with a little disdain, and it was from this period that one dates their tendency to make bold incursions into the classic domain of medicine. Wherever the idea of operative intervention cropped up in their minds they did not hesitate to act with a confidence in the efficacy of their weapons that may, perhaps, have been exaggerated [1905, p. 12].

The narrator of Thorwald's *The Triumph of Surgery* concludes his account of the decades following the advent of anesthesia by noting, with rhetorical flourish, that "Surgery would remain a poor thing, a deadly thing, until a second terrible menace was overcome: that of sepsis" (1957, p. 179). But, as Dubois intimates, neither the acceptance of antisepsis nor even the perfection of aseptic technique proved a surgical godsend. By promoting lengthy and extensive operations, it had the untoward result of exacerbating surgical shock and compromising the physiology of natural cell protection. The

American surgeon Robert Morris, whose career began in 1882 and spanned a full half century, looked back on the early aseptic era with special disdain:

> In the nineties it was customary for surgeons to treat cases of appendicitis in which there was infection of the peritoneum by making long incisions which caused shock. Incisions suitable for killing bears were being applied to weak patients. Surgeons made multiple incisions for purposes of drainage and these also caused shock. At that time gauze packing and large drains were used in great quantity. The mere presence of such foreign lumber in the abdominal cavity brought on shock and prevented the patient from readily summoning his own physiological resistance factors [1935, p. 155].

Morris twice mentions the problem of surgical shock, which, by the late 1880s, had become the leading cause of surgical mortality. The challenge of managing shock—the final barrier to the practical realization of the goal of surgically deep penetration—would await the pioneering animal experiments of the founder of "physiological surgery," George Washington Crile, a decade later. In a series of monographs published between 1899 and 1903, Crile established the correlation between reduced blood pressure and surgical shock, and, drawing on extensive laboratory investigations, reported on drugs that effectively combated the fluctuations in arterial pressure that occurred during surgery (English, 1980, pp. 83ff.).[10]

But even before Crile's research became widely known in the early years of our own century—and notwithstanding the mortality rate deriving from surgical shock—historians discern

---

[10] Of Crile's crowning contribution to the therapeutic management of shock, his *Blood Pressure in Surgery* (1903), English writes: "Crile offered the practicing surgeon for the first time a reliable means of diagnosing shock and monitoring its treatment in clinical cases. No longer would the surgeon need to rely on the weakened pulse or a sinking state of consciousness. Instead Crile presented a precise instrument and a rationale for its use. It was a contribution of the highest clinical order" (1980, p. 99). In research conducted during World War I, the Harvard physiologist Walter Cannon established that the decreased volume of circulating blood rather than falling blood pressure per se produced shock (pp. 137–139).

a sea change in the attitude of surgeons toward their specialty. The final decade and a half of the nineteenth century witnessed both the final triumph of Listerism and the emergence of the new science of bacteriology that underwrote this triumph. Bolstered by faith in bacteriology as a means of drastically reducing postoperative infections and buoyed as well by advances in surgical technique that led to successful operations for appendicitis, hernia, and intestinal cancer, surgeons increasingly espoused a triumphalist philosophy of "radical surgery" (Lawrence, 1992a, pp. 32–33). English (1980) believes that this self-characterization was ascendant among American surgeons by 1890 and defines it thusly: "By this phrase, they [viz., surgeons] signified their confidence in the merits of cutting, of removing the disease at its root, and of a bullish optimism that with surgery the patient could be saved but without an operation faced certain doom" (p. 20). It was only at this juncture in surgical history that surgeons acquired a radical confidence in the operative treatment of preexisting infections, including those of the abdomen, chest, and head. Whereas, a decade earlier, surgical wards were "ripe with pus," from the late 1880s on surgeons viewed the occurrence of postoperative infection and surgical fever as an exception to the rule of strict Listerian practice. In the context of this development, "to lose a patient from infection was becoming an unpardonable error reflecting poorly upon the surgeon's training, skill, and technique" (p. 30).

Radical surgery, which also went by the names of scientific surgery, physiological surgery, and experimental surgery, marked the modern ascendance of the surgical point of view, which, in turn, fell back on the surgical concept of disease (Lawrence, 1992a, p. 27). In Europe and especially in America, this point of view and this concept of disease have been associated with late nineteenth century "democratic heroism"—with the belief that surgeons were cultural heroes of democracy, since their operative skills brought healing to the many rather than the few. As surgery became "the medicine of democracy," so it acquired a newfound legitimacy that transformed it from the treatment of last resort to the therapy of choice (pp. 27, 31).

In noting the emergence of radical surgery, with its belief in the "merits of cutting" and its confident expectation of "removing the disease at its root," we are at the point of rejoining Freud and the surgical metaphor of psychoanalysis. For the surgical metaphor implicates a vision of surgery that has little in common with the nature and grounds of surgical practice prior to the late 1880s. Rather, Freud's metaphor grows out of a particular surgical vision that arose at a particular point in history; it enshrines the radical surgical ideal in the realm of talking therapy. How did this come to be?

"Surgery Was Different"
⚭

The understanding of surgery that Freud invoked in elaborating the surgical metaphor has several key biographical referents. Perhaps the most important one implicates his intense relationship to the Berlin internist and self-styled nose surgeon Wilhelm Fliess in the 1890s, but this relationship, in turn, is informed by the *image* of surgery and the surgeon that Freud imbibed during the period of his medical training. In what follows, we recur to the triumphalist tone appropriate to the strictly technical advances of surgery in the final quarter of the nineteenth century. This catalog of surgical breakthrough is not antithetical to the account of surgical history provided in the preceding chapter. Rather, it is a complementary perspective. We are no longer addressing the historical location of surgery within medicine, the operator's motives, or the healing efficacy of his ministrations and penetrations. Our concern now is with the growth of surgical skill and the resulting image of the surgeon on the eve of the era of radical surgery.

For the student Freud, as for medical students throughout Europe and America during the latter decades of the nineteenth century, surgery had become the apotheosis of the medical art and the surgeon the reigning monarch of the medical kingdom. If the nineteenth century writ large is "the century of the surgeon" (Thorwald, 1956), then the final quarter of the century witnessed the "triumph of surgery" (Thorwald, 1957) insofar as the progressive refinement of anesthesia administration and the advent of Listerian antisepsis and asepsis provided surgeons with a window of operative possibility that had never before existed. By making progressively lengthier and more elective procedures clinically possible, these developments gave surgeons the impetus both to develop a host of new procedures and to refine techniques adequate to these procedures.

By the early 1870s, it was becoming clear that surgeons had both a warrant and a technique for doing something when their medical colleagues could do nothing. And so it was that in an era of "therapeutic nihilism" (Johnston, 1972, chapter 15) in which scholarly diagnostics often was an end in itself, "surgery," in the words of the analyst Fritz Wittels, "was different" (Timmes, 1995, p. 25). Between 1873, when Freud entered medical school, and 1885, when he received his appointment as a privatdozent in neuropathology, the drumbeat of surgical advance built to a deafening crescendo throughout Europe and North America.

Already at the beginning of the 1870s there were notable breakthroughs: the first successful nephrectomies performed by Gustav Simon in Germany in 1870 and J. T. Gilmore of Alabama in 1872. In 1879, the Birmingham surgeon Lawson Tait, otherwise remembered as the first surgeon to remove an acutely inflamed appendix, initiated the era of gallbladder surgery with the successful removal of gallstones; three years later Carl Langenbuch, operating in the Lazarus Hospital in Berlin, demonstrated the feasibility of removing the entire calculus gall bladder.

From the mid-1870s, the Swiss surgeon Theodor Kocher and Freud's mentor Theodor Billroth pioneered thyroid gland surgery; in 1883, Kocher made the decisive advance, abandoning total removal of the gland for a partial removal that spared the patient the total absence of thyroid hormone that resulted in cretinism. Billroth, rightly deemed "one of the surgical giants of all time" (Ellis, 1996, p. 35), went on to achieve a succession of "firsts" across a broad surgical front. His breakthroughs in abdominal surgery, in particular, are a triumphal thread traversing the entire era, among them: one of the first colonic resections in 1879, the first successful gastric resection in 1881, and the first successful pancreatectomy for malignant disease in 1884.

The period of Freud's medical training likewise encompassed decisive breakthroughs in the understanding of brain functioning and the ensuing birth of modern neurosurgery. In 1870, three years before Freud began his medical training, the German physiologists Gustav Theodor Fritsch and Eduard Hitzig produced irrefutable experimental evidence of functional parcellation of the cerebral cortex, thereby laying to rest the unitary theory of regional brain functioning, which, under the aegis of Pierre Flourens, had dominated European medicine for the preceding half century (Clark and Jacyna, 1987, pp. 212ff.). A decade later, in August of 1881, the Third International Medical Congress in London was the scene of David Ferrier's powerful demonstration of the theory of cerebral localization put forth two decades earlier by the Parisian surgeon and anatomist Paul Broca, borne out by the experimental findings of Fritsch and Hitzig, and elaborated in the years to follow by the London clinician Hughlings Jackson. Three years later, two London physicians, the surgeon Rickman Godlee and the neurologist Hughes Bennett, offered the first dramatic realization of the promise of Fritsch and Hitzig's animal research by correctly diagnosing, locating, and surgically removing a cerebral tumor.

Scientific research enlarged upon these advances in praxis. In 1875, while Freud fitfully made his way through the preclinical curriculum of the University of Vienna, Claude Bernard published his *Leçons sur les anesthésiques,* the first experimental effort to achieve an understanding of the specific action of anesthesia on the central nervous system. Bernard's discovery of the combined effects of chloroform and morphine, spelled out in this same work, further enlarged the domain of nineteenth-century surgery by permitting anesthesia to be achieved with dramatically reduced doses of chloroform (Rey, 1993, pp. 175–178).

As Freud entered the period of his clinical training in 1876–77, he encountered clinical surgery as taught by one of the great medical authority figures of his life, the illustrious Theodor Billroth, whose achievements we have already touched on. Billroth had arrived in Vienna in 1867, the very year Joseph Lister, a surgeon from Edinburgh, announced his antisepsis method. To be sure, Billroth was a giant among European surgeons even before the introduction of Listerism. Between 1865 and 1870, for example, he was celebrated for perfecting ovariotomy technique to the point of eliminating the surgical risk of injuring the peritoneum (Lesky, 1976, p. 398).

Billroth's impact in Vienna in 1867 was immediate. Shortly after his arrival, he introduced systematic thermometry and launched a series of theoretical studies aimed at elucidating the role of microorganisms in wound diseases. And, with scalpel in hand, he went on to pioneer three fields of major surgery, with esophagus resection in 1871, laryngectomy in 1873, and, as noted above, gastrectomy in 1881.[1] The success of these new procedures testified not only to his surgical skill, but also to the rigorous physiological experimentation and thorough mastery of pathological anatomy that preceded each new surgical intervention (Lesky, 1976, pp. 397–398).

Following his surgical triumphs of the 1870s, Billroth's renown extended across the Atlantic; Americans joined their European colleagues in making Billroth's university clinic at Vienna's *Allgemeine Krankenhaus* a mandatory stop in their tours of the great European surgical clinics. To train under Billroth or under Kocher in Bern was to receive the best that Europe had to offer.[2]

Beginning with the winter session of 1876–77, Freud took four consecutive semesters of clinical surgery, all but the first with Billroth (Bernfeld, 1951, appendix, pp. 216–217). And of his three world-famous professors — Billroth, the dermatologist Hans Hebra, and the ophthalmologist Ferdinand von Arlt[3] —

---

[1] Ellis (1996, pp. 31–37) deems Billroth's successful gastrectomy of 1881, which followed the unsuccessful resections of the Parisian surgeon Jules Pean of 1879 and the Polish surgeon Ludwig Rydigier of 1880, one of the "operations that made history."

[2] "Dozens of American surgeons, now active, studied under him, and his name is a household word among us" (Mumford, 1908, p. 100). On the Americans who trained under Kocher, Billroth, and other European surgeons during the last three decades of the nineteenth century, see especially Bonner (1963, pp. 96–103).

[3] In his imposing contribution to medical history, *The Medical Sciences in the German Universities* (1876), Billroth situated Arlt (pp. 239–241) and Hebra (p. 243) within the historical development of their respective specialties. For his role in training Albrecht von Graefe, Arlt was one of three ophthalmologists deemed "the masters of the master, comparable with the teachers of Raphael and Mozart" (p. 240). Hebra, for his part, was counted "among the greatest teachers of modern times" (p. 243).

Billroth clearly held pride of place both during his training and throughout his life. It was Billroth who, at Breuer's urging, supported Freud's application for the Stipendium, or traveling grant, that took him to Paris and Charcot in 1885 (Jones, 1953, p. 74). And it was Billroth whose death in the winter of 1894 rated special mention to Fliess: "Billroth's death is the event of the day around here. How enviable not to have outlived oneself" (FFIL, p. 66).

Not to be overlooked in this chronology is the role of Josef Breuer, who likely made Freud's acquaintance in 1877, the very year Breuer himself, then in quest of a staff appointment to Vienna General Hospital, added the title "doctor of surgery" to his credentials.[4] Six years later, in 1883, this same Josef Breuer informed Freud of his treatment of the daughter of a well-to-do Viennese merchant, one Bertha Pappenheim, the famous "Anna O." of psychoanalytic lore, thereby introducing his young colleague to the so-called "cathartic" treatment method that served as precursor to the psychoanalytic method. By 1887, Breuer had effectively adopted Freud as his medical protégé, assigning Freud his nervous cases at a time when the younger man's reputation among his medical colleagues was at a decided low.

But during the time when Breuer was assuming the role of Freud's mentor, he was also becoming a valued junior colleague of Billroth's. And Billroth's estimation of Breuer grew during the 1880s: he not only offered to recommend Breuer for an associate professorship, the Extraordinariat, in 1884, but, like other senior medical faculty at the University, chose him as family doctor (Hirschmüller, 1978, pp. 27, 32). Indeed, Billroth placed himself in the hands of the experienced and competent (*Sachverständigen*) Breuer in coping with the progressive cardiovascular disease of his later years (Billroth, 1910, pp. 341, 458).

In matters scientific, the admiration was clearly mutual. Breuer's research on the cause of wound fever in the late 1860s

---

[4] "Candidates for positions in the public service [at the hospital], however, usually needed doctorates in both medicine and surgery, as well as a master's degree in obstetrics if possible" (Hirschmüller, 1978, p. 27).

was inspired by Billroth's work, and his findings confirmed the surgeon's belief that such fever was due to toxic substances released at the site of inflammation and not to reactive processes in the vegetative nervous system (Hirschmüller, 1978, pp. 52–53). Two decades later, when Breuer capped his research on the function of the semicircular canals in the labyrinth of the ear with a lengthy monograph on the function of the otoliths,[5] Billroth conveyed in writing the most heartfelt praise.[6]

Did Freud himself ever harbor surgical aspirations? Surely not, as far as we know. And yet his interlude of cocaine experimentation between 1884 and 1887 increased his proximity to surgery and surgeons in personally telling ways. Among Freud's therapeutic claims for cocaine use, his advocacy of cocaine as a treatment for morphine addiction figures prominently. But even this advocacy, so well known among Freud scholars, arose in the aftermath of a surgical procedure. And here we encounter Ernst von Fleischl-Marxow, the gifted and charismatic assistant of Ernst von Brücke, the premier medical researcher in Vienna. In the early 1880s, when Freud himself had gained entry to Brücke's laboratory as a student assistant, Fleischl became his mentor, friend, and acknowledged role model (Freud, 1925b, pp. 9–10).

Fleischl's sad demise has been carefully recorded by Bernfeld (1953) and Jones (1953). Fleischl was not only a gifted scientist in Brücke's laboratory but a "quite extraordinary character" whose gatherings attracted the avant garde of the Viennese medical world: Breuer, Freud, Exner, Chrobak, Czerny, and

---

[5] The otoliths are calculus formations within the membranous labyrinth of the ear.

[6] Hirschmüller quotes from Billroth's letter to Breuer of 23 March 1891, a portion of which I give here: ". . . I cannot refrain from telling you how excellent I consider your work to be, in both form and content. Everything unites there in one organic work of art — anatomical analysis and its physiological evaluation, experimental procedure, pathology, criticism. If the work had been carried out by a guild physiologist I would rate it very highly. I can only marvel that you yourself can have found the inspiration to do as much, when I consider your enormous commitments as a practicing physician which already tax you to near exhaustion in mind and body. The pure joy of scientific exploration and thought is manifest in every paragraph of your essay" (1978, p. 69).

Bettelheim, among others (Hirschmüller, 1978, pp. 31–32). In 1871, while conducting research in pathological anatomy, Fleischl contracted a life-threatening infection. While amputation of his right thumb saved his life, neuromata— tumors resulting from the enlargement of the ends of a nerve in the stump—resulted in excruciating nerve pain and led to a series of unsuccessful operations at the hands of Billroth himself. To control the pain, Fleischl resorted to morphine, to which he rapidly became addicted. And it was at this juncture that his young admirer and laboratory colleague Sigmund Freud intervened in his treatment by proffering a newly synthesized medicinal that held the promise, so Freud believed, of enabling Fleischl to overcome his morphine dependency.

In the full flush of his early enthusiasm for cocaine, Freud prescribed the drug, orally administered, to Fleischl in May of 1884. But Freud's hopes for the drug were never realized: Fleischl was successfully weaned from morphine, only to come under the grips of a more fatally intractable cocaine addiction within a week. Specifically, the huge doses of cocaine that Fleischl needed to control his morphine-induced symptoms quickly led to chronic intoxication followed by delirium tremens, the latter replete with hallucinations of white snakes crawling over his skin.

By 1887, when Freud's much publicized advocacy of cocaine for morphine addiction was eliciting harsh criticism in the medical press, Freud defended himself in the pages of the *Wiener Medizinische Wochenschrift* by noting that his recommendation of 1884 had pertained only to cocaine orally ingested and not cocaine administered by subcutaneous injection, a far riskier proposition.[7] And yet we know that

---

[7] Freud recurred to this defense in his associations to the dream of Irma's injection in *The Interpretation of Dreams* (1900). But, interestingly, he stopped short of recording any *objection* to Fleischl's hasty recourse to cocaine injections, noting only that he had "advised" Fleischl to use the drug orally (p. 115) and that he had "never contemplated the drug being given by injection" (p. 117). Jones discovered "no evidence of any protest on his [Freud's] part at the time," adding that some months later Freud himself was "advocating subcutaneous *injections* of large doses for just such cases as Fleischl's, i.e., withdrawal of morphine, and he presumably used them" (1953, p. 96, emphasis in original).

Fleischl, immediately on Freud's prescription of oral cocaine, contravened Freud and, without any apparent objection on Freud's part (Jones, 1953, p. 96), began to administer the drug via subcutaneous injection. We know further that Freud had been playing the surgeon in January 1885, when he tried to relieve the pain of trigeminal neuralgia in one of his patients by injecting cocaine into the nerve.[8] This experiment was unsuccessful, perhaps owing, as Jones (1953, p. 95) suggests, to Freud's "lack of surgical skill."[9]

But the absence of surgical skill did not prevent Freud from undertaking a similar experiment with Fleischl, whose suffering had only been compounded by cocaine addiction. In January 1885, Fleischl was in a pitiable state. When surgical interventions proved unavailing, Billroth, in a final, desperate attempt to ease the pain, subjected Fleischl's hand to electrical stimulation under narcosis. This treatment only intensified Fleischl's pain to the point that he was on several occasions found unconscious on the floor of his room. And so Freud himself entered the surgical fray with a new gambit: he undertook to relieve Fleischl's suffering with direct nerve injections of cocaine. Unsurprisingly, he was no more successful in easing the pain of neuromata than he had been in relieving his patient's trigeminal neuralgia.

If a lesson learned from the period of Freud's cocaine experimentation is that Freud was no surgeon, it is equally that he had reason to envy the surgeon. Some months before his unsuccessful recourse to nerve injections of cocaine, in the summer of 1884, he had recruited a colleague and acquaintance, Carl Koller, an assistant physician in the Vienna General

---

[8] Jones provides this otherwise unknown information (1953, p. 96), citing an unpublished letter from Freud to Martha Bernays of January 7, 1885. In point of fact, Freud was attempting to improve on a technique well known in his time: the modern hypodermic syringe, as developed by the Scottish physician Alexander Wood in the 1850s, was originally used to inject morphine into the peripheral nerves of neuralgia sufferers in order to induce a local analgesia. This remained the principal use of the hypodermic for the next quarter century and brought in its wake innumerable instances of morphine addiction (Howard-Jones, 1971).

[9] Cf. Thorwald: "[Freud] had so little surgical experience that in all probability he missed the nerve" (1957, p. 293).

Hospital's ophthalmic division, to help him undertake experiments on the systemic effects of cocaine. Koller, an aspiring ophthalmologist who, as a medical student, had heeded Arlt's call for a local anesthetic for eye surgery, had pursued this quest with animal experiments utilizing chloral, bromide, and morphine. The experiments were uniformly unsuccessful, but, as Koller recalled in 1928, "they had the good effect that my mind was prepared to grasp the opportunity whenever I should encounter a real anesthetic" (in Becker, 1963, pp. 273–274).

And so it was that, on ingesting cocaine, Koller was struck — as many before him, Freud included, had been struck — by the numbness of tongue that resulted from cocaine taken orally. In a moment of apparent epiphany, Koller realized that what Freud envisioned as an invigorating nerve tonic and quite probably an aphrodisiac (Swales, 1983, pp. 4–6) was in fact the local anesthetic he had long been seeking. In August 1884, he proceeded post haste to Salomon Stricker's anatomy lab, where, with the assistance of J. Gartner, Stricker's lab assistant, he topically applied a strong cocaine solution to the eyes, successively, of frogs, rabbits, dogs, and, finally, of Gartner and himself. He sealed his finding by persuading a patient in the eye clinic to undergo cocaine anesthesia, whereupon he secretly performed the first cataract operation in history under local anesthesia. The preliminary communication of his revolutionary finding was written in September and delivered by a colleague, a Dr. Brettauer of Trieste, at the Congress of German Oculists in Heidelberg on September 15 (Bernfeld, 1953, pp. 330–332; Thorwald, 1957, pp. 287–290). Koller provided a more elaborate description of his discovery to the Vienna Royal Imperial Society of Physicians a month later.[10]

Among those taken with Koller's discovery was William Stewart Halsted, a young American surgeon who, following graduation from the College of Physicians and Surgeons in New

---

[10] The English translation of this paper, which appeared in *The Lancet* (2:990–992, 1884) as "On the Use of Cocaine for Producing Anaesthesia on the Eye," is included in Cole's *Milestones in Anesthesia: Readings in the Development of Surgical Anesthesia, 1665–1940* (1965, pp. 141–148).

York in 1877, spent two years visiting the surgical clinics of European luminaries like Johann von Mikulicz, Ernst von Germann, Karl Thiersch, and of course Theodor Billroth. Following his return to New York, Halsted became interested in Koller's discovery of the anesthetizing effect of cocaine on the cornea, and, pursuing Koller's lead, he began experiments with his assistants, Richard J. Hall and Frank Harley, at Roosevelt Hospital. Struck by the long-lasting analgesic effects of cocaine solution injected first into and then under the skin, Halsted was emboldened to inject the drug directly into sensory nerves. Following an initial experiment in which the entire leg of an animal was numbed by cocaine injection into the sciatic nerve, he and his assistants undertook a series of anatomical studies to determine the precise locations at which pain-conducting nerves to the various extremities and organs could be effectively blocked. Through the discovery that cocaine injection anesthetized the entire area supplied by the branches of sensory nerves, Halsted was led to a second major discovery — a second major *surgical* discovery — attendant on Freud's endorsement of medicinal cocaine: that nerve block through cocaine injection could be utilized to achieve surgical anesthesia (Olch, 1975; Harvey, 1981, pp. 71–72); this marked the discovery of conduction or regional anesthesia.[11] Beginning in late 1884, Halsted and his group began employing cocaine-induced regional block in a variety of outpatient procedures, from the routine draining of abscesses and removal of nevi to more elaborate operations that included amputation of the penis, excision of the inferior dental nerve, and excision of

---

[11] Halsted's assistant, R. J. Hall, provided the first written account of cocaine-induced conduction anesthesia in the form of a letter to the Editor of the *New York Medical Journal* of November 26, 1884. Hall reported on two incidents of conduction anesthesia in which he himself figured as subject, initially for the removal of "a small congenital cystic tumor, situated directly over the outer third of the left supra-orbital ridge" by Halsted, and shortly thereafter "to have the left first upper incisor tooth filled." In the latter instance, he persuaded a "Dr. Nash, of No. 31 West Thirty-first Street" to perform an inferior dental nerve block. Hall's letter, which includes a summary of his and Halsted's early experiments on themselves, is reprinted in Cole (1965, pp. 149–153).

axillary lymph nodes.[12] Spinal block, successfully performed by James Leonard Corning in 1885 and first employed in surgery by August Bier in 1898, was the capstone of this discovery. Halsted, best known for his pioneering introduction of surgical asepsis in New York hospitals and subsequent development of the department of surgery at Johns Hopkins University between 1886 and 1889, succeeded where Freud, owing to "lack of surgical skill," simply failed.[13]

And so Freud's ill-fated period of cocaine experimentation, which claimed his friend Fleischl as a victim, culminated in two surgical triumphs in which Freud played no part. Bernfeld's otherwise useful investigation of this episode exemplifies "Whig history" applied to the psychoanalytic domain; he exculpates Freud by viewing his cocaine-related failures as harbingers of later analytic triumphs. In this manner, he turns Freud's investigatory failures on their head via an encomium:

> Yet, there is no indication that Freud would have invented local anesthesia even if he had devoted himself to the study of cocaine

---

[12] The tragic personal aftermath of these surgical successes was the cocaine addiction of Halsted, Hall, and two other assistants, all of whom became habituated to cocaine during their personal experimentation of 1884. Halsted's lifelong struggle with addiction has been ably investigated by Olch (1975). In the context of our concerns, it is worth mentioning that the trajectory of Halsted's addiction was opposite that of Freud's friend, Ernst von Fleischl. During a period of voluntary hospitalization at the Butler Hospital in Providence in 1886, Halsted was weaned from cocaine but became dependent on morphine. Olch's archival research sustains the claim that Halsted never overcame his morphine addiction and went on to achieve his remarkable status as "*a* Dean if not *the* Dean of American surgery . . . while harnessed to the specter of morphine addiction" (p. 486).

[13] In point of fact, the story of the surgical application of cocaine does not end here. There is a *third* notable discovery that occurred the following decade. In 1896, George Washington Crile, the American surgeon whose pioneering research effected a clinical revolution in the management of surgically induced shock, reported experiments on dogs, probably conducted before 1894, in which both topically applied cocaine and atropine blocked stimulation of the vagus nerve (which slows the heart rate) and its branches. This discovery significantly reduced the complications of laryngeal surgery as it was practiced at the time (English, 1980, p. 68). Crile had visited Billroth's surgical clinic in 1893 during his tour of German hospitals and clinics; Billroth, we recall, achieved early surgical renown for performing the first laryngectomy two decades earlier, in 1873.

with thoroughness and concentration. Freud's thoughts were not on surgery. By vocation a brain anatomist, he wanted to make the best of his situation. Since he had to be a physician, he wanted to be "a good doctor," one who relieves pain and restores the patient to normal well-being. He did not wish to be the dreaded surgeon, who cuts and hurts cruelly—although for the good of the patient [Bernfeld, 1953, p. 335].

But Bernfeld himself adduces evidence that calls into question the adequacy of this explanation. In 1884, pace Bernfeld, Freud wished to be a "good doctor" far less than an accomplished researcher, with fame and income adequate to his exalted ambitions and, no less importantly, to his urgently invested marriage plans. Freud was no surgeon, but he would gladly have reaped the surgeon's harvest in the matter of cocaine. "We may safely assume," Bernfeld concedes, "that he was disappointed and angry, at least with himself" (1953, p. 332) on learning in October 1884 of Koller's discovery of local anesthesia. In point of fact, Freud was profoundly disappointed, and, within several days of learning of Koller's breakthrough, he himself resorted to cocaine to overcome the resulting depression (Thorwald, 1957, p. 292). Bernfeld points out, further, "the subtle and hardly noticed in-fighting" between Koller and Freud that followed in the matter of Koller's acknowledgment of Freud's monograph, On Coca (1953, p. 334).

As to Halsted's perfection shortly thereafter of cocaine-induced nerve block, it turns out that Freud's lack of surgical skill was by no means transparent to Freud himself. To the contrary, Freud "often prided himself on his skill and luck with the needle and, for instance, advised [the ophthalmologist Leopold] Königstein on the finer points of technique" (Bernfeld, 1953, p. 349). Indeed, Freud had learned the technique of the hypodermic needle from one of his medical chiefs at the General Hospital, Franz Scholz, who allegedly played an important role in the early development of injection technique. Freud went on to employ the needle for some 10 years.[14] We

---

[14] Jones (1953, p. 96) writes that "It was his [Freud's] then chief, Professor Scholz, who had recently perfected the technique of the hypodermic needle, and doubtless Freud acquired it from him." He then cites an unpublished

know that morphine injections represented the "artificial means" by which Freud routinely "hastened the end" of the hysterical attacks of Frau Anna von Lieben, his most important patient, his *Hauptklientin*, between 1889 and 1893 (Swales, 1986, pp. 46, 51).[15] And, finally, we know of Freud's pride in possessing an injection technique that prevented his ever having caused infection — this latter fact being an important interpretive thread in "The Dream of Irma's Injection" with which he launched *The Interpretation of Dreams* (1900, p. 118). So in 1884, we may reasonably conclude, Freud would have willingly played the surgeon if the fame attendant to the medicalization of cocaine followed from its surgical employment. His absence of surgical sensibility and surgical technique redounded to his disadvantage; in the matter of medicinal cocaine, the surgeons prevailed and Freud himself was "relegated to a footnote" (Bernfeld, 1953, p. 332).

A poignant aftermath to Freud's cocaine episode occurred six months after Koller's discovery of the anesthetic properties of cocaine in eye surgery. On April 5, 1885, the elderly Jakob Freud called on his son Sigmund, complaining that his vision in one eye had deteriorated. Freud was inclined to make light

---

letter from Freud to Martha Bernays of 7 January 1885 in claiming that "he [Freud] employed it [the hypodermic needle] a good deal in the next ten years for various purposes." Alas, the nature of Scholz's contribution to hypodermic technique is a puzzle I could not solve. Scholz receives only a single, cursory mention by Lesky (1976, p. 355), where it is noted that Freud's training as secundarious (i.e., a resident) at the Vienna General Hospital from October 1882 through August 1885 included work "in the departments of Nothnagel and Meynert, and in the Fourth Department of Medicine headed by Franz Scholz." Scholz receives no mention in the two histories of early hypodermic usage I was able to locate (Howard-Jones, 1971; Haller, 1981). Nor was his identity and contribution known to the three knowledgeable historians of nineteenth-century medicine and surgery whom I contacted: Thomas Bonner, Christopher Lawrence, and Ghislaine Lawrence, the last, incidentally, the author of a superb essay on the history of surgical instrumentation (G. Lawrence, 1992). For one turn-of-the-century clinician's first-hand commentary on hypodermic technique, perhaps revelatory of those aspects of technique Freud learned from Scholz, see Davenport (1987, p. 72).

[15] See Swales's (1986, pp. 72–73, n57) consideration of the "distinct possibility" that Freud used drugs to facilitate the induction of hypnosis during his first decade of clinical practice.

of the symptom, but Koller, who was present at the time, examined the eye and diagnosed glaucoma. The following day, Leopold Königstein successfully operated on Jakob Freud. Fittingly, Koller administered topical cocaine anesthesia, assisted by Freud.[16] In his associations to the "Dream of the Botanical Monograph" of March 1898, which we discuss below, Freud recalled Koller's gracious comment at the time, that Jacob Freud's surgery "brought together all of the three men who had had a share in the introduction of cocaine" (1900, p. 171). But the "shares" were hardly equal, and Koller's remark, however well intended, must have reminded Freud of the fame he had narrowly missed. One is hard-pressed to imagine a more personal ratification of the surgical harvest of Freud's cocaine research. One surgeon wielded the scalpel that saved his father's eye; the other reaped the fame for discovering the anesthesia that made the surgery painless. Freud, the surgeon manqué, stood by and assisted.

---

[16] Jones (1953, p. 87) citing an unpublished letter from Freud to Martha Bernays of April 6, 1885, provides the information about Jakob Freud's vision complaint and Koller's diagnosis of glaucoma. The episode is also discussed by Grinstein (1980, p. 51).

"I Wish I Were a Doctor"

∞

It is not surprising, then, that for the neuropathically minded young Dr. Med. Freud, introduced to the surgeon's craft by Billroth, dreaming of success from nerve injections of cocaine, and fresh from the rigors of dissecting crayfish nerve cells in Brücke's laboratory and fetal medulla oblongata in Meynert's laboratory, surgical cutting became the metaphor for self-analysis. Nor is it surprising that Freud's intense relationship to the Berlin physician Wilhelm Fliess in the 1890s—his transference dependency, we may say—became wrapped up in his idealization of surgery as the ameliorative cutting that was beyond his modest medical endowment and that promised to heal in ways that mere psychology could not. Fliess was an academically ambitious general practitioner, whose medical studies at the Friedrich-Wilhelms-Universität in the early 1880s brought him into contact with the leading scientific lights of his time—Hermann Helmholtz, Emil du Bois-Reymond, Rudolf Virchow, and Carl Reichert. He made Freud's acquaintance, possibly through an introduction by Josef Breuer, during a three-month visit to Vienna in the late summer and early fall of 1887 (Swales, 1982, p. 4).

Freud's relationship with Fliess, his special friend and confidant of the 1890s, has been studied with great earnestness by historians and psychoanalysts over the years. And well it should be, given the momentous period in Freud's development when the friendship was at its most intense. For it was during this period of time, from approximately 1894 to 1900, that Freud not only became estranged from Josef Breuer, till then his mentor and professional patron, but devised a new psychotherapeutic procedure, dubbed "psychoanalysis," which he began

49

announcing to his medical colleagues. More intriguing still, during the latter part of this period, Freud proceeded to employ the new procedure on his own person—or rather on his own mind—in the manner of a "self-analysis," one fruit of which was his extraordinarily self-revelatory magnum opus of 1900, *The Interpretation of Dreams*. And then, with these accomplishments already laid up for posterity, Freud and Fliess became bitterly disaffected with one another.

Psychoanalysts have traditionally understood the ending of this strange and intriguing relationship as a product of Freud's self-analysis. Through his systematic psychological self-investigation, so it has long been held, Freud eliminated the basis of his intellectual and emotional reliance on Fliess; the self-analysis "resolved the transference," to borrow the psychoanalytic idiom. This understanding of the friendship, which makes Fliess entirely epiphenomenal to Freud's ascent to self-understanding and scientific maturity, has been revised over the past three decades, thanks in large part to the research of the historians Frank Sulloway and Peter Swales and the psychoanalyst Max Schur. Whereas Sulloway (1979) rescued Fliess's intellectual reputation from oblivion and Swales (1982) reconstructed his professional development, Schur (1966), relying on then unpublished correspondence between Freud and Fliess, earlier documented several significant episodes in which Freud's dependence on the Berlin internist-cum-surgeon went beyond the simple exchange of ideas.

Following publication of the complete Freud–Fliess correspondence in 1985, we are able to document fully what Schur first adduced: that Freud was extraordinarily dependent on Fliess for medical advice regarding not only his patients but his family members and himself as well.[1] Throughout 1894, Freud repeatedly pitted Fliess's judgment against that of Breuer,

---

[1] As early as June 28, 1892, Freud acknowledged that "my respect for your diagnostic acumen has only increased further," and by the fall of 1892 he already placed great stock in Fliess's diagnosis at a distance. See, for example, the case of Mr. F. and Fliess's diagnosis, which neither Freud nor the family physician could confirm, of flat-footedness (FFlL, pp. 33–34). Fliess's medical authority, in turn, was intensified by Freud's serious cardiac crisis of 1894 (Schur, 1972).

whose long-standing personal and financial support had come to elicit Freud's increasing resentment. In April, beset with diagnostic uncertainty about the gravity of his cardiac symptoms, Freud deemed Fliess "more competent than anyone else to make a differential diagnosis in these delicate matters" — delicate matters that left him "confounded in what to make of my condition" (FFlL, p. 69). Two months later, in the fullness of his dissatisfaction with Breuer, with his "apparent contradictions" and lack of concern (p. 85), Freud turned again to his special friend from Berlin:

> I would be endlessly obliged to you, though, if you were to give me a definite explanation, since I secretly believe that you know precisely what it [viz., Freud's cardiac condition] is, and that you have been so absolute and strict in your prohibition of smoking—the justification for which is after all relative—only because of its educational and soothing effect [FFlL, pp. 85–86].

When Fliess chastised Freud for resuming smoking again, his authority was not to be questioned even if his recommendations could be temporized; his word alone sufficed to "rob" Freud "of [his] enjoyment of tobacco." With respect to the medical management of his continuing cardiac symptoms, Fliess remained the authority, the consultant without equal: "Should I take digitalis frequently or rarely? I promise to obey" (p. 87).

Over the summer of 1894, there is an effortless segue from Fliess's medical authority to his surgical authority. And surgery, in the context of the Fliess relationship, is always nose surgery, namely, cutting into the turbinate bones[2] and the sinuses. Eventually, Fliess, with seeming disregard of the important role of the turbinates in nasal physiology, would come to advocate

---

[2] The three turbinates (superior, middle, and inferior) are elongated laminae of bone that divide the nasal cavity or "fossa" into three areas or "meati." Each turbinate consists of a scroll-like bony skeleton covered with a thick mucous membrane. The turbinates emanate, respectively, from the ethmoid bone (superior and middle turbinates) and from the superior maxilla and palate (inferior turbinate) (Morrison, 1948, p. 232; Ballenger, 1969, pp. 2–3).

surgical excision of the middle turbinate for a variety of nonrhinological reasons.[3] How did this come to be?

Fliess, we have long known, was among the last great proponents of nineteenth-century "reflex theory"—a set of ideas coalescing in the belief that a given organ, via nervous connections running down the spine, could exert its influence at distant sites within the body (Shorter, 1992, pp. 40ff.). Fliess's particular variant of this theory, which originated with the work of the Breslau rhinologist Friedrich Voltolini in 1871 and gained followings in Germany, Austria, and the United States in the 1880s, focused on the nose; hence the designation "nasal reflex theory." The central interlocking ideas were that thickening of nasal mucosa over the turbinate bones or conchi could "reflexly" cause remote disease, and that such disease, in turn, was treatable by reducing the engorgement of the rich bed of veins in these nasal structures (Shorter, 1992, pp. 64–65). In a series of publications beginning in 1893, Fliess claimed to have located actual "genital" and "stomach" sites on the nasal mucosa and reported dabbing the former with cocaine as a treatment for painful menstruation (dysmenorrhea).[4]

The belief that reflex irritation of nasal mucosa was specifically connected to the genitals and could cause neurosis was

---

[3] In modern rhinology, surgery of the turbinates, up to and including partial turbinectomy, is a treatment of last resort for severe allergic or "hyperplastic" rhinitis that does not yield to conventional treatment. The latter always addresses the patient's predisposing allergies and may also entail removal of obstructive polyps, correction of nasal septal deviations, and submucosal cauterization of the inferior turbinate. Turbinate surgery is undertaken to remove obstructing tissue that persists despite such measures: "If much hyperplastic tissue remains along the inferior borders of the inferior or middle turbinates after adequate cauterization and obstructive symptoms persist, the excessive redundant tissue may be removed by means of straight or curved nasal scissors or snare. Care should be taken to leave the turbinates themselves and the nasal mucous membrane in as nearly intact condition as possible, otherwise marked disturbances of the nasal physiology might occur" (Ballenger, 1969, p. 105).

[4] As Sulloway (1979, pp. 147–152) has documented, Fliess's notion of a nasogenital relationship was independently arrived at by the Baltimore laryngologist John Noland Mackenzie in 1884 and endorsed at century's end by no less a medical personage than Richard von Krafft-Ebing. Further, as late as 1914, "Fliess's ideas on nasogenital disorders were still being openly discussed and zealously defended on an evolutionary as well as on a clinico-medical basis" (p. 151).

especially congenial to Fliess and for a time to Freud as well. More generally, Freud was not only enthusiastic about Fliess's "discoveries" in the domain of nasal reflex theory but was fully accepting of the treatment recommendations that followed from them—up to and including indications for nasal surgery. In this latter respect, I propose, Freud's transference dependency on Fliess was fueled by an idealization of surgeons and surgery, which, as we have seen, was rooted in the period of Freud's medical training. On August 29, 1894, on the eve of Fliess's own turbinate/sinus surgery for relief from severe headaches, Freud gave way to passive wonderment before the surgeon's— any surgeon's—blade. He confessed to Fliess:

> I wish I were a "doctor," as people say, a physician and a great healer so that I could understand such matters and would not have to leave you in strange hands and in such circumstances. Unfortunately I am not a doctor, as you know. I must rely on you in this as in everything else; I must hope that you also know how to treat yourself and that you can be as successful in your own case as in those of others (myself included) [FFlL, p. 95].

Five months later, on the eve of Fliess's arrival in Vienna to examine and operate on one Emma Eckstein, of whom more below, Freud mused about Fraulein Eckstein's imminent operation in comparably submissive terms. Would Fliess's operation help Eckstein? Did Freud have the right to expect so much from it? He confessed to Fliess that "my lack of medical knowledge once again weighs heavily on me. But I keep repeating to myself: so far as I have some insight into the matter, the cure must be achievable by this route. I would not dare to invent this plan of treatment on my own, but I confidently join you in it" (FFlL, p. 107).

The idealizing trend in Freud's surgical estimation of Fliess was likely bolstered by the collegial rapport of Breuer and Fliess. An analogy with Billroth suggests itself: just as Breuer's admiring friendship with Billroth could only have reinforced Freud's high estimation of his surgical mentor, so it was with Fliess. We know that Breuer was in friendly correspondence with the German internist-cum-nose-specialist, at least from the beginning of 1894, and that their relationship led to reciprocal referrals: while Fliess asked Breuer to attend to the medical problems of Fliess's mother-in-law, Pauline Bondy,[5] Breuer referred his own patients, including his daughter Dora, to Fliess for otolaryngological evaluation and, on Fliess's recommendation, nose surgery.

The ten letters from Breuer to Fliess included as an appendix to Hirschmüller's study of Breuer suggest the routine nature of Breuer's referrals. In March of 1895, when Fliess was still recuperating from one of his periodic bouts of influenza, Breuer asked his colleague to "be so kind as to let me know when you are back at work, so that I can dispatch my people to B[erlin]" (in Hirschmüller, 1978, p. 313). Breuer's letters discuss four such referrals, and there is an especially touching letter of March 19, 1895 from Dora Breuer to Fliess, written because her father had informed her of Fliess's "inquiry as to how things are with my nose." Young Fraulein Breuer preferred to write to Fliess herself,

> since Papa can have no idea how happy I am that you have done this for me. I don't wheeze any more, and the buzzing and occasional deafness in my ears has ceased. I am so happy, and sometimes I think how awfully stupid I must have looked always going round with my mouth open. I only hope that Selma B. [another of Breuer's referrals] is just as fortunate when she gets back from Berlin. Thank you very, very much [p. 314].

Freud's idealization of Fliess, likely abetted by his knowledge of Breuer's own amicably trusting relations with the Berlin nose surgeon, frames the sad story of Emma Eckstein, the daughter of a Viennese industrialist whom Freud was treating gratis for hysterical symptoms early in 1895.[6] Intent on determining

---

[5] In point of fact, Breuer had served as family physician to the Bondy family and thus came to know Ida Bondy, Fliess's future wife, when she was a child (Hirschmüller, 1978, p. 416n).

[6] The story of Eckstein was first brought to light by Max Schur in 1966 in "Some Additional 'Day Residues' of 'The Specimen Dream of Psychoanalysis.'" Schur had access to the then unpublished correspondence of Freud and Fliess that documents this episode and its aftermath. Eckstein, be it noted, has her own minor role in the history of psychoanalysis. Prior to the period of her invalidism, she wrote articles and a booklet on the sexual enlightenment of children—with Freud's support and even participation. Following her nine-month analysis with Freud in the mid-1890s, she

whether there was a contributory "nasal origin" to what he construed as hysterical abdominal symptoms, Freud summoned Fliess to Vienna, where the latter recommended and performed surgery of the turbinate bone and one of the sinuses.

Prior to Eckstein's surgery, it now appears, Fliess's ministrations in cases of alleged "actual neuroses" had been noninvasive, being limited to applications of cocaine and cauterization. But with Eckstein, he apparently leapt to major surgery and, in line with published reports of his experience at the time, undertook to remove the patient's left middle turbinate bone (Masson, 1984, pp. 60).[7] Then, as was customary during the 1890s, he tightly packed the site of the operation—in this case the nasal cavity—with gauze impregnated with a weakly disinfectant iodine solution, iodoform.[8]

The operation proved far from successful, and, when Eckstein's swelling and persistent pain were followed by massive

---

remained in contact with him over the following decade and, in 1905, appealed to him, unsuccessfully, to take her back into analysis. Freud, while declining to resume analytic work with her—especially on the gratis basis she insisted on—nonetheless retained some small involvement in her medical management in ensuing years. He prescribed boric acid for her on at least one occasion in 1910 (Masson, 1984, p. 245), presumably in the context of severe vaginal hemorrhages that led to gynecological evaluation and subsequent hysterectomy. On Eckstein, see Masson (1984, pp. 233–250) and Swales (1997, p. 126).

[7] Masson (1984, pp. 75–78), drawing on Fliess's publications of the period, summarizes the peculiar (to say the least) reasoning that underlay Fliess's belief that the "neuralgic alterations" caused by nasal reflex neurosis could be surgically remedied in this manner.

[8] Iodoform, or tri-iodomethane (CHI_3), was first used as an antiseptic in 1878 (Schmitz et al., 1993, p. 23), and gauze impregnated with iodoform was commonly used during the 1890s to pack the abdominal cavity after appendectomy. The surgeon Robert Morris, an outspoken critic of this procedure, recounted that "In addition to ordinary packing and drains, iodoform gauze was commonly used, and this had a special death rate of its own because of insidious iodoform poisoning—the symptoms of which are so like those of sepsis that deaths were set down to the account of sepsis when really due to iodoform" (Morris, 1935, p. 156). Despite such incidents, the use of iodoform as a topical wound dressing continued right through the 1960s, when it was replaced by mercurochrome. In the 1940s and 50s, before the widespread availability of antibiotics for childhood infections, pediatricians and family doctors routinely swabbed the throats of ill children with iodine preparations; indeed, tincture of iodine is still available at well-stocked pharmacies (William Stepansky, personal communication).

hemorrhage and a fetid odor, Freud reluctantly but anxiously called in Robert Gersuny, the prominent Viennese surgeon with whom Freud had wanted Fliess to consult before undertaking Eckstein's operation (FFlL, p. 106) and who may well have been Fliess's own surgeon (p. 197n).

Gersuny examined Eckstein and inserted a drainage tube on March 4. When Freud was awakened in the morning of March 6 and informed of the resumption of his patient's pain with profuse bleeding, he again sought immediate surgical help. When Gersuny proved unavailable until the following evening, Freud summoned another Viennese otolaryngologist, Horaz Ignaz Rosanes. Rosanes was no stranger to Freud; an adolescent companion who spent time the summers of 1872 and 1873 with Freud, Rosanes matriculated to the University of Vienna, where he remained part of Freud's "wider circle" (FSL, p. 71) and, as such, was the object of a number of disparaging barbs in Freud's letters to Eduard Silberstein.[9] Rosanes rushed to Eckstein's bedside, where his postsurgical ministrations led to the following extraordinary discovery:

R[osanes] cleaned the area surrounding the opening, removed some blood clots which were sticking to the surface, and suddenly pulled at something like a thread. He kept right on pulling, and before either of us had time to think, at least a half meter of gauze had been removed from the cavity. The next moment came a flood of blood. The patient turned white, her eyes bulged, and her pulse was no longer palpable. However immediately after this he packed the cavity with fresh iodoform gauze, and the hemorrhage stopped. It had lasted about half a minute, but this was enough to make the poor creature, who by then we had lying quite flat, unrecognizable. . . . So we had

---

[9] Two examples will suffice. From a letter to Silberstein of August 28, 1873: ". . . I am glad that your company will render superfluous that of the amphibian Rosanes, who has nothing of the student save certificates, nothing of the dreamer save lack of judgment, nothing of the nobleman save indolence, and for the rest has cold blood and a pointed nose" (FSL, p. 45). And from a letter to Silberstein of November 8, 1874: "Wahler and Rosanes are distinguishing themselves neither by their industry nor by their indolence; in Wahler life seems to be falling asleep, in Rosanes to continue its somnolence. I hope that you will refrain from referring to this denunciation in your letter to them" (p. 71).

done her an injustice. She had not been abnormal at all, but a piece of iodoform gauze had gotten torn off when you removed the rest, and stayed in for fourteen days, interfering with the healing process, after which it had torn away and provoked the bleeding [Schur, 1972, 56–57; FFlL, pp. 116–117].

Through careful examination of Freud's ensuing reports to Fliess on Fraulein Eckstein's condition, as revealed in the Freud–Fliess correspondence (then unpublished, but to which Schur had access), the late Max Schur explored the meaning of the episode in terms of Freud's transferential idealization of Fliess and the subsequent loosening of this positive transference. According to Schur, Freud's strained exoneration of Fliess's surgical negligence took the form of successive displacements, wherein the culprit in this surgical mishap was, variously, Freud himself (for urging Fliess precipitously to operate in Vienna), the iodoform gauze (which, in Freud's wording, simply "had gotten torn off"), and the consulting surgeon (for thoughtlessly pulling at the exposed threads of gauze). Everyone, so it seemed, was responsible except Fliess himself:

> You handled it as well as possible. The tearing off of the iodoform gauze was one of those accidents that happen to the most fortunate and cautious of surgeons. . . . Of course no one blames you in any way, nor do I know why they should. And I only hope that you will come as quickly as I did to feel only pity. Rest assured that I felt no need to restore my trust in you. I only want to add that I hesitated for a day to tell you all about it, and that then I began to be ashamed, and here is the letter [Schur, 1972, p. 58].

The Emma episode proved a crucial signpost in Freud's journey of self-discovery. Here, I wish to highlight a complementary dimension of the episode: its revelatory character as an index of Freud's complex relationship to surgery and surgeons. Schur, less taken with Freud's complicity with Fliess's surgical recklessness than with the absorption of the Eckstein incident into Freud's self-analytic process, stressed the degree to which the incident helped Freud work through, and ultimately resolve, his transference dependency on Fliess. In this regard, he followed Jones, for whom the unusual aspects of Freud's "passionate friendship" with Fliess paled before the extraordinary dissolution of that friendship through "the heroic task of exploring his own unconscious mind" (1953, p. 316). Neither looked to the episode as a signpost pointing to the surgical metaphor. But this collateral meaning is surely present. In the aftermath of Fliess's bungled operation, when Eckstein's condition further deteriorated, it was only the surgeons who could set matters right. The regrettable lesson learned was that only surgeons could make good the carelessness, even incompetence, of other surgeons. In the aftermath of Fliess's bungled operation, but for the "swift intervention" of Rosanes and Gersuny, the surgeon's surgeons, Emma Eckstein "might well have died" (Masson, 1984, p. 66).

"I Never Did Any Harm
With My Injections"
⟨∞⟩

The Eckstein incident is a telling barometer of Freud's transference dependency on Wilhelm Fliess and the medico-surgical context in which this transference was enacted. Throughout the 1890s, Freud's and Fliess's intellectual twinship was mirrored by their shared nasal pathology, with Freud suffering from empyema of the sinuses and Fliess from suppurative rhinitis. In their correspondence, the health of their respective noses is discussed "at self-indulgent length" (Anzieu, 1975, p. 142). As Anzieu goes on to observe:

> They were, so to speak, bound together by their noses, a bond made all the stronger by cocaine: Freud revealed the substance to medicine, and only just failed to discover its anesthetic properties; Fliess urged his patients, Freud's patients and Freud himself to undergo treatment of the affected parts of the nose with a local application of cocaine [p. 142].

In matters of nasal pathology, Fliess was not only Freud's mentor but his personal physician. It is thus unsurprising that Fliess took the occasion of his trip to Vienna in February 1895, when he examined and operated on Emma Eckstein, to examine Freud and cauterize his bothersome turbinate bones (Anzieu, 1975, pp. 142, 144).

This convergence—Fliess as authoritative consultant and Fliess as trusted personal physician and surgeon—suggests that, throughout the 1890s, Freud's professional self-worth and personal well-being had medical referents that drew him into the world of surgeons and surgery. It is in this context that we

59

turn to Freud's celebrated dream of Irma's injection of July 24, 1895. This "specimen dream" may be crucially implicated in Freud's discovery of the analytic method and process (Blum, 1996), but it is equally revelatory of the surgical preoccupations that subtended the birth of psychoanalysis.

Beginning with Erikson's (1954) pioneering examination of the dream in terms of issues of life cycle and ego identity, the Irma dream has generated a substantial secondary literature, much of it explicitly biographical.[1] Our brief reprise seeks to highlight one little-explored tributary of the river of biographical insights flowing from the dream. I refer to the status of the dream as the capstone of the decade of surgical consciousness that began with the period of cocaine experimentation and continued into the period of medicosurgical dependency on Fliess. To borrow the language of the British analyst Wilfred Bion, the dream functions as a "container" of the protracted medicosurgical self-questioning that was a principal legacy of the cocaine episode and continued into the period of intense friendship with Fliess.

Freud dreamed what commentators have long-since designated "the dream of Irma's injection" during the night of July 23–24, 1895. The dream takes as its manifest protagonist "Irma," who, we now know, was Anna Hammerschlag, the family friend and soon-to-be godmother of Anna Freud and one of Freud's first—and favorite—analytic patients during the mid-90s.[2] The residue of the Irma dream concerned the residual somatic symptoms that remained in the wake of Freud's analytic treatment of Hammerschlag, as reported by Freud's friend, the pediatrician Oskar Rie. Following a visit with Hammerschlag

---

[1] Anzieu (1975) and Grinstein (1980) are high points of the literature that follows Erikson (1954). Blum (1996) usefully reviews a portion of the more recent journal literature.

[2] "Irma" was originally believed to be none other than Emma Eckstein, a claim first made by Schur (1972), shared by Roazen (1975), and carried over most recently by Blum (1996). But the weight of converging biographical evidence now points decisively to Anna Hammerschlag (Peter Swales, personal communication), and this in fact was the judgment of Anzieu (1975, p. 134), Krüll (1979), and Masson (1984). Masson reports that Anna Freud, in conversation, confirmed that "Irma" was in fact Anna Hammerschlag (p. 205n).

and her family at a summer resort, Rie visited Freud and informed him that Anna, his former patient, was "better, but not quite well," a remark that Freud construed as a veiled reproach (1900, p. 106) directed at his treatment methods. Significantly, in view of the dream that followed, Rie then related that during this brief visit with the Hammerschlags, he "had been called in to a neighboring hotel to give an injection to someone who had suddenly felt unwell" (p. 115).

Rie, be it noted, was a colleague of some standing. He had attended Freud's lectures at the University of Vienna in 1886–1887 and shared authorship of the "Clinical Study of Half-Sided Cerebral Paralysis of Children," which the two published in 1891 (Mühlleitner, 1992, p. 271). He also served as Freud's assistant on the pediatric-neurology service of Vienna's Kassowitz Institute for Children's Diseases from 1886 to 1896; Freud had sufficient confidence in him to use him as his children's pediatrician. It is thus understandable that Rie's remark about Irma's unresolved symptoms should have left a "disagreeable impression" (p. 106) and prompted Freud to justify his nontraditional treatment of Anna Hammerschlag. He set out to write her case history that very evening, intending to submit it for review, and presumably approval, to a far higher authority than Oskar Rie: Josef Breuer.

The dream to which Rie's collegial disclosures and Freud's strategy of exoneration gave rise is, among other things, a reprise on the issues of medical and surgical competence that emerged during the period of Freud's cocaine experimentation and medicosurgical dependence on Fliess. The manifest dream transposes Freud to the role of surgical consultant, namely, the examining otolaryngologist (i.e., Fliess) who peers down the throat of Irma and discovers scabs on the turbinate bones. Freud associates to his own "troublesome nasal swellings," the "extensive necrosis of the nasal mucous membrane" of another patient, and finally to the Fleischl episode and the "serious reproaches" brought down on him for prescribing cocaine (1900, p. 111).

The self-analytic insights about these "reproaches" carry with them a recapitulation of other instances of diagnostic uncertainty and medical mishap. There is Irma's "intimate woman friend" whom Breuer examined and found to have a "diptheritic membrane" but whom Freud suspected of hysteria (1900, p. 110). And there is reference to another "woman patient" in whom Freud induced "a severe toxic state" by repeatedly prescribing sulphonal, then thought to be a "harmless remedy." In this case, too, we learn of Freud's recourse to the authoritative Breuer, the "experienced senior colleague" to whom he turned for "assistance and support" (p. 111) in this trying matter. Finally, there is the case of the "young man with remarkable difficulties associated with defecating," whom Freud again diagnosed as hysteric and felt comfortable sending off on a sea voyage. When he received a "despairing letter" from the young man, then in Egypt, who reported a fresh attack diagnosed as dysentery, Freud stood by his diagnosis, but with an equivocation born of previous errors of medical judgment. "I suspected that the diagnosis was an error on the part of an ignorant practitioner who had allowed himself to be taken in by the hysteria," he wrote. "But I could not help reproaching myself for having put my patient in a situation in which he might have contracted some organic trouble on top of his hysterical intestinal disorder" (p. 114).

Via the dreamwork, Freud's medical self-reproaches elicit a spirited denial that borrows from the surgeon's technical arsenal. To wit, in subjecting medical colleagues and "supervisors" (Blum, 1996) to ridicule, the dream underscores the fact that Freud deemed himself good with the needle. In the manifest dream imagery, it was the pediatrician Rie who stood accused of "thoughtlessly" giving Irma an injection, and with a syringe that likely "had not been clean" (p. 107) at that. Freud associated this dream element to "an old lady of eighty-two to whom [he] had to give an injection of morphia twice a day." On learning that she had contracted phlebitis while in the country, Freud assigned blame to the country physician then attending her; the phlebitis resulted from "an infiltration caused by a dirty syringe." Freud himself stood blameless. "I was proud of the fact," he notes, "that in two years I had not caused a single infiltration; I took constant pains to be sure that the syringe was clean. In short, I was conscientious" (p. 118). Freud's exemplary technique with the syringe came to his rescue in the latent dream thoughts, where it exculpated him from any responsibility for Irma's continuing somatic difficulties and thereby served the wish-fulfilling function of the dream. In the manifest dream imagery and the thoughts accompanying it, "Irma's pains had been caused by Otto [i.e., Rie] giving her an incautious injection of an unsuitable drug—a thing *I* should never have done. Irma's pains were the result of an injection with a dirty needle, like my old lady's phlebitis—whereas *I* never did any harm with my injections" (p. 119).

"Harm with my injections" is likely overdetermined. It represents the harm occasioned by psychological treatment— what would evolve into the psychoanalytic method—in the presence of serious organic pathology. Correspondingly, it conveys Freud's medicosurgical foreboding about what he had or had not done in those instances when he had ranged outside the domain of talking therapy. In this sense, Freud's complicity in Fleischl's use of cocaine injection is the shadow of his avowed innocence as a diagnostician and prescriber, an innocence that encompassed Anna Hammerschlag's alleged organic pathology, his young man's alleged dysentery, his prescription of sulfunol, and his recourse to morphia injections. And Freud's insistence on physicianly rectitude, on his own "harmless injections," may even allude to the great surgical discovery that was attendant to the writing of *On Coca* in 1884 but nonetheless passed him by—Carl Koller's discovery that local injections of cocaine rendered eye surgery painless, providing the surgeon with ample time and a stationary surgical field, hence making common surgical procedures relatively harmless as far as patient and surgeon were concerned.

Freud's "botanical monograph" dream of early March 1898, more than two-and-a-half years after the dream of Irma's injection, bears eloquent testimony to the enduring quality of these surgical preoccupations. On this occasion, the legacy of the cocaine episode had become interwoven with them. In association to the dream image of a monograph on a plant, Freud associated post haste to his own monograph on the coca plant, "which had drawn Carl Koller's attention to the anesthetic properties of cocaine." He had been reminded of "this business of the cocaine" several days before having the dream, when he came across a Festschrift honoring the pathologist Solomon

Stricker and observed that, among the achievements of Stricker's laboratory itemized therein, was "the fact that Koller had made his discovery there of the anesthetic properties of cocaine" (1900, p. 171).

From here, Freud associated to a walk the evening preceding his dream with Leopold Königstein, Freud's "choice of ophthalmologists" in the matter of cocaine research, and the one who initially contested Koller's priority in the surgical application of topical cocaine; Königstein, we recall, had operated on Freud's father for glaucoma in April of 1885, on which occasion Koller, assisted by Freud, administered the cocaine anesthesia. And who should Freud and Königstein have encountered during their conversation but Professor Gartner and his wife, the very J. Gartner who, as Stricker's lab assistant, had assisted Koller in the original animal experiments with topical cocaine—and had not stopped short of lending Koller his own eyeball as an experimental object—in August of 1884.

This intriguing cluster of cocaine revenants constituted a central day residue of the botanical monograph dream. But, more, it culminated in a daydream about cocaine the morning after the dream. Freud recounted it in this way:

> I had thought about cocaine in a kind of day-dream. If ever I got glaucoma, I had thought, I should travel to Berlin and get myself operated on, incognito, in my friend's [Fliess's] house, by a surgeon recommended by him. The operating surgeon, who would have no idea of my identity, would boast once again of how easily such operations could be performed since the introduction of cocaine; and I should not give the slightest hint that I myself had had a share in the discovery [1900, p. 170].

Freud immediately discerned the relationship between this daydream and his father's glaucoma surgery 13 years earlier. But he did not explore in his dream analysis the meaning of the transposition, since it was now Freud who, struck with glaucoma, submitted to surgery at the hands of the anonymous eye surgeon to whom Fliess referred him—at the hands, that is, of a surgeon of such skill and authority that Freud need not bother himself with the surgeon's identity or the grounds of the procedure to which he submitted. A surgeon, that is, like Fliess himself.

Anzieu (1975, p. 291) suggests that the daydream, along with the botanical monograph dream itself, alludes to Freud's recent disagreement with Fliess over bilaterality and bisexuality. In the glaucoma daydream, he submits, Freud "identifies with his father and sees Fliess as the ungrateful Koller, who later took all the credit for the discovery" of the anesthetic properties of cocaine. Perhaps. Certainly, by this time (viz., March 1898) Freud's relationship with Fliess was beginning to encounter difficulties, with the issue of priority at least latently present. But we remain closer to the manifest content of the daydream and closer to Freud's medicosurgical dependency on Fliess in simply observing that, in the daydream, Freud has again entrusted himself to the surgeon Fliess, just as he comfortably entrusted his father to his friend, the surgeon Königstein, in 1885.

Surgery and matters of surgical judgment continued to bear the interpersonal weight of Freud dependency on Fliess in 1898. Several weeks before dreaming the botanical monograph dream, in late April, Freud had resigned from the editorial board of *Wiener klinische Rundschau* in protest over a dismissive review of Fliess's volume of the previous year, *The Relationship Between the Nose and the Female Sexual Organs*; in the same letter, he expressed pleasure that Fliess had taken over the medical care of "poor Mizi," his sister Marie Freud (FFlL, pp. 310–311). By early May, Freud was trying to schedule Fliess's evaluation of his daughter Mathilde for throat surgery; he hoped Fliess would find time for her when he next journeyed to Vienna at Whitsun, "and you may then, perhaps, recommend the necessary throat operation, which Hajek can carry out here" (FFlL, p. 313; cf. p. 314).

There is no question, then, that Fliess's surgical judgment remained uncontested during the same period that theoretical tensions and concerns about priority began to drive a wedge between Freud and Fliess. Indeed, one could argue, complementary to Didieu, that medicosurgical reliance on Fliess represented Freud's best strategy for containing ambivalence toward Fliess, a last bastion of denial of the strains of an intellectual companionship whose erosion was underway.

The fateful endpoint of this erosion is alluded to more than a year later in Freud's "Self-Dissection" dream of May 1899.

Here Freud's disengagement from Fliessian surgery is signaled by the realization that psychoanalysis can proceed without medicosurgical anchorage, that it provides a self-contained rationale for a genre of psychic surgery uniquely its own. The dream takes place at the very time *The Interpretation of Dreams* "is suddenly taking shape"—a period when Freud finally became reconciled to the compromising personal disclosures that publication would entail (FF1L, p. 353). So reconciled, Freud engaged his final task pursuant to publication, the task Fliess had set him (p. 355)—the review of dream literature out of which he would compose the introduction that framed his magnum opus. "After the literature," he advised Fliess, "there will be deletions, insertions, and the like, and the whole thing should be ready for the printer by the end of July, when I go to the country" (p. 353).

In the dream, Ernst Brücke, Freud's first laboratory mentor, has assigned him a strange task: "it related to a dissection of the lower part of my own body, my pelvis and legs, which I saw before me as though in the dissecting-room, but without noticing their absence in myself and also without a trace of any gruesome feeling" (Freud, 1900, p. 452). Freud associated from this self-dissection to the self-analysis he had undertaken, the *psycho*surgical project that would be shared with the public in *The Interpretation of Dreams*: "The task which was imposed on me in the dream of carrying out a dissection *of my own body* was thus my *self-analysis* which was linked up with my giving an account of my dreams" (p. 454, emphasis in original). The absence of "gruesome feeling" attendant to the task of self-dissection further signaled Freud's effort to overcome the resistance, the "feeling of distaste," that had led him to postpone the printing of the final dream manuscript for over a year (p. 477). It is the stuff of hagiography to suggest that, with the publication of *The Interpretation of Dreams*, Freud overcame his dependency on Fliess and became his own man. But, in the context of the medicosurgical events of the 1890s and the protracted self-questioning attendant to them, it is perhaps forgivable to suggest that, via the decision to proceed with publication of the dream book, Freud articulated ownership of a method through which he became his own surgeon.

"These Abdominal Matters
Are Uncanny to Me"
∞

If we turn now to the period 1912–15, when Freud wrote the papers on technique, we find actual surgical goings-on in the lives of Freud, his colleagues, and his patients. These events, intriguingly recounted in Freud's correspondence with Jones, Ferenczi, and Abraham, provide a veritable surgical subtext to the papers on technique in which Freud invoked the surgical metaphor.

During this period, surgery—and the prospect of surgery—complicated Freud's personal and professional life in a variety of ways. Early in 1912, Freud's professional peace was disturbed by the news that Ludwig Binswanger had undergone surgery (an appendectomy), during which the surgeon discovered and excised a highly malignant tumor. The surgeon, in accord with conventional wisdom of the time, held out little hope of a cure. Binswanger thereupon prepared for the worst. He confided the gravity of his condition to Freud alone, and Freud responded with this touching acknowledgment: "An old man like me who shouldn't complain (and has decided not to complain) if his life comes to an end in a few years feels especially aggrieved when one of his flourishing young friends, one of those who is meant to continue his own life, informs him that his life is in danger" (FL, p. 286; cf. Schur, 1972, pp. 262–263).

In early September of 1912, Freud was forced to cancel a trip to London to visit Jones, owing to the consequences "of a badly performed appendicitis-operation" on his eldest daughter, Mathilde: "I came up to Wien from Bozen a short time after the operation and I had to resolve not to go away until we see the end of the fever and the illness" (FJC, pp. 153–154; cf. p. 156). When he was able to resume his summer holiday in Rome later that month, Freud was suffering from gastrointestinal pain; we may gauge the severity of his discomfort from a letter to his wife, Martha, in which he owned up to trouble "recur[ring] every two days," though, he added, "it is infinitely better than it was" (FL, p. 292). Freud's "trouble" is a reference to symptoms associated with long-standing spastic colon, a condition that prompted him to travel to Karlsbad to take "the cure" on a regular basis (Schur, 1972, p. 133).

In the months that followed, Freud began the analysis of Loe Kann, Ernest Jones's common-law wife, whose morphine addiction and urological symptoms not only complicated the treatment, but also caused him considerable anxiety. In July of 1913, he confessed to Jones that Kann was causing him concern

> not with respect to a nervous condition but to an organic one. As the swelling in her legs would not subside, I finally had her consult one of our younger internists, Dr. R. Kaufmann, whom I regard as excellent. He has diagnosed that the feverish condition in May, which Hitschmann and Fleischmann traced to urine poisoning caused by bending of a ureter, was due to, or led to, a thrombosis of a vein deep in the abdomen. . . . I do not understand too much about this and may therefore be a little more anxious than necessary, but all these abdominal matters are uncanny to me [FJC, pp. 210–211].

Loe's recurrent kidney attacks prevented her making progress "in the Morphia struggle" (FJC, p. 252) and caused Freud to grow pessimistic about the possibility of therapeutic progress. Surgical intervention(s) apparently followed (pp. 262, 273), so that, by the winter of 1914, Freud, accepting Kaufmann's diagnosis of left-sided pyelitis (inflammation), proclaimed her "a mixed case." "Consoled by the concession of organic disease," he explained, "she no more denies the additional hysteria. As she is in a bad phase just now she makes no progress in giving up morphia" (p. 261).

By this time, Freud's analytic updates to Jones had taken on the character of medical reports. On March 25, 1914, he reviewed the results of Loe's most recent medical exam ("pyelitis, cystitis, bad function of the right kidney") and commented: "it gave no explanation for the constant left-sided pain (tortion, cicatrical tissue or hy[steria]) and did not clear up the condition of the left ureter, supposed to be dilated and fit to retain concrements" (FJC, p. 271). In the summer of 1914, Freud, by now despairing about Loe, was inclined to accept Jones's oft-stated conviction that "the far bigger part" of Loe's pain was hysterical (p. 290), but he remained unable to wean her from morphia dependency for her allegedly hysterical kidney attacks.

A year later, with World War I now raging, Jones brought closure to the episode by bringing Freud up to date on Loe's status. He reported her "pretty well," but still subject to "some sciatica and kidney attacks. A skiagram [x-ray] shows a large stone in the left kidney, but there is no talk of [further] operation" (FJC, p. 311).

Interestingly, no sooner had Loe's medical condition ceased to be a topic of regular correspondence than Jones alluded to his own medical problems. "My operation is at the end of this week," he cryptically announced in a letter of December 15, 1914. To which Freud replied, "I naturally do not know what you mean, and conclude that a letter was lost, but judging from your tone, it cannot be serious. As you can imagine, my medical practice has been reduced to a minimum of two to three hours a day" (FJC, p. 309).

How revealing that Freud, confronted once more with uncanny matters outside the realm of psychological treatment, placed himself in league with his colleagues. He too had become a doctor with a "medical" practice rather than a psychoanalyst with an analytic practice.

The thread of surgical dialogue in Freud's correspondence with Jones between 1912 and 1914 is paralleled by an even more protracted discussion of surgical issues during the same period in Freud's correspondence with Sándor Ferenczi, the most perspicacious but vulnerable of Freud's early followers. At the beginning of October 1912, while Freud was still preoccupied with his daughter's postsurgical recovery, he was apprised of a new series of medicosurgical problems by Ferenczi. He wrote Freud of intestinal discomfort, which he attributed to "(latent) hemorrhoidal conditions." Ever the analyst, Ferenczi deemed his stomach pain "the missing reaction to the final break with Elma" and went so far as to acknowledge that his rectal self-examinations "may have been hidden organ-erotisms" (FFC, 1, p. 407). Here Ferenczi was alluding to psychophysical sequelae to an ill-fated romantic involvement with Elma Pálos, the elder daughter of his patient and future wife Gizella Pálos. Elma had begun her own treatment with Ferenczi in the fall of 1911 and by the beginning of December had won Ferenczi's heart (p. 318). In a letter of December 30, 1911 he informed Freud of his intention to marry her.

Ferenczi had the presence of mind to direct young Elma to Freud for further treatment, and Freud indeed proved helpful in preventing a marriage based on what amounted to fleeting infatuation. As the process unfolded, however, Ferenczi's emotional turmoil heightened his preoccupation with his own bodily functioning, indeed took him to the threshold of full-blown hypochondriasis. Two months after informing Freud of his Elma-related stomach pain, he reported a more onerous constellation of symptoms: swollen glands that made him and a "specialist" suspect syphilis, and thereupon "deep depression, several sleepless nights with heart palpitations (tachycardia), weight loss, muscle weakness" (p. 438). In the wake of this scare, Ferenczi developed a new and unsettling respiratory symptom: "Cheyne-Stokes, which lasted for a time beyond my waking state" (FFC, 1, p. 438).[1] Hoarseness and general muscle weakness (which Ferenczi dubbed "myasthenia") compounded the sleep disturbance. But Ferenczi believed he had found the key to the symptom complex:

> Every time I fell asleep, my breathing became shallow, my pulse got bad, and after three to four hours' sleep I awoke (without anxiety) with a strange breathing, reminiscent of Cheyne-Stokes, which lasted for a time beyond my waking state. . . . Finally, a few days ago I was able to determine that I am breathing badly while lying and sleeping because my *breathing*

---

[1] Cheyne-Stokes respiration refers to a form of periodic breathing, usually a result of severe illness but very occasionally occurring in deep normal sleep, in which a cyclical waxing and waning of depth of respiration leads to intermittent periods of apnoea, the total suspension of breathing.

through the nose is insufficient. It has already been that way for a long time, but it manifested itself *now* because of the partly psychically determined muscle weakness and weight loss [FFC, 1, p. 438, emphasis in original].

Both symptom clusters induced Ferenczi to seek surgical consultation. The intestinal pain seemed to resolve itself with medical intervention, as the consulting surgeon, Ferenczi's friend Miksa Schachter, voiced agreement with the internist's diagnosis of "a case of resorption phenomena; the source of the infection could have been the fissura ani (possibly a small abscess in the urethra)" (FFC, 1, p. 422). So by April of 1913, Ferenczi was content to equate his intestinal pain with "neurasthenic conditions" that were the consequence of "severe circulatory disturbances," which, in turn, resulted solely from Ferenczi's "large paunch." Nothing was called for other than an abdominal bandage, which "immediately did away with all my intestinal disturbances and improved my breathing and circulation" (p. 478).

But the breathing-related sleep difficulty was another matter. In a letter of December 7, 1912, Ferenczi had informed Freud that the nose specialist Zwillinger had diagnosed "a relative stenosis [constriction] of both nasal meati [cavities] and applied cocaine and menthol, whereupon breathing became easier and I had my first good night after weeks of sleeplessness. The rhinologist advised an operation (removal of a part of the nasal septum)" (FFC, 1, p. 438).

And so, to Freud's apparent chagrin, Ferenczi continued to pursue a surgical remedy, advising Freud in March of 1913 that his "nightly sleep disturbances will have to be ameliorated by an intervention on the turbinate bones of my nose" (FFC, 1, p. 476).

The parallel with Emma Eckstein is strikingly obvious. Nasal surgery on the turbinate bones was again to be undertaken to relieve symptoms that may well have been hysterical in origin. After all, Freud had reacted to Ferenczi's medical revelations by reminding him that "a hypochondriacal trait is unmistakable in the case history," and Ferenczi himself willingly comprehended his poor health of the time as "a bodily reaction to the failure of the marriage project" (FFC, 1, p. 467). And true to the Eckstein precedent, Ferenczi's nasal surgery had little if any effect on the symptoms that occasioned it. On May 3, 1913, he advised Freud of the outcome of the surgery in a way that linked his two symptom clusters, that revolving around the breathing-induced sleeping disturbance and that revolving around persisting intestinal discomfort:

> The operation on my nose has not brought about any significant improvement. — Breathing through my nose is still impeded at times; warmth is especially harmful to me. When I get warm, a kind of 'capillary paralysis' of my skin ensues. The veins in my arms swell up, the nasal turbinate bones disrupt my breathing. All that seems to go together with the blockages in my colon, because the distention of my belly, which often occurs, may produce the same vasomotor phenomena. — Every night I wake up around 3:30–4 o'clock with heart palpitations, which soon abate after the expulsion of intestinal gases; but usually I can't go to sleep anymore afterwards, and then I am tired during the day and incapable of spontaneous work [FFC, 1, p. 480].

To which Freud, by now growing impatient, could only offer an admonition that echoed the verdict he and Fliess had privately reached after the surgical trials and near death of Emma Eckstein two decades earlier: "Now try to get to work again. I don't think that there is anything seriously organically wrong with you" (p. 482).

But Ferenczi's nose problems — or at least his conviction that his symptoms had a nasal origin — persisted. In early August he informed Freud that he would "possibly spend two to three days in Vienna to get my nose straightened out before the vacation" (FFC, 1, p. 503), and five months later, in January of 1914, he reported feeling quite well since his most recent nose surgery, "even though the possibility cannot be excluded that additional (small) repairs to my turbinate bones will be necessary" (p. 530). Such repairs were indeed undertaken, and precious time in Vienna — time otherwise reserved for Freud — was subsequently spent "in nasal matters" (p. 530), as Ferenczi underwent several "smaller interventions in my much-abused organ of scent" (p. 533). Only on January 29, 1914 did Ferenczi finally begin a letter by expressing the hope "that I will hereby initiate a series of letters which will not deal with illness (I mean my own)" (p. 535).

And what of Freud's own health during the period in which he worried about Loe Kann's medical condition and endured Ferenczi's litany of medical complaints and reports of Fliessian surgical interventions? On August 5, 1913, the very date Ferenczi wrote Freud of his plans to delay his vacation by spending several days in Vienna to get his nose "straightened out," Freud related to Ferenczi his own intestinal woes: "I am unmistakably in a toxic condition similar to the one you saw me in last year, and even more similar to the one I had at the beginning of the first Karlsbad cure" (FFC, 1, p. 504). The "toxic condition" denotes one of the periodic flare ups of Freud's spastic colon.

In May of 1914, an upper respiratory infection and fatigue prompted Freud to journey south for a few days rest (Schur, 1972, p. 287), where he remained "unwell and without energy for work." And a week later, recurring to the gastrointestinal symptoms, he informed Karl Abraham that his "last bout of intestinal trouble caused my specialist to take the precaution of carrying out a rectoscopy, after which he congratulated me so warmly that I concluded that he regarded a carcinoma as highly probable. So this time it is nothing, and I must struggle on" (FAL, p. 176). And on November 12, 1914, he complained again of intestinal discomfort that was only temporarily allayed by the soothing spring waters of Karlsbad: "I am tormented by my own particular intestine, which has shaken off the effects of Karlsbad after four months" (p. 205).

As if in counterpoint to Freud's admission of gastrointestinal pain, with the prospect of surgery it entailed, Abraham, drafted into military service, wrote Freud repeatedly of his own transformation into a wartime surgeon at the German military hospital in Grunewald. On August 29, he reported having "plenty of work, mainly surgical" (FAL, p. 194), and a month later he gave Freud an account of his wearying routine as surgeon/analyst following a transport of wounded soldiers to the hospital: "I had to get up at 4:30 a.m., was standing in the operating theater without a break till 2 p.m., and then spent some hours in my own practice in the afternoon" (p. 196).

Around this same time, be it noted, Ferenczi too was recruited into the armed forces. Beginning in October of 1914, he was assigned to the town of Pápa where, as a physician with the Hungarian Hussars, he was called on to "bandage and lance boils, treat coughs and stomach aches, and examine the personnel who come in or are about to go on leave" (FFC, 2, pp. 19–20). So Ferenczi functioned as a generalist, albeit one occasionally called on to pick up the scalpel. But with Abraham the wartime transformation had a decidedly surgical cast. On March 13, 1915, he reported being transferred from Grunewald to Allenstein, where he anticipated a routine of surgical work (FAL, p. 214). By the beginning of June, he was "living in the hospital as a medical officer on night duty," and in July he was more explicit still about his new surgical identity: "The hospital work takes up almost all my time. My duties as psychiatrist are, by the way, only a side-line. In the main, I have become a surgeon—not only an assistant or dresser, but an operating surgeon. The psychoanalyst in me stands amazed while I operate on a hydrocele or carry out a rib resection for empyema. But war is war" (FAL, p. 226; cf. p. 229).

"Much Skill, Patience, Calm, and Self-Abnegation"

≈

In a pregnant passage from his "Postscript to a Discussion on Lay Analysis" (1927a), Freud owned up to the self-knowledge that he had "never really been a doctor in the proper sense." He "became a doctor through being compelled to deviate from my original purpose," and the triumph of his life lay "in my having, after a long and roundabout journey, found my way back to my earliest path." Yet, Freud continued, "I scarcely think, however, that my lack of a genuine medical temperament has done much damage to my patients. For it is not greatly to the advantage of patients if their doctor's therapeutic interest has too marked an emotional emphasis. For them, it is for the best if the doctor works coolly and as correctly as possible." (pp. 253, 254).[1]

In the manner, that is to say, of the surgeon. Schafer, in an interpretive commentary of 1983 on the papers on technique, put the strongest possible ego-psychological gloss on Freud's medicosurgical resolve, taking it as the signpost of "a disciplined approach in which considerations of what will be most helpful to the analysis, and therefore to the analysand, will always be foremost in the analyst's mind." In recommending that the

---

[1] The Standard Edition translation of the last sentence is "They are best helped if he carries out his task coolly and keeps as closely as possible to the rules" (1927a, p. 254). I have retranslated this sentence more literally. Freud's German reads: "Für ihn ist es am besten, wenn der Arzt kühl und möglichst korrekt arbeitet" (1927b, p. 291). Surgery per se is not mentioned, but it remains the informing image.

analyst remain cold, Schafer continued, Freud "was thinking of the surgeon's skill and decisiveness. One might say that he was distinguishing between sentimental or maudlin analysis and analysis ruled by disciplined compassion" (1983, p. 23).

Coolness, precision, skill, discipline—the words all circle around a vision of the analyst as master of a dangerous invasive procedure, one in which the laying open of unconscious contents may lead the operator to lose his head and proceed waywardly, as in wild analysis. But why exactly the *surgical* metaphor? Why is it the *surgeon's* skill and decisiveness that represent the model of a disciplined approach to analysis? Surely, coolness, precision, skill, and decisiveness evoke a wealth of metaphors, including the military, legal, and political metaphors that Freud invoked in various descriptions of psychological processes, especially the operation of defenses. Why were such evocative *nonsurgical* images never used to describe the analyst's attitude or activity? Why, for example, did Freud not erect technique on the foundation of the military metaphor, with the analyst/field commander coolly and decisively surveying the enemy's entrenched defenses and underlying vulnerabilities as he rallies the patient's ego-syntonic troops to battle? Or why not the legal metaphor, with the analyst, as prosecuting attorney, coolly and skillfully maneuvering around and beneath defenses so that the accused is led to reveal, unwittingly and in his own words, his act, his "crime," his fantasy?

The historical material adduced earlier does not answer this question, but it broadens our understanding of the life circumstances out of which the surgical metaphor arose and, in so doing, permits cautious surmises about the various motives —conscious and unconscious—informing what we may now designate Freud's "choice of metaphor."

The surgical metaphor represents one tributary of Freud's lifelong idealization of medical authority figures: Billroth, Breuer, and Fliess. More especially, it enabled Freud to make good his medical identity in the context of his "lack of genuine medical temperament" (Bernays, 1940, p. 340). By means of the surgical metaphor, analytic technique partook of the mystique of surgical intervention; it promised to heal in the absence of therapeutic intent. Indeed, like surgery, it promised to heal despite the patient's failure to perceive a therapeutic intent in either the personality of the analyst or the procedural requirements of the surgicoanalytic method. In fact, it promised to heal in the face of the patient's anathema, in the form of transference, to the analyst and his stringently withholding method. Indeed, the inevitability of transference only bolstered the analyst's surgical resolve, as the interpretive management of transference obliged the analyst–surgeon to muster "much skill, patience, calm, and self-abnegation" (Freud, 1926a, p. 227). The fact that, during the war years, so valued a colleague as Abraham actually became a surgeon likely redounded on Freud's belief that analysts, in their own way, were surgeons.

Then, too, the surgical metaphor is perhaps the last bastion of Freud's idealization of Fliess. While Freud successfully worked through his idealization of Fliess as diagnostician, researcher, and counselor par excellence, his reliance on the surgical metaphor suggests a remaining enclave of what analyst's term "positive transference." Through the metaphor, that is, Freud remained in touch with the uncanny in Fliess, whose mystifying nasal interventions presumed to go where psychology could not—to the very pathophysiological substratum of hysteria. As the personal relationship with Fliess waned, I suggest, Freud's idealization of the surgically "uncanny" came to encompass surgeons in general, one important biographical catalyst for the diffusion being Freud's dependence on the authoritative consultants who remedied Fliess's negligence in the surgical aftercare of Emma Eckstein in 1894.

Surgery and the Papers on Technique

If we turn now to the period of the papers on technique, a series of surgical happenings, summarized above, appears to have mobilized Freud's appreciation of surgeons and surgery. Freud entered the fall of 1912 preoccupied with the "badly performed" appendectomy of his eldest daughter, Mathilde. During this same time, Ferenczi began apprising him of both his intestinal disturbance and his sleep-related breathing difficulties. Both symptom clusters occasioned surgical consultations, with the latter eventuating in recommendations for nasal surgery, including "an intervention on the turbinate bones of my nose"

(FFC, 1, p. 476). Ferenczi, we recall, underwent turbinate surgery in May of 1913, with an outcome no more positive than that of Emma Eckstein.

During the same period that Freud skeptically pondered Ferenczi's Fliessian turn, he was confronted with the serious medical condition of Loe Kann, whose recurrent kidney attacks entailed repeated surgical interventions during 1913 and 1914. Kann's significant organic disease not only called forth another round of dependence on the surgeons—"all these abdominal matters are uncanny to me" (FJC, p. 211)—but were mirrored by Freud's own recurrent intestinal symptoms (FFC, 1, p. 504; FAL, p. 205), which entailed their own prospect of surgery (FAL, p. 176).

With the outbreak of hostilities in World War I in 1914, Freud experienced a final call from the surgical beyond. Karl Abraham, ever Freud's stalwart soldier for the psychoanalytic cause, now became a solder for the German cause and, as such, developed into a bona fide surgeon, an "operating surgeon" alongside whom the erstwhile analyst in Abraham could only "stand amazed" (FAL, p. 226). Could there have been a more dramatic concretization of Freud's belief that the analyst, disciplined dissector of the unconscious, was in fact a surgeon?

But there is a more pointedly Fliessian echo in Abraham's wartime transformation. For Abraham, following up on a colleague's introduction, had actually made Fliess's acquaintance in February of 1911. Freud encouraged Abraham to meet this "remarkable, indeed, fascinating man," albeit with a warning: "He will certainly try to sidetrack you from psychoanalysis (and, as he thinks, from me) and to guide you into his own channel" (Freud to Abraham, February 1911, in H. Abraham, 1974, p. 48). And, true to Freud's estimation of Fliess, Abraham emerged from his first meeting with Fliess with "the impression of a penetrating and original thinker." To be sure, he reassured Freud, Fliess appeared to lack "real greatness," but he could not withhold a glowing estimation that belied Freud's concern:

> He met me without prejudice, has meanwhile visited me in turn, and I must admit that he made no attempt to draw me over to his side in the way you feared. I have learned many

interesting things from him, and am glad to have made his acquaintance—perhaps the most valuable I could make among colleagues in Berlin [Abraham to Freud, in H. Abraham, 1974, p. 48].

Abraham, we know, was at the time interested in the theory of periodicity. "But far deeper," his daughter Hilda recounts, "was his admiration for Fliess as a great clinician and diagnostician, which was his own ideal for himself" (H. Abraham, 1974, p. 49). Hilda Abraham does not mention her father's estimation of Fliess as a surgeon. And yet, Fliess's clinical and diagnostic gifts had long subserved, had justified his recourse to, nasal surgery. And so we may ask: Could Abraham's esteem for Fliess the clinician have been dissociated from admiration for Fliess the nose surgeon? Perhaps for Abraham, but certainly not for Freud. There is no evidence that Freud ever believed Abraham was influenced, much less duped, by Fliess. And yet, Abraham's friendship with Fliess, which only intensified in the postwar years,[2] teamed with Abraham's own surgical role in the war, likely heightened the idealizing trends that entered into Freud's choice of metaphor in the papers on technique.

Ferenczi's journey to Vienna for nasal turbinate surgery, Loe Kann's uncanny gastrointestinal ailments, Freud's own gastrointestinal pain and fear of carcinoma, Abraham's transformation into a wartime surgeon—we have here a series of evocative revenants (see Schur, 1972) hovering around surgery, surgeons, and Fliess. The surgical metaphor is in part the distillate of these revenants; it suggests both Freud's identification with the surgeon and his dependence on the surgeon. It is the performative analogue of his lifelong belief in neurophysiology

---

[2] In the portion of her unfinished biography published in 1974, Hilda Abraham wrote suggestively that her father's "closer relationship to Fliess in the post-war years from 1919 to 1925 will need more detailed discussion later. . . . We can merely say at this point that Abraham maintained his independent opinion in his relationship to Freud, a factor we have underlined as so important a condition for his allegiance. This quality remained intact in my father's relationship to Wilhelm Fliess up to the last few months of his [viz., Abraham's] fatal illness, when the need for a helpful, omnipotent father interfered at times with his critical judgment" (p. 49).

as the ultimate explanans of the mental apparatus, the residuum of *The Project for a Scientific Psychology* of 1895.

But, finally, Freud's appropriation of the surgeon's attitude was only a metaphorical acquisition. The analysts, doctors though they were, remained dependent on real surgeons, and their mounting experience of surgery and surgeons—as medical colleagues, as patients themselves, even as occasional assisting operators—would reflect back on the adequacy of the metaphor as the central analogy for the psychoanalytic procedure. As the analysts experienced more of surgeons and surgery, that is, they had reason to reconsider the surgical nature of their own therapeutic enterprise. This was true for Freud and true for his closest followers, Ferenczi among them.

"Midwifery of Thought"

∞

Ferenczi's exploding symptomatology of the prewar years, especially his preoccupation with "nasal matters" in 1913, only intensified with the outbreak of hostilities. During 1915 alone, he conveyed to Freud, now bearing the sobriquet "my [Ferenczi's] physician" (FFC, 2, pp. 67, 81), a litany of medical complaints that traversed his stomach (pp. 54–55, 67, 103), trachea (p. 55), ears (p. 87), and stool (p. 103). Early in 1916, he characterized his condition as one of "constant fluctuation" and offered the following itemization: "Somatic: heart palpitations, tachycardia (always, even at night, 120 and higher), feeling of heat, thirst. (Dr. Levy found nothing in the internal organs.) Psychic: tiredness, total lack of endurance, unbelievable, tormenting impatience, e.g., in the theater, in the evening, during the last analytic hour, etc. Trembling" (p. 112).

For Ferenczi, still actively wrestling with the nature of his feelings for "Frau G." (Gisela Pálos) and her "renounced" daughter Elma, a psychosexual interpretation seemed in order, and he ventured the opinion that his symptoms collectively represented "a poisoning of the psychosomatic organism with libidotoxin" (FFC, 2, p. 112). But Ferenczi added a medical afterthought that proved more to the point: his symptoms also reminded him of "morbus Basedowi" or, in our contemporary lexicon, Graves' disease, the hyperactivity of the thyroid gland from which he was actually suffering.[1]

---

[1] The original designation, Basedow's disease or morbus basedowi, credits Carl Adolf Basedow of Merseburg, Germany, who wrote the first monograph on exophthalmic goiter in 1840. Basedow identified the three cardinal symptoms of hyperactive thyroid gland: swelling of the goiter, exophthalmos (bulging eyeballs), and tachycardia (abnormally rapid heartbeat), conjointly referred to as the Merseburg triad (Robinson, 1931, p. 436).

A month later, Ferenczi recurred to his "disturbed nasal breathing" as standing "in the center as the nucleus of my ailments" (FFC, 2, p. 118). The libidinal significance of the symptom as a "turning away from Frau G." was now relegated to a secondary role, for his shortness of breath had recently increased significantly, and Zwillinger, the nose specialist who had diagnosed stenosis of the nasal meati in the fall of 1912, now "ascertained that the operation on my nasal septum was not successful, and a membrane is obstructing the nasal passages" (p. 118). And so Ferenczi's nose again upstaged his heart and stomach, not to mention his thyroid, as the site of his pathophysiological ruminations, and, following Zwillinger's advice, he planned to travel to Berlin to consult Gustav Killian, "the best nose specialist in Germany" (pp. 118, 120).

Freud's reaction to what he termed Ferenczi's "physiological derivatives" was dismissive. The nose problems, he believed, had everything to do with Frau G., and "one must be able to decide whether one loves a woman or not even with stuffed-up nostrils" (FFC, 2, p. 119). This voice of analytic authority may have played a role in Ferenczi's decision to forego the trip to Berlin (p. 125), even though he was by then constrained to assist his nasal breathing "by artificial enlargement of the nostrils" (p. 120).

Following three weeks of analysis with Freud in June 1916, Ferenczi was able to report that his nasal symptoms and sleeplessness "almost all disappeared" (FFC, 2, pp. 135, 139), but the symptomatic respite proved short-lived. Basedow concerns resurfaced in the correspondence in mid-October (p. 141), and a month later Ferenczi wrote of an "accentuation of the Basedow symptoms," including nighttime breathing difficulty (p. 151), with subsequent reports of severe heart palpitations (pp. 154, 159, 163) and nasal disturbances (p. 159).

Freud, with undisguised annoyance, continued to insist that Ferenczi's symptoms were disingenuous, an instrument of resistance in his protracted and painfully indecisive courtship of Frau G. (FFC, 2, p. 162). Unsurprisingly, Freud 's "categorical assertions"[2] served only to intensify Ferenczi's morbid

---

[2] "You seem to be making much too much out of your Basedow," Freud chided Ferenczi in a letter of November 26, 1916 (FFC, 2, p. 162). And

preoccupations. By the end of November, he confessed that Freud's judgment had led to "a worsening of my condition." His "hypochondriacal ideas" had strengthened to "to the point of anxiety," and he now felt that his Basedow symptoms pointed to cancer of the thyroid gland (p. 164).

The year 1917 did not bear out this last premonition, but it did witness an exacerbation of Ferenczi's medical concerns. In the final week of January, an X-ray and physical examination suggested pulmonary tuberculosis, and, following the advice of his internist, Ferenczi planned a recuperative stay in the mountains outside Budapest (FFC, 2, p. 177). By the second week of February, he was writing Freud from a hotel in Semmering, where he had placed himself under the care of a Dr. Kraus, a Basedow specialist and friend of an analytic colleague, Eduard Hitschmann (p. 183). By the end of the month Ferenczi had gained admittance to the Semmering Sanitarium, where he convalesced for the next two and a half months. His recovery was medically uneventful but emotionally draining. During his recuperation at the sanitarium, Ferenczi witnessed the admittance of his beloved friend and Budapest colleague Miksa Schachter, who was gravely ill with tuberculosis and diabetes. Ferenczi was obliged to watch his friend waste away amid the incessant snowstorms of the Semmering winter (p. 185, n1). A hopeless case, Schachter was rushed home to die in peace, and after Ferenczi was notified of his death in late April, he wrote Freud to "ameliorate" his depression in the wake of the passing of the man who was second only to his father as a loved and revered model (p. 199).

Ferenczi's touching tribute to this nonanalytic father figure went unacknowledged by Freud, who, indeed, persisted in

---

even after Ferenczi's internist Levy confirmed the diagnosis shortly thereafter, Freud's tone had not changed. In a letter of shared frustration to Ferenczi's intended, Gizella Pálos, on January 23, 1917, Freud wrote of his failure to induce Ferenczi "to do anything decisive," irritatedly viewing the latter's physical symptoms as merely the latest instrument of his passivity and indecision: "Then this stupid, trifling, but nevertheless undeniable organic affliction, morbus Basedowi, came and has permitted him to free himself from the snare in which I was hoping to catch him. It troubles me deeply that he should have no more of you and of life than before. But I can do nothing" (p. 176).

making light of Ferenczi's tuberculosis and Graves' disease.[3] He would have preferred Ferenczi to emulate his own attitude of stoical forbearance in the face of bodily suffering exacerbated by the hardships of war. Nineteen seventeen was far from an easy year for Freud, whose own catalogue of medical tribulations, doubtless aggravated by bitter cold and severe food shortages, included prostate troubles, rheumatism (FFC, 2, p. 205), recurrent intestinal infections (pp. 207, 237), and an acute upset stomach (p. 231). When, in early November, Freud smoked away the last cigar of his depleted stock, he wrote Ferenczi of heart palpitations and an increase in the "painful swelling" of the gums that he had noticed "since the meager days" (p. 245). Freud himself realized that this last symptom could be ominous; the parenthetical "(carcinoma? etc.)" following the report of swelling gums is plain in import (cf. Jones, 1955, p. 192). But Freud labored on, even as Ferenczi indulged his "moderate case of morbus Basedowi" in the mountains of Semmering.

As Ferenczi regained his strength in the late spring of 1917, he came into contact with the countryman destined to become his analytic soul mate in the remaining years of the war. I refer to Anton von Freund, the wealthy Hungarian industrialist whose friendship with Ferenczi was cemented by his status as the psychoanalytic movement's staunchest convert and most financially generous benefactor. The inheritor of one of Budapest's thriving breweries, Freund had made Freud's acquaintence in 1916, when both he and his wife received a brief period of psychoanalytic treatment (Mühlleitner, 1992, p. 107). Thereafter, Freund remained in friendly contact with Freud;

---

[3] Following Ferenczi's report of his "catarrh" associated with tubercular disease, Freud wrote: "I heard about your diagnosis with regret, without ascribing the same significance to it as you. Illnesses of this kind now seem to be uncommonly frequent and certainly don't always mean anything serious. It also turned out with Anna that in breathing the apex of one of her lungs comes through less clearly, otherwise nothing" (FFC, 2, p. 179). And, in a reassuring letter to Gizella Pálos two weeks later, Freud reported: "He shows a moderate case of morbus Basedowi without any dangerous complication, has every prospect of recovery in two to three months, and doesn't need to assign any particular role to the illness in the economy of his life" (p. 181).

indeed, he joined Ferenczi in smuggling food and cigars into Vienna to ease Freud's misery during the final years of the war (Harmat, 1988, p. 63). More significantly still, he began directing his philanthropic largesse in the direction of psychoanalysis. With the war still raging, he collected one and a half million kronen for humanitarian relief in Budapest and then, with the approval of the city's mayor, earmarked the money for the foundation of a psychoanalytic institute, which, under Ferenczi's scientific leadership, would not only teach psychoanalysis but make treatment available to the city's indigent, its "poor neurotics," through an outpatient clinic (Freud, 1920c, pp. 267–268).

No sooner was Ferenczi back in Budapest after his convalescence than he began hearing from Freund, by then deeply involved with the psychoanalytic movement. They initially collaborated in finding Freud suitable lodgings for his summer vacation of 1917 (FFC, 2, p. 208), and by January of the new year, Freund was comfortable enough to approach Ferenczi about bringing a child relation, likely his daughter Vera, to him for treatment (p. 258).

But these circumstances do not exhaust Ferenczi's attachment to Freund; they merely circumscribe it. For as it turns out, Freund was critically ill. Surgical removal of a testicular tumor in February of 1918 led to fears of recurrent sarcomas, and Freund, with a penchant for hypochondria, grew delusional. When Ferenczi was called in to see him shortly after the surgery, he found the brewer in the grips of what he breezily termed an anxiety neurosis. But his description of Freund's condition suggested something far more serious. "Today I saw him," he wrote Freud, "and unfortunately determined an acute incipient psychosis. The symptoms are composed of hypochondriac-paranoid-delusional fantasies and hypomanic manifestations of excitation, as well as, at times anxiety" (FFC, 2, p. 266). Ferenczi found the brewer lying in bed revising his will. Convinced that brain metastases of the sarcoma had set in and that his end was near, Freund excitedly introduced Ferenczi to his "plan," whereby the latter would take over the "prophylactic-psychoanalytic treatment" of his young daughter after Freund's demise.

Freund, it becomes clear, was not merely a convert to the psychoanalytic cause. He had become a comrade-in-arms, a homo religioso for whom, as Ferenczi explained to Freud, "psychoanalysis has taken the place of theism; he harbors the same feeling for it as for the deity, and it is ordained to assume this place for all humanity" (FFC, 2, p. 266). He had become, that is, much like Ferenczi himself. Like Ferenczi, Freund suffered from a serious medical condition but was prone to hypochondriacal embellishment of, and morbid preoccupation with, his various signs and symptoms. Like Ferenczi, he understood the reality of his condition but still clung to the hope that the entire disease process was psychogenic and hence subject to psychoanalytic cure (p. 266). Finally, like Ferenczi, Freund was totally committed to Freud—to his person, his physical well-being, his creature comforts, and his doctrine—and like Ferenczi he lived for his brief interludes of analysis with the master.

Freund's generous bequest to the psychoanalytic movement was intended as a tribute to his new religion. For Freud and Ferenczi, this generosity to the cause promised to make good the deprivations of the war years, and their shared concern about Freund's physical condition during this period was more than solicitous; it was heartfelt and touching.

Psychoanalysis, undertaken mainly by Ferenczi and episodically by Freud, was a key element of their ministrations. It was employed at first to help Freund overcome his morbid preoccupation with rampant metastases, but was ultimately reduced to a vehicle of comradely support and, during Freund's brief pain-free intervals, of diversion.

And so Ferenczi and Freud engaged the matter of surgery yet again, both analytically—since the prospect of magical surgical cure entered into Freund's resistance—and medically—since surgery alone held any prospect of prolonging Freund's life. For Ferenczi, especially, the burden of Freund's illness was great and led to a recrudescence of his own physical symptoms. In the winter of 1918, as Freund wrestled with his fear of brain metastases and consulted Theodor Kocher's *Surgical Handbook* to learn his prognosis following surgical removal of the testicular tumor (FFC, 2, pp. 266, 267), Ferenczi announced his own "relapse." He was, he advised Freud, experimenting with belladonna to remedy his "vagotonia" (p. 268), which, he now believed, added neurasthenic symptoms to his Basedow complex, the two jointly contributing, via some "unexplained connections," to his "strange combination of cardiac, intestinal, nasal, and sleep disturbances" (p. 271).[4]

During the spring and summer of 1918, it fell to Freud to analyze Freund's "postoperative psychosis" (FFC, 2, p. 272), the goal of treatment being to resolve hypochondriacal delusions that, following Freund's testicular surgery, had, as Ferenczi reported, grown luxuriant. Or so Freud and Ferenczi wanted to believe. When Freund returned to Vienna for further treatment at the end of 1918, it was a measure of previous treatment success that Freud could report him "in bad, but only neurotic, condition," adding, "I hope to bring him far along this time, provided that nothing organic pulling the strings makes a fool of us" (p. 321). And five days later, he wrote Ferenczi that "Toni is better, a full neurosis" (p. 323).

But analyzable neurotic or not, Freund was fatally ill, a fact that Freud fought with an analytic resolve that could only have bolstered his analysand's denial. By January of 1919, Freund was suffering from a periostitis (FFC, 2, p. 325)—an inflammation of the fibrous membrane covering the surfaces of bones—and in April Ferenczi pronounced him "quite hypochondriacal again," with "strong pains, which are localized in the back and the liver area" (p. 346). When Freud, owing to his own prostate troubles, declined a journey to Budapest to be with the dying Freund, Ferenczi proceeded as he thought best, joining Freund in calling in "an adept surgeon, who suspects a small kidney stone and is having a precise X ray taken" (p. 349).

By late May, gratification that Freund had withstood his medicosurgical ordeal without recourse to "psychosis" finally gave way to fatalism about the inevitable end. Freund was by

---

[4] Three years earlier, in a letter to Freud of February 8, 1913, Ferenczi had speculated that vagotonia (i.e., increased tonicity of the vagus nerve) provided a biological explanation of neurasthenic symptoms (FFC, 1, p. 467).

then sick from radiation treatment and complaining of paresthesias in the stomach (FFC, 2, p. 353). For Ferenczi, the matter was now in the hands of "the internist and the surgeon," according to whom "the fact and the nature of the increase in volume which has been ascertained are beyond a doubt" (p. 355). Another surgical consultation followed at Freund's behest, and surgeon and internist jointly ascertained "*one* tumor the size of a hen's egg on the posterior wall of the abdominal cavity, retroperitoneal, situated above the aorta" (p. 359). Ferenczi's fantasies of analytic melioration yielded to ruminations of surgical cure, and he "pressed for a consultation with a Viennese surgeon. I thought to myself: maybe a desperate attempt at a radical cure can be made! But inwardly I was convinced of the improbability that a surgeon can attempt this" (p. 359).

Predictably, no surgical remedy was to be had for poor Freund, and by the end of November 1919, Ferenczi was content to hope that his dear friend would be spared "all too great pains." "The doctors must fulfill his demand for euthanasia," he advised Freud, and added, "He has complete justification for it" (FFC, 2, p. 370). A final round of radiation therapy, including the insertion of a radium capsule via a drain (pp. 371, 372), accomplished nothing, and by December 11, even Freud deemed his condition hopeless (p. 372).

Ferenczi's sense of loss was doubtless greater than Freud's. His letters reveal his increasing closeness to Freund during the final months, when Freund's condition depressed him "unspeakably" (FFC, 2, p. 350). By the end of April, he admitted to Freud the great effort required "to show that I am calm and in a good mood. We have become much closer to each other lately—it is all the more painful to know that he is suffering so" (p. 353).

To consult with the surgeon, to yield to the surgeon, to fantasize radical surgical cure, all the while praying the patient be spared "all too great pain"—this, for Ferenczi, was the legacy of Freund's protracted ordeal. And, predictably, Ferenczi emerged from the war years a changed analyst: hardened by war and rededicated to Freud's surgicoanalytic method, but sensitized to pain by his own physical and emotional tribulations of the period, capped, tellingly, by the suffering and death of Anton von Freund.

It is especially Ferenczi's passivity that blossomed in the postwar years, by which I mean not merely the characterological fact of his passivity but his ownership of that passivity in therapeutically productive ways. For it was a passivity that Ferenczi felt constrained to integrate with the requirements of Freud's surgicoanalytic technique. How did he effect this integration? By exploring Ferenczi's use of the surgical metaphor in papers written after the war, we readily discern his strategy.

In the Ferenczi of the postwar years, we behold a kinder, gentler surgeon, yet one prepared to deliver the patient of unconscious contents with forceps in hand. Analysis had become a psychological form of childbirth, with the patient constrained to "comport himself passively during this 'midwifery of thought'" (1921, p. 200). The guiding metaphor remained surgical, but now obstetrical:

> The doctor's position in psychoanalytic treatment recalls in many ways that of the obstetrician, who also has to conduct himself as passively as possible, to content himself with the post of onlooker at a natural proceeding, but who must be at hand at the critical moment with the forceps in order to complete the act of parturition that is not progressing spontaneously [1919a, pp. 182–183].

Active interference on the analyst's part was a measure of last resort, just as obstetric forceps "should only be used in extreme need and whose unnecessary employment is rightly condemned by medical art" (1921, p. 208). And when are the forceps called for? Here Ferenczi mixed metaphors while remaining ensconced within the operating suite:

> Just as in experiments on animals the blood pressure in distant parts can be raised by the ligature of large arterial vessels, so in suitable case we can and must shut off psychic excitement from unconscious paths of discharge, in order by this 'rise of pressure' of energy to overcome the resistance of the censorship and of the 'resting excitation' by higher psychic systems [1919b, p. 197].

The analogy between active intervention and the tying off of blood vessels is entirely in keeping with *The Development of Psychoanalysis*, which Ferenczi wrote with Otto Rank in the summer of 1922. There the analyst's task was envisioned as "watching the process of the automatic unwinding of the libido—which, like the organic process of healing, takes place within a definite time and contains crises" (Ferenczi and Rank, 1923, p. 6). Only at those points of crisis, when neurotic resistance blocked the unwinding process, was the analyst obliged to "intervene and correct it." Ferenczi understood analytic activity as "correcting neurotic forms of discharge"; the analyst effected the correction by behaving "as a sort of catalyzer," one whose verbal directives and injunctions served to restore the "artificially induced process" of libidinal unwinding (pp. 8, 14). For Ferenczi, this occasional recourse to prescriptive advice and explicit prohibitions in the interest of overcoming resistance marked a refinement of Freud's technique, which never departed, at least in theory, from a consistently nonjudgmental, interpretive response to the patient's free associations.

Already in 1922 Ferenczi stressed that such crisis-induced directives—the calling card of what he subsequently termed the "active technique" of psychoanalysis—were episodic and infrequent. In their absence, the analyst's task was to remain "rather passive in the face of the repetition of the libido overflow and to act as it were as the object or rather the phantom of the process" (Ferenczi and Rank, 1923, p. 8). The circumscribed realm of analytic "activity" did not authorize "overwhelming the patient with commands and prohibitions," the latter tantamount to a type of "wild activity" (p. 43). Three years later, in 1925, Ferenczi returned to surgical analogizing by chiding younger colleagues who saw his endorsement of "active technique" less as an adjunct to midwifery than as a warrant for preemptive surgical strike. Specifically, he dissociated himself from those who, shying away from obstetrical passivity, believed that active technique relieved them of the need "to travel the hard road of the ever more complicated analytic theories." Such colleagues were not content with analytic midwifery, since they believed that "a courageous 'active' slash could loosen the most difficult therapeutic knot at a stroke" (1925, p. 218).

When, in his clinical diary of 1932, Ferenczi reflected on the outcome of his clinical experiments with "mutual analysis,"[5] he turned once more to the surgical metaphor in an effort to comprehend with analytic specificity the rationale of his own noninterpretive disclosures. With his patient R.N., he overcame analytic stalemate by frankly acknowledging a formerly suppressed feeling that "the whole treatment will go wrong and that she will end up insane or commit suicide" (p. 37). It was his struggle to articulate a belief that was, in the nature of things, painfully disillusioning, to overcome what he later termed his "terrorism of suffering" (p. 53), that appeased his difficult patient. She well knew "how much pain this cruel task caused me. (She already knew long ago that because of similar internal obstacles I disliked performing surgery and whenever possible avoided postmortem examinations as well)" (p. 38). Two weeks later, he reported coping with his patient B.'s accusations of being a murderer by openly admitting the inadequacy of his ministrations, by "not making any secret of my own feelings on the subject." Here analytic cruelty, like benevolent surgical cruelty, subserved a benevolent therapeutic resolve. Ferenczi described it thusly:

> If one knows that this hangman's work is inevitable, that in the end it does help the patient, and if one overcomes the resistance against such cruelty, which can vary in strength; if one does or allows to be done the necessary analytical explorations—then one will not shrink from the radical interventions that will result in the patient's disengagement. After all, the child too must be separated from its mother by scissors: delaying this operation may be injurious to both the mother and the child (analyst and patient) [1932, p. 53].

---

[5] In Ferenczi's "mutual analytic" experiments of the 1930s, his patients' own psychoanalytic surmises about their analyst (viz., Ferenczi) were allowed into the treatment process in the interest of improving the analyst's functioning and thereby strengthening the therapeutic relationship. Ferenczi, in the belief that his patients might provide important insights into his vulnerabilities and therapeutic limitations, took the experiments to the extreme of providing patients with his own free associations and self-disclosures, on the basis of which the patients would venture interpretations about Ferenczi's own wishes, anxieties, and conflicts. For recent reappraisals of Ferenczi's experiments in mutual analysis, see Ragen and Aron (1993) and Fortune (1996).

Surgery, scissors, operations. We are back in the operating suite, but now with a reticent surgeon whose subjective terror of suffering—his own and his patients'—edges toward a "relational" apprehension of the analytic field in which penetrating analytic interpretation is seen to require a double-edged sword—or blade.[6] Analytic technique is now freighted with the moral responsibility of completing an operation that makes reciprocal emotional demands on analyst and patient and, further, leaves the patient vulnerable in the absence of empathically supportive surgical aftercare.

It is on the basis of this construal of analytic process that Ferenczi faults Freud, whose "analytic technique creates transference, but then withdraws, wounding the patient without giving him a chance to protest or to go away; hence interminable fixation on the analysis while the conflict remains unconscious" (1930, p. 210). The therapeutic answer, for Ferenczi, lies less in exposing the wound than in the therapeutic ministrations that follow its uncovering:

> Once the patient is freed from these fetters, he protests against the sadistic procedure; but if the patient really feels that we will in fact take care of him, that we take his infantile need for help seriously (and one cannot offer a helpless child, which is what most patients are, mere theories when it is in terrible pain), then we shall be able to induce the patient to look back into the past without terror. More proof that the lasting effect of the trauma stems from the absence of a kind, understanding, and enlightening environment [p. 210].

And there is still more to Ferenczi's surgical ruminations. There are cases, he observes, where even the most beneficent aftercare will not suffice. Here preanalytic steps must be undertaken to ensure a viable surgicoanalytic field. In short, there is a need for preanalytic anesthesia to permit the "traumatic analysis" that will lay bear the traumatic wound, even before it can become transferentially engaged. Ferenczi has in mind traumatized patients who have "never relaxed sufficiently

---

[6] Aron and Harris (1993, pp. 1–35) provide an informative overview of the relevance of Ferenczi's work in general to contemporary "relational psychoanalysis."

into free association, let alone to the point of intellectual and emotional semiconsciousness or unconsciousness. To make it possible for such patients to make contact with "the real upheavals in their lives," Ferenczi must deaden their sensitivity to the analytic probe. He reasons that

> since the traumas probably took place in an artificially induced (narcotic) state of unconsciousness and paralysis (of the body and mind) it might be appropriate to anesthetize the patient with ether or chloroform, in order to anesthetize the traumatic pain to such a degree that the circumstances related to the trauma would become accessible. From such a procedure the emergence of significant pieces of material evidence may be expected, which the patient will not be able to deny or minimize even after waking up [1932, p. 138].

In Ferenczi's gentle obstetrical scruples — scruples that embrace even the use of major anesthesia to ease traumatic pain and facilitate trauma-related recall — we see the only bona fide transformation of Freud's surgical metaphor of which I am aware. It is the exception to the rule. Analysts since Freud have not worked — or played — with the metaphor in creative ways. Rather, as we noted at the outset, they have invariably taken *Freud's* surgical metaphor as capturing, objectively and timelessly, the surgeon's modus operandi. Nor have analysts, with rare exceptions, even *engaged* the metaphor in the interest of deepening their understanding of Freud and psychoanalytic history. They apprehend the metaphor statically, and they cite it passingly, whether to endorse, qualify, or repudiate it.

In our own time, it is fair to say, the rejection of the surgical metaphor constitutes an aspect of a broader epistemic agenda: a skeptical questioning of the very relationship of psychoanalysis to medical models of disease and treatment. Is the retreat from medicosurgical analogizing therefore unique to contemporary psychoanalytic theorizing? Far from it. The process of distancing psychoanalysis from surgeons and surgery — indeed, from the medical model in general — begins with Freud himself and the small circle of medical colleagues who initially found the surgical model congenial enough. There is another story to tell, and it begins with World War I and the lessons learned from it.

PART II

⸎

THE METAPHOR IN RETREAT

"German War Medicine
Has Taken the Bait"
❧

In publications following World War I, the surgical metaphor
surely does not vanish from sight. We concluded Part I by
considering one particular variant of the metaphor that emerged
in the postwar period, Ferenczi's obstetrical model of therapeutic action, his re-visioning of the psychoanalytic procedure
as a "midwifery of thought." Freud was never to follow Ferenczi's
lead. He never felt impelled, that is, to transform the metaphor
in accord with an evolving understanding of the nature of the
psychoanalytic procedure. Rather, Freud would retreat almost
entirely from surgical thinking and the surgical metaphor. It is
now our task to trace this retreat and to explore some of the
reasons that underlay it.

   The retreat is evident at once in "Lines of Advance in Psychoanalytic Therapy" (1919a), where Freud does not drop the
metaphor entirely, but assigns it an entirely unexceptional status
within the family of analogies evoked by the analytic procedure.
Here Freud is mainly concerned with the metaphoric insufficiency of any one characterization of analytic therapy. He
begins by acknowledging the reasonableness of the analogy
between "the work by which we bring the repressed mental
material into the patient's consciousness" and "the work carried
out by chemists on substances which they find in nature and
bring into their laboratories" (p. 159), only to underscore the
limitations of this or any other analogy: "What is psychical is
something so unique and peculiar to itself that no one comparison can reflect its nature," he insists. And then, with respect
to the chemical analogy at hand, he continues: "The work of

psycho-analysis suggests analogies with chemical analysis, but it does so just as much with the intervention of a surgeon or the manipulations of an orthopedist or the influence of an educator" (p. 159).

Only with respect to the ameliorative potential of analytic intervention does the surgical metaphor appear to retain a certain pride of place. Looking wishfully to a future in which public clinics would extend psychoanalytic care to the poor, and guided more specifically by his vision of the Institute that would grow out of Anton von Freund's promised bequest, Freud anticipates the time when

> the conscience of society will awake and remind it that the poor man should have just as much right to assistance for his mind as he now has to the life-saving help offered by surgery; and that the neuroses threaten public health no less than tuberculosis, and can be left as little as the latter to the impotent care of individual members of the community [p. 167].

Of course, it is clear that the notion of analyst as surgeon has been radically transformed and devalued in relation to the claims set forth earlier in Freud's papers on technique. To be specific, surgery has relinquished any claim to metaphoric specificity, much less primacy, in regard to the psychoanalytic procedure and the psychoanalytic attitude. What is left in its place is an analogy, propagandistic in character, between the therapeutic *promise* of analysis and the life-saving *help* of surgery. Psychoanalysis, Freud now seems content to argue, resembles surgery only with respect to the therapeutic potency it brings to bear within its particular domain of intervention — the mind and its problems.

What has happened here? Why has the "strong" use of the metaphor, which is in evidence as late as the *Introductory Lectures* of 1917, given way to the "weak" analogizing of 1919? We will spend the next several chapters considering the professional and personal factors that help account for this transformation. We begin with a topic of clinical conversation throughout the Great War and during its immediate aftermath. I refer to the "war neuroses" and the psychoanalytic contribution to their understanding.

The unparalleled human carnage of the Great War was compounded by a degree of human psychological wreckage wholly unknown in previous wars. Prior to the Great War, the most common psychic disability associated with war was homesickness or, as the French in the Napoleonic Wars called it, *nostalgie*, a war-induced condition of intense separation anxiety (Rosen, 1975; Leed, 1979, p. 164). But the combat conditions of World War I elicited hysterical and psychosomatic symptoms that, in both sheer variety and frequency of occurrence, were entirely unprecedented.

Historians offer different perspectives on the disjunction between World War I and previous wars, but their explanations tend to be complementary. The Great War, of course, signaled the emergence of industrial warfare, with the transformation of battlefield anxiety attendant to a loss of personal control over the conditions and actualities of combat. It was especially the frontsoldier's immobility in the face of possibly imminent mutilation, dismemberment, and death that has been linked to the horrific scale of neurotic breakdown (Leed, 1979, pp. 180ff.).[1] As Leed observes,

> the dominance of long-ranged artillery, the machinegun, and barbed wire had immobilized combat, and immobility necessitated a passive stance of the soldier before the forces of mechanized slaughter. The cause of neurosis lay in the dominance of material over the possibilities of human movement. In a real sense the neuroses of war were the direct product of the increasingly alienated relationship of the combatant to the modes of destruction [p. 164].

The psychologically debilitating nature of mechanized warfare was compounded by the sheer duration of the combat

---

[1] As Leed (1979) goes on to explain, the knowledge that human agency underlay the mechanized, impersonal violence of trench warfare only intensified the intolerability of life on the front: "Always the randomness of death at the front, the impersonality of violence, was qualified by the recognition that it was men who were operating these machines, men who made and continued the war, men who sought the death of the immobilized men in the trenches. This combination of the impersonality, randomness, and human agency behind the mechanized violence of war was uniquely destructive of the psychic defenses of combatants" (pp. 180–181).

conditions to which Allied and Axis troops alike were exposed. The experience of front line service during the war, in which soldiers and officers lived with the prospect of imminent death for prolonged periods of time, was simply unprecedented; prior to the Great War, soldiers typically experienced a comparable degree of threat only during siege operations (Haythornthwaite, 1992, p. 55). To the unremitting anxiety of trench duty—an anxiety, we may say, of inhumanly acute chronicity—was added a degree of privation, including lack of decent rations and sleep, entirely unknown in any realm of civilian life.

The psychological damage attendant to these conditions could not be ignored by the warring nations. Psychiatric casualties were granted official recognition for the first time in military history, and they were not long in coming. As early as August of 1914, British medical war records reported instances of men "broken" by their experiences in the British retreat from Mons; a month later, Gordon Holmes, a nerve specialist at base hospitals in France, reported "frequent examples of gross hysterical conditions which were associated with trivial bullet and shell wounds, or even with only slight contusions of the back, arms, and legs" (in Gilbert, 1994, p. 61).

It was during the prolonged fighting on the Somme in the fall of 1916 that the sheer number of psychiatric casualties prompted an official response. As droves of soldiers retreated from the battlefield with shattered nerves and reported themselves sick, they were queried about what had happened. "Shell shock" was the usual response. The self-diagnosis was colorful and accurate enough to stick: many of the symptoms reported by these soldiers indeed took as their "initiating influence the psychic and physical horrors of life among exploding shells" (Mills, 1919, p. vi). As the number of shell-shocked soldiers during the Battle of the Somme mounted into the thousands, both armies opened special centers directly behind the front for the diagnosis and treatment of this new and unsettling malady (Gilbert, 1994, pp. 275–276).[2]

---

[2] It was deemed essential to military discipline to evaluate shell-shocked soldiers in the actual battle area, with evacuation to a base undertaken only as a matter of last resort (Babington, 1997, p. 87).

There is a voluminous literature on these issues of diagnosis and treatment, of which Eissler (1986) provides a fair sampling. The principal methods of treatment in hospitals behind the front lines were "drugs combined with diet and hydrotherapy; painful faradization; suggestion and hypnosis; the persuasion method after Dubois; and the psychoanalytic method and its modifications" (Eissler, 1986, p. 299, relying on Schüller, 1919, p. 974). Classified according to "the degree to which they depended on authoritarian discipline, and subordination of the patient and the infliction of pain versus voluntary collaboration between patient and physician," these methods embodied radically different therapeutic philosophies, with Fritz Caveman's method of electrotherapy ("faradization") occupying one end of the spectrum and Ernst Simmel's "method of modified psychoanalysis" the other (Eissler, 1986, p. 299).

For the analysts drafted into medical service during World War I, the neuropsychiatric problems of the battlefield provided new confirmation of psychoanalytic ideas and were therefore seized on as valuable propaganda for the psychoanalytic movement writ large. The battlefield, it should be stressed, was not envisioned as a new clinical arena for testing psychoanalytic claims, nor did it prompt the analysts to modify those claims in significant ways. Rather, the war neuroses were viewed as directly confirmatory of what the analysts had known right along. With the outbreak of war, as Freud acknowledged, the explanation gained from the neuroses of peace could be "applied quite generally to war neurotics" (1920d, p. 212).

Abraham, in particular, repeatedly sought to bolster Freud's sagging spirits by apprising him of the corroborative character of his wartime experiences. As early as the winter of 1915, even as he labored under the workload of a wartime surgeon, he reported seeing "a number of traumatic neuroses, well known to us from peacetime, in a typical form" (FAL, p. 210). Ten months later, when he had finally quit his war hospital's surgical unit, he wrote of "some interesting findings about the origin of paralyses in the war-wounded," and in the following spring, he apprised Freud that his psychiatric work had given him "excellent proof of the correctness of your theory on paranoia" (FAL, pp. 230, 250). Around this same time, Ferenczi, newly arrived in Budapest to direct the unit for "nervous war invalids" at the Maria Valerie Hospital, joined in the effort by writing Freud of the revivifying effect of the lecture on war neuroses he had presented to the hospital staff: "After the lecture, which was received with much applause . . . I *suddenly* felt very well" (FFC, 2, p. 113, emphasis in original).

Freud's spirits received a sharper boost when in February of 1918 he received a copy of a slight brochure authored by Ernst Simmel, an obscure German psychiatrist superintending a military hospital for war neurotics in Posen (now Poznan), Poland. Simmel's hospital was originally devoted to the treatment of shell-shocked soldiers by hypnotic suggestion, but following a series of treatment failures, Simmel and his supervisor, Adolf Schnee, sought to extend their approach by what Schnee termed the "psychoanalytical cathartic method" (Eissler, 1986, p. 321).

The brochure that Freud received in the winter of 1918 presented the grounds and results of this bold gambit. Bearing the title *"War Neuroses and 'Psychic Trauma': Their Mutual Relationship Presented on the Basis of Psychoanalytic Hypnotic Studies,"* the brochure did indeed propound a psychoanalytic understanding of, and treatment approach to, war neuroses. That the understanding was rudimentary and the treatment approach "cathartic"[3] did not temper Freud's excitement over this recognition by a military psychiatrist outside his coterie of followers. It was "unreservedly on analytic ground even though it is essentially a 'cathartic' work," he informed Ferenczi (FFC,

---

[3] Simmel's approach was simply to hypnotize war neurotics, take them back to a singularly traumatizing battlefield event, and rely on the hypnotically induced reexperiencing of the event to release the repressed emotion, the "strangulated affect," that fueled the neurotic symptoms, thereby liberating the soldier from his symptoms. This is precisely the cathartic method of treatment proffered by Breuer and Freud in the *Studies on Hysteria* of 1895 and superseded over the following two decades by the development of the psychoanalytic method, which relied on free association and interpretation and a revised theory of therapeutic action.

2, p. 264), and he expatiated more fully on its significance to Abraham:

> This is the first time a German physician, basing himself firmly and without patronizing condescension on psychoanalysis, speaks of its outstanding usefulness in the treatment of war neuroses, backs this with examples, and is also completely honest on the question of sexual etiology. It is true that he has not gone the whole way with psychoanalysis, bases himself essentially on the cathartic standpoint, works with hypnosis, which is bound to conceal resistance and sexual drives from him, but he correctly apologizes for this because of the necessity of quick results and the large number of cases with which he has to deal. I think a year's training would make a good analyst of him. His attitude is correct [FAL, p. 269].

Abraham shared Freud's "amazement" at Simmel's pamphlet, which echoed, so he claimed, many of his own hospital experiences. No sooner had he received Freud's missive than he set out to track down Simmel and recruit him for the analytic cause (FAL, p. 271). In the months to follow, he would give Freud periodic updates on Simmel's progress toward conversion, which essentially revolved around persuading him to move beyond the protoanalytic "Breuer-Freud point of view" and, more particularly, to overcome his resistance to the sexual etiology of the neuroses—wartime and otherwise (pp. 280, 293, 298, 299–300).

Of course, Freud was under no illusions about the adequacy of Simmel's psychoanalytic understanding. In the matter of the war neuroses, however, he seemed more than willing to countenance theoretical regression in the service of the cause. The point, he held, was that Simmel's pamphlet both reflected and promoted German psychiatric interest in analysis; its publication showed that "German war medicine has taken the bait" (FFC, 2, p. 264). Ernest Jones, who would present his own paper, "War Shock and Freud's Theory of the Neuroses," to the Royal Society of Medicine's Psychiatric Section two months later, was predictably unwilling to yield analytic pride of place on war neuroses to his colleagues, much less to an analytically unschooled psychiatrist from Posen. Simmel had little to say, he wrote Freud in March of 1919, "but is no doubt useful propaganda" (p. 337). Just so. Propaganda was precisely the point right along.

The analysts' contribution to the war effort and the therapeutic satisfaction attending it dominated the Fifth International Psycho-Analytic Congress that convened in Budapest at the end of September in 1918. It was here that Freud read the paper on "Lines of Advance in Psycho-Analytic Therapy," which, among other things, signaled the tactical retreat of the surgical metaphor. But the Congress included, more significantly, a symposium on "The Psycho-Analysis of War Neuroses," which brought together the papers written earlier in the war by Simmel and Ferenczi, and one prepared especially for the Congress by Abraham. To the three conference papers was added Jones's recent paper on "War Shock," and the small collection, together with Freud's brief introduction, was published in 1919 as *Psychoanalysis and the War Neuroses*, the inaugural volume of the newly established *Internationale Psychoanalytischer Verlag*, the International Psycho-Analytical Press.

In his introduction to this volume, Freud, who had never treated a case of shell shock (FJC, p. 334), claimed that the role of psychoanalysis as a treatment adjunct for soldiers suffering from shell shock, now analytically understood to be war-induced traumatic neuroses, had already attracted considerable interest by the time of the Budapest Congress. Indeed, it was owing to this interest, Freud noted, that "official representatives from the highest quarters of the Central European Powers were present as observers at the papers and other [Budapest] proceedings" (1919b, p. 207). Apparently the official observers, unnamed by Freud,[4] were duly impressed with what they heard, since "the hopeful result of this first contact was that the establishment of psychoanalytic centers was promised, at which analytically trained physicians would have leisure and opportunity for studying the nature of these puzzling disorders

---

[4] The medical representative of the Austrian Army General Staff was Alfred Georg Hermann Fritz Casten, Colonel, ret., M.D., a Berlin neuropsychiatrist (Eissler, 1986, p. 65n).

and the therapeutic effect exercised on them by psychoanalysis" (p. 207).[5]

Of course, the end of the war shortly after the Congress prevented the implementation of these proposals, but Freud took heart nonetheless from the episode, which "was not without an important influence on the spread of psychoanalysis." Physicians formerly lacking any introduction to analysis had, as army doctors dealing with war neuroses, been propelled into "closer contact" with analysis, and this with good reason:

> Some of the factors which psychoanalysis had recognized and described long before as being at work in peace-time neuroses — the psychogenic origin of the symptoms, the importance of *unconscious* instinctual impulses, the part played in dealing with mental conflicts by the primary gain from being ill ('the flight into illness') — were observed to be present equally in the war neuroses and were accepted almost universally. Simmel's studies show, too, what successes could be achieved by treating war neurotics by the method of catharsis, which as we know, was the first step toward the psychoanalytic technique [1919b, pp. 207–208, emphasis in original].

Freud spent the rest of his introduction aptly considering the differences between traumatic war neuroses and "the ordinary neuroses of peacetime," and thence the implications of the former for "the libido theory of the neuroses." Here the experience of war seemed to represent an exception to, rather than an application of, the theory of sexual etiology. But Freud took exception to the seeming exception. Just as libido theory, via the notion of narcissistic libido, an "entirely legitimate development of the concept of sexuality," had cast its net wide

---

[5] Freud reiterated his optimistic gloss on the Budapest Congress and the promise of establishing psychoanalytic treatment centers for the war wounded in February 1920 in the "Memorandum on the Electrical Treatment of War Neurotics," prepared at the request of the Austrian Commission investigating dereliction of duty among Austrian officers (1920d, p. 215). And he recurred to it again in testimony given on the first day of the Commission's investigation of alleged abuses at the psychiatric hospital of Julius von Wagner-Jauregg (in Eissler, 1986, p. 64).

enough to subsume dementia praecox, paranoia, and melancholia, so too it would prove adequate to the explanation of traumatic neuroses in war and peacetime alike. In the case of war neuroses, he surmised, the danger of external violence might manifest itself as the ego's fear of an internal enemy, so that "the theoretical difficulties standing in the way of a unifying hypothesis of this kind do not seem insuperable" (1919b, p. 210).[6]

Now the psychoanalytic contribution to the *understanding* of war neuroses may have been a real one, but its role in the actual *treatment* of shell shock was peripheral to the point of insignificance. The 589 case histories from the war literature compiled by Elmer Southard and published in 1919 as *Shell-Shock and Other Neuropsychiatric Problems* put the role of psychoanalysis in proper perspective. In introducing this massive work, which drew on the literature of all the belligerent powers, the Philadelphia neurologist Charles Mills offered this comprehensive itemization of the various therapeutic procedures resorted to by authors of the case reports:

> Miracle cures are wrought through many pages. Mutism, deafness and blindness, palsies, contractures, and tics disappear at times as if by magic under various forms of suggestion. Ether or chloroform narcosis drives out the malady at the moment when it reveals its true nature. Verbal suggestion has many adjuvants and collaborators—electricity, sometimes severely administered, lumbar puncture, injections of stovaine into the cerebrospinal fluid, injections of saline solution, colored lights, vibrations, active mechanotherapy, hydrotherapy, hot air baths

---

[6] This very point was stressed by Jones in "War Shock and Freud's Theory of the Neuroses." He appealed to Freud's "striking suggestion that the developed dread sometimes found in situations of real danger is derived, not from the repressed sexual hunger that is directed towards external objects, as is the case with morbid anxiety of the peace neuroses, but from the narcissistic part of the sexual hunger that is attached to the ego, and I venture to suggest that we may here have the key to the states of terror with which we are so familiar in the war neuroses." And further: "It seems to me probable that the intolerance of narcissistic sexual hunger which leads to dread in the presence of real danger is to be correlated with the inhibition of the other manifestations of the fear instinct, with the accumulated tension characteristic of the mode of life in the trenches" (1918, pp. 57–58).

and blasts, massage, etc. Painful and punitive measures have their place—one is inclined to think a less valuable place than is given them by some of the recorders. In some instances the element of suggestion, while doubtless present, is overshadowed by the material methods employed. Persuasion and actual physical improvement are in these cases highly important. Reeducation is not infrequently in evidence. The patient in one way or another is taught how to do things which he had lost the way of doing.

It is interesting to American neurologists to note how frequently in the reports, especially of French observers, the "Weir Mitchell treatment" was the method employed, including isolation, the faradic current, massage, and Swedish movements, hydrotherapy, dietetic measures, reeducative process, and powerful suggestion variously exhibited, especially through the mastery of the physician over the patient. It is rather striking that few records of Freudian psychoanalytic therapy are presented [Mills, 1919, p. xv].

And what does "Freudian psychoanalytic therapy" amount to in those few records to which Mills refers? Little that is recognizably Freudian. Among the British, we find Captain William Brown's specious equation of analysis with "autognosis" —"a method of giving the patient self-knowledge, by revealing to the patient through his own confessions the cause of mental change leading to his symptoms" (Southard, 1919, pp. 702, 901). Equally specious among "analytically" derived approaches was W. R. D. Rivers's therapy of "rationalization of war memories," in which Rivers formulated the therapeutic plan of directing psychiatric casualties to find a redeeming feature in the traumatic experiences implicated in their symptoms. Following this approach, one victim of shell shock was advised "no longer to try to banish the memories [associated with the symptoms], but to try to transform them into tolerable, if not pleasant, companions" (p. 712), while another "was now advised to give up repressing, to read and talk a little about the war, and to accustom himself to thinking about war experiences" (p. 713).

The most the analysts could extract from the Southard compendium were the occasional avowal of "the psychogenic nature of shell-shock" (p. 675) and the equally occasional report of hysteria as an "appendix" to traumata (p. 582). The Freudian testimony of a few British psychiatrists—Forsyth's belief that shell-shock cases eventually turned into "everyday neurosis" (p. 702) or Eder's belief that the "mechanisms" of war shock were the Freudian mechanisms of hysteria (p. 702)—were more than offset by those who decried analysis on account of time limitations (Adrian and Yealland, in Southard, 1919, p. 702), who warned against offhand explanations of war neuroses "as hysteria, wish-fulfillment, and simulation" where organic signs were present (Oppenheim, in Southard, 1919, p. 361), and who reported cases in which hypnotism and "psychoanalysis" were simply ineffective (Purser, in Southard, 1919, p. 677).

A further gloss on the minuscule role of psychoanalysis in the treatment of war neuroses arose in the aftermath of the Great War, for the nature and treatment of shell shock was very much implicated in the national self-questioning that followed the cessation of hostilities. Throughout the 1920s, the British public, suspecting that many soldiers found derelict in the performance of duty were suffering from shell shock (Babington, 1997, p. 136), evinced great uneasiness about military executions for cowardice and desertion. Austrian self-questioning followed a different route. In 1919, spurred by agitation in the popular press, Austria's provisional National Assembly appointed a commission to investigate alleged war crimes among Austrian military officers.

Among the principal topics of inquiry was the Austrian medical service's use of electrotherapy, or faradization, in treating war neuroses. A week before the National Assembly empowered this commission to investigate whether commanding Austrian officers "can be accused of gross mismanagement in the command of military bodies, or of other serious violations of their duties" (in Eissler, 1986, p. 11), *Der Freie Soldat*, a socialist weekly, had characterized faradization as *Die elektrische Foler*—the electrical torture—and deemed its regular employment "one of the revolting chapters in the story of the Austrian army medical services in the treatment of war neurotics" (p. 14). This and comparably sensationalistic reports culminated in publication of extracts from the diary of one Walter Kauders, a junior officer in the Austrian army who suffered a cerebral injury from an exploding shell on the Austrian front in 1914, received a variety of diagnoses over the following three years (including neurasthenia and traumatic neurosis), and was eventually transferred to the Vienna University Clinic in November 1917. Kauders's diary, which recalled a variety of abuses and dwelled especially on electrotherapy and isolation therapy, both of which he had experienced personally, induced the commission to investigate no less a personage than Julius von Wagner-Jauregg, the esteemed psychiatry professor at the University whose responsibilities had long included directorship of the psychiatric clinic of Vienna's *Allegemeine Krankenhaus.*

The investigation of Kauders's charges against Wagner-Jauregg, especially the latter's reliance on traumatizing faradization in the treatment of war neurosis, has been subject to lengthy review by Eissler (1986). Here I cite this episode in forensic psychiatry only because it provides further evidence of the clinical irrelevance of psychoanalysis to wartime realities.

Eissler is understandably at pains to dismiss the testimony of witnesses before the commission whose antipsychoanalytic animus was, by the time of the investigation, a matter of record. But not even Eissler can impute malevolent bias to the remarks of Wagner-Jauregg's assistant Otto Pötzl, an adherent of analysis and member of the Vienna Psychoanalytic Society from 1919 to 1933. Pötzl testified that

> theoretically I am an adherent of psychoanalysis, but I should like to remark that from a practical point of view nothing can be gained from it in wartime. On this I wish to insist. . . . But I have to state that it is impossible to use it in a mass operation in a ward of war neuroses. . . . I am convinced that it needs far more involvement on the part of the physician and far more determination on the part of the neurotics than either the doctor in the presence of mass demands or the war hysteric, who does not want to go back to the war, can bring to it [in Eissler, 1986, pp. 87, 93–94].

Wagner-Jauregg himself, speaking in his own defense, was characteristically brusque in observing that the conditions in military hospitals made psychoanalytic treatment impossible.

Analysis could not be employed, he held, because it "often takes God knows how long." And further, the fact that hospitalized war neurotics frequently spoke foreign languages, a reality that "has been admitted by Professor Freud," presented an insuperable obstacle (Eissler, 1986, p. 67).

More stridently dismissive was Emil Raimann, a former assistant to Wagner-Jauregg who, like Freud, served as an expert witness at the hearing. Raimann, to be sure, was hostile to psychoanalysis, and he did not mince words in his testimony. Freud, he began, "has never seen war neuroses," and, further, Freud's representation of the Budapest Congress as a signpost of official acceptance of the psychoanalytic treatment approach to war neurotics was specious:

> I have read the report of the past psychoanalytical congress in Budapest in 1918, in which there is a summary of what the entire psychoanalytical school has accomplished with war neuroses. . . . the outcome was that two of Freud's closest pupils came to the conclusion that psychoanalysis was not possible in practice and the only one to report on such a treatment was not reporting on psychoanalytical treatment but on a rapid procedure of suggestion [Eissler, 1986, p. 92].

If psychoanalysis were indeed applicable to the casualties of war, Raimann mused, why had Freud himself not entered the fray, why, that is, "did he [Freud] not do it differently [i.e., show how psychoanalysis could be modified to accommodate the actual conditions in the mental wards of military hospitals] and show us how to cure war neuroses by psychoanalysis?" (p. 92).

Eissler deems Raimann's question "invalid," a reflection of anathema to psychoanalysis that antedated the war years. "Had not Freud shown how peacetime neuroses are cured?" Eissler counters. "And in spite of that had not Raimann warned people to avoid the treatment?" (1986, p. 107). But such reasoning is a variant of the very ad hominem strategy that Eissler otherwise abjures. There is no epistemic reason why an opponent of analysis cannot accurately report on circumstances that weigh against the meaningful application of the psychoanalytic method as Freud and his followers understood it. For Raimann's question, when all is said and done, is entirely to the point. Freud did not concern himself with the war neuroses in any substantive way, and he certainly never set out to demonstrate to Austrian military psychiatrists "how to cure war neuroses by psychoanalysis." This is to say that he did not show how a bona fide psychoanalytic treatment approach incorporating the psychoanalytic (as opposed to the hypnotic-cathartic) method could accommodate the realities of life in military hospitals — realities that weighed so heavily against the possibility of any form of intensive, long-term treatment.

Given these realities, what of the specific import of psychoanalysis with respect to the war neuroses? How did it achieve a significance that transcended its marginal, even bastardized, applicability to wartime conditions? In addressing these questions, we must reiterate that the war neuroses did not elicit the progressive development of psychoanalytic treatment approaches.[7] To the contrary, the analysts found they could most profitably address shell shock by invoking the "cathartic" point of view developed by Breuer and Freud in the 1890s. Let us

---

[7] Eissler, in a strained defense of Freud's unimpressive (in my judgment) performance at the investigation of Julius Wagner-Jauregg, demurs from this assessment. He writes that Freud, in his testimony before the Austrian commission, "laid himself open to attack by talking about psychoanalysis and not emphasizing sufficiently how he wanted the word understood. His opponents, and Pötzl too, took advantage of this omission, and they spoke of psychoanalysis exclusively in the sense of the classic technique, which, if only because of the time it takes, could not be used in a military hospital at that time. *It was clear that Freud was envisaging a far wider conception, for he had advanced as an example of psychoanalytical technique Simmel's therapy, which was based on psychoanalytic insight, adapted to the circumstances and therapeutically successful.* Neither the expert witness nor the other witnesses who were attacking psychoanalysis went into that matter" (1986, p. 112, emphasis added).

Now, Freud certainly endorsed Simmel's wartime appropriation of Breuer's hypnocathartic method because it was politically useful to the psychoanalytic movement, but to suggest that Freud thereby envisioned a wider concept of *psychoanalytic* technique is specious. At the hearing, Pötzl and the "opponents" spoke of psychoanalysis "exclusively in the sense of the classic technique" because that technique is precisely what psychoanalysis *meant* in 1920. In reality, Freud, while delighted with Simmel's psychoanalytic "attitude," was patently dismissive of what passed as his "technique." He did not demur from Jones's cynical assessment that Simmel had little to say "but is no doubt useful propaganda." As noted earlier, he did remain hopeful that, under Abraham's tutelage, Simmel would eventually renounce his primitive "Breuer-Freud point of view" and become a psychoanalyst.

now examine more closely how this preanalytic method was grafted onto a psychoanalytic viewpoint by those of Freud's followers most directly involved with the treatment of war neuroses. Perhaps in considering their appropriation of Freudian theory to the *explanation* of war neuroses we shall reengage the surgical metaphor.

Simmel's contribution to the collection on *Psychoanalysis and the War Neuroses*, which derived from his monograph of 1918, was altogether explicit about the kind of "psychoanalytic" intervention that had proven relevant to cases of shell shock. He reported on "a combination of analytical-cathartic hypnosis with analytical conversations during the waking state, and dream interpretation carried out both in the waking state and in deep hypnosis." The approach apparently had much to commend it; in his reported cases of hypnosis followed by regression to the specific event or set of events that had precipitated war neurosis, Simmel claimed to produce symptomatic relief after "an average of two or three sittings" (1921, p. 30). This, for Simmel, was "mental analytic therapy," a modality that enabled shell-shocked soldiers to overcome the splitting of personality attendant to the conflicting demands of wartime service; not surprisingly, the active conflict was between the "undischarged mental material" following from the "compulsory discipline" and "psychic and physical exhaustion" of battlefield conditions, on one hand, and the "abnormally heavy demands" of military performance, on the other (p. 33).

Hypnosis, in this scheme of things, promoted catharsis pure and simple. Through the hypnotically induced reenactment of battlefield events, replete with the full affect of their first occurrence, shell-shocked soldiers instantaneously arrived at an understanding of the formerly repressed motives underlying their symptoms. Once the knowledge of events gleaned from hypnosis was conveyed to the patient, the "crowning point" of treatment immediately ensued. It consisted of "securing the spontaneous cooperation of the neurotic who, freed of his emotional inhibition, and now in harmony with himself, has, through his wider mental field of vision, a greater scope for the activity of his will power" (p. 33).

Reflecting back on his treatment approach to war neurotics a quarter century later, Simmel was clear about the intuitive manner in which he had proceeded during the war years. And in his own retrospective, the procedure itself looks even less analytic-cathartic than the publications of 1918 and 1921 suggest. Writing in 1944, Simmel recalled his systematic efforts to establish a "direct bridge" between his patients' sleeping and hypnotic states, whether by using dream content to induce hypnotic repetitions of traumatic war scenes, asking patients to interpret dream symbols while under hypnosis, or actually providing posthypnotic suggestions that patients, by dreaming, supplement memory fragments that arose under hypnosis. Particularly striking is his admission that the nature and extent of soldiers' ability to relieve traumatic experiences under hypnosis "depended very much on [his] personal attitude during the hypnotic situation." This attitude incorporated not only "reassurance by suggestion," but also the provision of an "actual enemy" (in the form of a stuffed dummy) on whom hypnotized soldiers could discharge the "aggressive instinctual energies" called forth by hypnosis (pp. 243–244). The curative process began with the mobilization of the patient's rage to the point of partially mutilating or completely destroying the dummy. It was capped by a final act of suggestion, in which Simmel told the patient, under hypnosis, that "he had killed his enemy in a dream, and need not feel guilty about it." Small wonder, then, that Simmel did not impute any particular *psychoanalytic* significance to the procedure as he developed it and employed it during World War I. Quite the opposite: "Only through the enlargement of our psychoanalytic ego psychology, which we have gained in the meantime (thanks to Freud), am I able to define theoretically the principle of my therapy at that time" (p. 243).

Ferenczi's consideration of "Two Types of War Neuroses" in the volume on war neuroses was descriptively richer than Simmel's presentation, but it too was wedded to the language of catharsis. Ferenczi's specific contribution is only the presentation of a rudimentary typology of war neuroses attendant to the varieties of cathartic blockage. There are cases, he found, that constitute *"conversion hysterias* in the sense of Breuer and Freud" (1917, p.129, emphasis in original); in such cases, the analyst witnessed a fixation of the nervous energy, the "inner-vation," that was dominant at the moment of war-related trauma and its conversion into morbid symptoms in one part of the body. Ferenczi had in mind instances of paralysis in which the nature of the contracture of an arm or leg, for example, corresponds exactly to the position or movement of that extremity at the moment of shock.[8] In addition to these "monosymptomatic" cases, there were the more numerous cases of shell shock in which soldiers developed generalized tremors or disturbances of gait; further, when they tried to walk, or to walk without support, they experienced classic symptoms of anxiety— palpitations, increased pulse rate, profuse sweating—often accompanied by hyperaesthesia (hypersensitivity) of the senses. Here Ferenczi discerned classic anxiety hysteria, in which a motor disturbance functioned "as an expression of phobia that serves the purpose of preventing an outbreak of anxiety" (p. 135).

Ernest Jones, who thought poorly of Simmel's and Ferenczi's contributions to the Budapest Congress, could muster only faint praise for the effort of Karl Abraham. It was "very good descriptively," he wrote Freud, "but deficient on the theoretical side" (FJC, p. 337). Here Jones is wrong. Abraham's contribution to the Budapest Congress, "Psychoanalysis and the War Neuroses," is theoretically bolder than those of Simmel and Ferenczi, since Abraham is not content to highlight the continuity between the traumatic neuroses of ordinary life and those of wartime in terms of the unconscious and the "cathartic" release of the repressed; rather, he stresses the commonalties at the level of a specifically sexual etiology. Like the traumata of everyday life, that is, the traumata of the battlefield operated on the libidinal economy; to wit, they induced "a regressive change in the direction of narcissism" (Abraham, 1921, p. 60).

---

[8] Among Ferenczi's examples: "The man whose right arm is contracted at an obtuse angle was concussed by the shell just as he was sliding *his rifle into the 'stand easy' position*. This position corresponds exactly with that imitated by the contracture" (1917, p. 127, emphasis in original). And further: "This soldier with the permanent contracture of the left calf recounts how he was cautiously descending a steep mountain in Serbia, and, while *stretching his left foot downwards* to find a support, was concussed by an explosion and rolled down. Here, too, therefore, there is a 'petrification' due to shock, in the attitude that had just been adopted" (p. 129, emphasis in original).

Thus, for Abraham, the incidence of war neuroses fell back on predisposing factors of a totally conventional sort. Even before war neurotics experienced the trauma of the battlefield, he held, they were incipiently neurotic, in a word, "emotionally unstable, especially with regard to their sexuality":

> Some of them were unable to fulfill their duties in everyday life; others were able to do so, although they showed little initiative or driving power. In all cases sexual activity was restricted, and libido inhibited by fixations. Many of them had already before the war shown poor or limited potency. Their relationship to the female sex was disturbed by partial fixation of the libido in the developmental phase of narcissism to a greater or less extent. Their social and sexual functioning was dependent on certain concessions to their narcissism [p. 61].

The specific stressors of wartime—"the renunciation of all narcissistic privileges" entailed in the readiness to sacrifice oneself for the common good, the readiness to commit acts of aggression and even to kill, and the necessity of living "in an almost exclusively male environment"—these factors interacted synergistically with a "narcissistic" predisposition to produce libidinal disequilibrium. The result was the recurrent symptomatic picture of war neuroses, in which tremors, fits, and hysterical convulsions assumed a significance that was both narcissistic and feminine. Why the latter? Because "many patients show the traits of complete feminine passivity in the way they abandon themselves to their suffering" (p. 62).

With Abraham, no less than with Simmel and Ferenczi, we seem to be far from surgery and the surgical metaphor. But this is precisely the point. The war neuroses spurred the analysts to re-vision the analytic attitude in the light of new circumstances that underscored the limitations, indeed the radical inadequacy, of medicine and surgery as therapies for the war-wounded. The analytic approach, even in the distorted "cathartic" guise elicited by battlefield conditions, was increasingly seen as a counterpoise to a surgical mentality that rested content with organic repair. As the analysts came to juxtapose their approach to battlefield trauma with the ministrations of wartime surgeons, they had progressively less need to appropriate a surgical model of psychoanalytic intervention. And as the analytic procedure relinquished its mimetic dependency on surgery, the surgical metaphor began to retreat from analytic consciousness.

We glean this development most clearly in Abraham's "Psychoanalysis and the War Neuroses." Abraham was far more skeptical about surgery than Freud had been in "Lines of Advance in Psychoanalytic Therapy." He not only refused to appropriate the surgical metaphor, but even called into question what Freud had expressly endorsed: the adequacy of surgery's "life-saving help" as a template for the possibilities of psychoanalytic intervention. For Abraham, the very *incompleteness* of surgical remedies served to underscore the epistemic autonomy of the psychoanalytic procedure and the theoretical insights that it subserved. And he was thereby led to evoke his own surgical experiences during the war in a new light, namely, as observational data sustaining a psychoanalytic understanding of those whom surgeons could save but not cure:

> On a ward in a general military hospital I had to treat four soldiers who had all suffered a severe injury to the right eye by splinters from the same grenade. All four had already undergone enucleation of the eye in another hospital. They were in no way depressed, but were in a carefree and cheerful mood On the day they each received an artificial eye, a strange scene took place. The men exuberantly skipped about, danced, and laughed, just like children working themselves up into a frenzy of joy. There is no doubt that this, too, was a regression to narcissism, albeit of a restricted type [1921, p. 64].

> In 1915, whilst I was working in a surgical ward, a man was treated for a bullet wound in the penis. The operation, carried out by a well-known surgeon, was very successful. Two years later the same patient came to my psychiatric ward. Having previously been psychologically normal, he now showed a paranoid mental illness. Questioning revealed that as a consequence of his injury he had developed complete genital insensibility. Here, too, the psychosis seemed to be closely connected with the loss of masculine potency [p. 65].

"I Have Been Through Hell"

∞∞∞

And what of Ernest Jones, whom last we saw embroiled with Freud in the medicoanalytic treatment of Jones's common law wife, Loe Kann, in 1914–15. By June 1915, Loe had quit her analysis and, with Freud in attendance, married one Herbert Jones in Budapest. Several weeks later, Ernest Jones, now amply satisfied with the entire course of events, advised Freud that Loe was "happy and pretty well on the whole," though still suffering from sciatica and kidney attacks. This would be the first of his continuing updates on the medical, analytic, and domestic status of Kann and her new husband (FJC, pp. 313, 317), as Jones was loath to relinquish the role of analytic *pater familias* to Loe and her husband.

Jones's bond to Loe was in keeping with his own penchant for unconventional domestic arrangements. Even before Loe quit her analysis with Freud and married Herbert Jones in the spring of 1915, Ernest had been living with Loe's companion, Lina, a liaison that lasted until the beginning of 1917. Lina's unpublished correspondence suggests she was "overwhelmingly" in love with Jones (Brome, 1983, pp. 111–112), and her presence was no doubt powerful consolation to Jones during the war years. "Lina is still with me," Jones informed Freud in March of 1916, "and I am as happy and contented as anyone can be in war time" (FJC, p. 316).

But not contented enough, it appears, to resist the charms of Morfydd Owen. In 1916, Jones's British colleague, Eric Hiller, introduced him to the gifted Welsh musician who would shortly become his first wife. A pianist, vocalist, and composer, Owen was widely viewed at the time as a Welsh national treasure in the arts. A prodigy, she had been a scholarship student at the

Welsh Royal Academy of Music, where she became an associate professor by the age of 24. Jones's whirlwind romance led to a marriage proposal after three brief encounters. Perhaps, as his biographer suggests, he was swept away by her "soulful face with its withdrawn beauty" and envisioned her a soulmate whose artistic sensibility would complement his own practical scientific bent (Brome, 1983, p. 112).

In any event, the marriage proved no less troublesome than Jones's sundry other *liaisons impulsives*. Owen was 12 years his junior and apparently immature; her "mental evolution," Jones euphemistically observed, "had not proceeded evenly in all directions" (Jones, 1959, p. 254). In point of fact, Jones was put off not merely by her strong attachment to her father, whom she felt she had deserted by marrying Jones, but by her "very simple-minded religious beliefs," with the inconvenient schedule of church observances they entailed.

Still the marriage promised to overcome these difficulties. "As time went on," Jones observed, "love began to tell, and her ideas broadened," which is to say, Morfydd relinquished her ideas for those of her "practical scientific" husband.[1] But just as their happiness "grew more and more complete" (1959, p. 254), and after a mere 18 months of marriage, tragedy struck. In the summer of 1918, Jones begins, "We were paying a summer visit to my father in Wales, and I was looking forward to taking her over my familiar Gowerland; though a native of the same country, she had never visited that beautiful peninsula."

> On the way down I wanted to buy her a box of chocolates, which for some reason, she declined; it was poignant to reflect later that it would probably have saved her life. Life and great issues are always at the mercy of meaningless trivialities. Soon after arriving she fell obscurely ill, and it was a couple of days before it became plain that there was an appendicitis, which

---

[1] "As time went on, however, love began to tell, and her ideas broadened. As may be imagined, my notion of adjustment in such matters consists in persuading the other person to approach my view of them, and that is what gradually and painlessly happened" (Jones, 1959, p. 254).

was going on to form an abscess. An operation was urgently indicated. I spent four or five hours at the telephone trying to reach [the surgeon Wilfred] Trotter; communications late in 1918 were poor, both by telephone and by rail. He advised me to secure a local surgeon and not risk the delay of waiting till he could come the next day; it was, of course, a simple operation. She did not do well, however, and after a few days became delirious with a high temperature. We thought there was blood poisoning till I got Trotter from London. He at once recognized delayed chloroform poisoning. It had recently been discovered, which neither the local doctor nor I had known, that this is a likelihood with a patient who is young, has suppuration in any part of the body, and has been deprived of sugar (as war conditions had then imposed); in such circumstances only ether is permissible as an anesthetic. This simple piece of ignorance cost a valuable and promising life. We fought hard, and there were moments when we seemed to have succeeded, but it was too late [1959, pp. 254–55].

That Jones's understanding of what had transpired hung on the authoritative verdict of a great surgeon, his lifelong friend and brother-in-law Wilfred Batten Lewis Trotter, comes as no surprise. In 1900, pursuing graduate medical studies at London's University College Hospital with his characteristically ferocious ambition, the 21-year-old Jones, intent on a career in neurology that would benefit from experience in "surgical neurology," received the hospital's highly competitive House Surgeonship under the pioneering British neurosurgeon, Sir Victor Horsley. As House Surgeon, Jones quickly became friends with Trotter, seven years his senior, then Surgical Registrar and "a man to whom Horsley could safely leave any operation whatever, and he did so as often as possible" (Jones, 1959, p. 100). Jones's boundless admiration for the man who, second only to Freud, "mattered most in my life" (1959, p. 101) blossomed in the context of shared surgical endeavor. The two operated together, sometimes under dramatic circumstances. In his autobiography, Jones recounts two instances in which patients with crushed legs required double amputation: "Trotter would amputate through one thigh while I did the other; it is a pretty formidable operation, but both patients recovered" (p. 100).

Trotter was a polymath whose knowledge came to embrace psychoanalysis and group psychology.[2] It was Trotter who had first brought Freud to Jones's attention; indeed, he accompanied his one-time surgical colleague to the first International Psychoanalytic Congress in Salzburg, Austria in April 1908. Unlike Jones, who at the time was still able to relish the role of onlooker, Trotter was ill at ease and absented himself frequently from the proceedings. At the Congress banquet, he found himself seated between Jones and the youthful Fritz Wittels, who regaled him with "jejunely facetious remarks about the hysteria of some Greek goddess." Sufficiently put off with Wittels's puerile psychobabble and unimpressed with the Congress in general, Trotter turned to Jones and muttered: "I console myself with the thought that I can cut a leg off, and no one else here can" (Jones, 1959, p. 168).

Of course, in the matter of Morfydd Owen, it was precisely Trotter's surgical identity that rose to the fore in Jones's account. Would that Trotter had been on hand to evaluate Jones's wife, to choose the anesthesia, and to perform the appendectomy. Even at a distance Trotter's clinical acumen was equal to the case, but his diagnosis of chloroform poisoning came too late either to alter the course of events or to mask their significance for Jones.

Obscure illness. Hurried operation. Choice of anesthesia. A hard fight alongside the surgeon. For Jones in 1918, the theater

---

[2] Trotter's *Instincts of the Herd in Peace and War*, published in 1916, was one of very few psychological studies to use the Great War as a catalyst for deeper reflection on human nature. Jones apprised Freud of the book (FJC, p. 316), had Loe Kann send him a copy (p. 318), and subsequently commended the work to him (p. 372). When Freud himself turned to the topic of group psychology after the war, Trotter's notion of a primary herd instinct coexisting with the instincts of self-preservation, nutrition, and sex was given respectful, albeit critical, consideration (Freud, 1921, pp. 118–121).

Trotter, whose surgical authority had mattered so much to Jones in 1918, was ultimately destined to bring this same authority to bear on no less a patient than Freud himself. In February of 1939, shortly after Freud's relocation in England, Trotter was called on by Freud's personal physician, Max Schur, to evaluate a suspicious lesion in the back of Freud's mouth (Schur, 1972, pp. 517–518). He thereby became the last of a series of distinguished surgeons to scrutinize Freud's oral cavity (Romm, 1983a, pp. 127–131). Trotter, apprised by biopsy that Freud's suspicious lesion was indeed a recurrence of malignant epithelioma, advised against any further surgery on a dying patient whose 16-year surgical ordeal by then lay behind him.

of life and death was not the theater of the mind but the operating theater. And here the analyst in Jones, so resourceful and persistent in sparking his young wife's "mental evolution," stood helpless before her operative plight. Nor was Jones's helplessness the helpless wonderment with which Freud had earlier gazed on Fliess and relied on Fliess: rather, it was helpless frustration in the face of the limits of the surgeon, in this instance, the tragic limits of a "local surgeon" whose "simple piece of ignorance" propelled Jones into a grief without limits, "the most painful experience of my life" (1959, p. 255). Three months after Morfydd's death on September 7, 1918, Jones was again embroiled in psychoanalytic politics and able once more to "look forward in life." Yet, he confided to Freud, "I have been through hell itself these last three months. It has been an indescribably terrible experience, signifying more even than a tremendous loss—owing to my inner psychical situation and the poignant circumstances of my wife's death" (FJC, p. 326).

As matters turned out, the untimely death of Morfydd Owen created only the briefest of hiatuses in Jones's convoluted romantic history. Even during the 18-month marriage to Morfydd, Jones had become entangled with his analysand Joan Riviere in a personal relationship that had quickly spiraled out of control.[3] And in October 1919 he married Katherine Jokl, a Viennese "who combined voluptuous good looks with the intellectual ability to master the intricacies of a Ph.D." (Brome, 1983, p. 124). Jones had met Fraulein Jokl during a trip to Switzerland in the summer of 1919. True to his abiding impetuosity, he dined with his future wife on the day of their meeting, sent her flowers the following day, and casually proposed marriage during a walk in the Dolder Woods a day later.

---

[3] "Whether during the years 1916/18 Jones had become enamored of another woman and was once more struggling to control his torn loyalties, or whether it was simply that a patient fell hopelessly in love with him during psychoanalytic transference and persuaded herself that Jones reciprocated that love, can only be determined by a close reading of her [Riviere's] letters" (Brome, 1983, pp. 113). Discreetly, Brome goes no further in his assessment, but his analysis of the correspondence in question suggests the latter possibility (pp. 114ff.)

"I Am No More What I Was"

∞

In February of 1923, Freud, an inveterate cigar smoker whose nicotine dependency had played an obvious role in his cardiac crisis of 1894, detected what he casually termed a "leucoplastic growth" on his jaw and right palate. He suspected an "epithelioma"—a usually benign surface tumor—though his diagnosis "was not accepted." He had been "assured on the benignity of the matter but as you know, nobody can guarantee its behavior when it be permitted to grow further" (FJC, p. 521). With these casual revelations to Ernest Jones, the surgical metaphor enters a new and harsh personal domain: that of the surgical trials and tribulations that would tax Freud's wit, intellect, and physical stamina for the remaining 16 years of his life. It is not only in its continuing surgical aftermath that the jaw cancer of 1923 commands attention. Freud's behavior on making his initial self-diagnosis and his behavior on learning the definitive diagnosis illuminate from a telling vantage point the hold of the surgeon on the dissector of the unconscious.

Three decades earlier, in May 1893, Stephen Grover Cleveland, reelected 24th President of the United States the preceding fall, detected a "rough spot" on the roof of his mouth.[1] When this ulcerating lesion of the palate did not clear up and generated increasing discomfort, he brought it to the attention of the White House physician, Major Robert Maitland O'Reilly, who initiated local treatment with iodides and bichloride of

---

[1] This account of President Cleveland's cancer draws on W. W. Keen's first-hand reminiscences of the surgical course of events, published in the *Saturday Evening Post* in 1917, supplemented by several contemporary commentaries (Brooks et al., 1980; Aziz, 1995; Hoang and O'Leary, 1997).

mercury while enlisting immediate surgical consultation. Surgical evaluations by William W. Keen of Philadelphia's Jefferson Medical College and Joseph Decatur Bryant of New York City in mid-June, followed by evaluation of two biopsied specimens by several pathologists, including Johns Hopkins Hospital's William Welch, all pointed to a diagnosis of malignant epithelioma. Excision of the President's tumor, which we now know to have been a "verrucous carcinoma"[2] of the hard palate and gingiva (Brooks et al., 1980, pp. 19–20), took place in secrecy aboard the yacht *Oneida*, whose lounge had been converted to an operating suite. Shortly after noon on July 1, as the yacht cruised up New York's East River toward the President's summer home on the coast of Massachusetts, a surgical team led by Bryant removed Cleveland's entire left maxilla, disinfecting the resulting cavity with Theirsch's solution and packing it, as was the practice of the time, with iodoform gauze.

This swift journey to surgical intervention resulted in radical cure. Cleveland's recovery from his surgery (including a follow-up operation on July 17, also on board the *Oneida*) was so swift, and his accommodation of the vulcanized rubber prosthesis prepared by New York prosthodontist Kasson Gibson so complete, that he was able to address a special session of Congress on August 7 without incident; no one detected any change in the President's voice which, with the prosthesis in place, so one of his surgeons recounted, was "excellent, even its quality not being altered" (Keen, 1917). And Cleveland's ability to address Congress with utter clarity and conviction was of some moment at this particular juncture of American history: his

---

[2] The diagnosis of Cleveland's neoplastic lesion was arrived at in 1976, when the pathologists Gonzalo Aponte and Horatio Enterline microscopically and radiologically evaluated the preserved portion of Cleveland's tissue specimens, first biopsied in 1893. Verrucous carcinoma is a highly uncommon low-grade malignant tumor; it accounts for only two to four percent of all oral carcinomas, is usually treatable by surgery alone, and offers an excellent prognosis (Brooks et al., 1980, p. 20). Although Luce (1983) has considered the diagnosis of verrucous carcinoma for Freud, Romm's comprehensive study leaves no doubt that Freud's oral cancer was the far more common and, alas, far more metastatic, squamous cell carcinoma.

address calmed the nation's financial markets, then in the midst of the Panic of 1893, and eventuated in Congress's repeal of the destabilizing Sherman Silver Act of 1890. Drawing on the best that modern surgery of 1893 had to offer, Cleveland fulfilled the pressing obligations of high office seven weeks after major oral surgery and three weeks after the follow-up procedure. He lived out his remaining 15 years completely free of any recurrence of the cancer.

With Freud, we behold a strikingly dissimilar course of events—studded by a series of delays and deceptions—culminating in a far less sanguine outcome. Why, Max Schur asks, did Freud initially take no steps to have his growth—far more ominous than Cleveland's, as it turned out—examined? Why did he not consult the more esteemed of his physician-friends: the family pediatrician Otto Rie, the internist Felix Deutsch, the cardiologist Ludwig Braun, the surgeon Julius Schnitzler, the latter "a brilliant and very experienced diagnostician" (Schur, 1972, p. 348)? Why did he wait until the second week of April to consult a colleague, and only a marginally suitable colleague at that—the analyst-dermatologist Maxim Steiner?

Schur cannot answer these questions, but in recalling the "tragic chain of deceptions" that followed Freud's untoward delay, he leads us to an understanding of the way in which Freud's attitude toward surgeons and surgery led him to engage the demoralizing period of his own operations. Neither of the two physicians to whom Freud first appealed would share with him the grave pathology each beheld. And what they beheld was a common malignant lesion of the oral cavity, a squamous cell cancer, probably located at the right glossopalatine arch.[3] The dermatologist Steiner recommended an excision and therefore, as far as Schur is concerned, "obviously recognized the lesion for what it was." But he was content to advise Freud only that his growth was a leukoplakia. When Felix Deutsch visited Freud several days later, Freud "took him aside as he

---

[3] The glossopalantine arch is "a fold of tissue situated at the back of the mouth which, with its companion—the palatopharyngeal or posterior palantine arch, form the pillars of a nest in which the palatine tonsil lies" (Romm, 1983a, p. 34).

was about to leave and asked Deutsch to look at his mouth, remarking: 'Be prepared to see something you won't like'" (Schur, 1972, pp. 350–351). Deutsch too immediately recognized an advanced malignancy but, like Steiner, was content to mislead the patient. He pronounced Freud's growth a "bad leukoplakia" due to smoking and advised, like Steiner, that it be surgically removed. The choice of surgeon was obviously broached and the name of Professor Marcus Hajek was mentioned, presumably by Deutsch, whereupon Freud voiced his misgivings: Hajek was the brother-in-law of the surgeon Julius Schnitzler, a member of Freud's weekly card-playing circle; Freud knew Hajek personally and, so Schur informs us, was aware of Hajek's ambivalent attitude toward him. The choice was thereby left open, with the matter in Freud's hands.

For Schur, "the days that followed had the quality of a grotesque nightmare" (1972, p. 351). Deutsch made repeated phone calls urging Freud not to delay surgical consultation. Freud, so Schur believes, took these urgings as indications of the far graver diagnosis that Steiner and Deutsch had independently arrived at but withheld from him. He was thereby induced to schedule ambulatory surgery with Marcus Hajek, the very surgeon about whom he had earlier voiced misgivings. Unbeknownst to his family, Freud, accompanied by Deutsch, traveled to the outpatient department of a private hospital headed by Hajek on April 20, 1923.[4] As Deutsch later recalled,

We drove to the hospital together with the understanding that he [Freud] would be at his home immediately after the operation. But he lost more blood than was foreseen and as an emergency he had to rest on a cot in a tiny room on a ward of

---

[4] It is interesting to contrast this course of events — diagnosis of a probably malignant lesion through physical examination by an internist and dermatologist, followed by the scheduling of ambulatory surgery with a rhinologist—with the contemporary management of an oral cancer of the magnitude of Freud's. In 1983, Luce observed that "the evaluation of such a patient [viz., with Freud's cancer] would consist of an examination under general anesthesia, nasopharyngoscopy, and direct laryngoscopy to define the full extent of the lesion and, in addition, to search for a possible second synchronous primary. A treatment program for a lesion as advanced as Freud's might include preoperative chemotherapy, then operative resection followed by immediate reconstruction" (p. 715).

the hospital, since no other room was available, with another patient who, by tragicomic coincidence, I might say, was an imbecile dwarf [1956, p. 280].

Freud's first operation did not go "entirely smoothly" (Schur, 1972, p. 352). Moreover, only after the operation was Freud's family first advised of his "outpatient" procedure and asked to bring to the hospital what he would require for an overnight stay. On arriving at the hospital, Schur relates, " 'Frau Professor' Freud and [his daughter] Anna found Freud sitting on a kitchen chair, covered with blood. There was no nurse or physician in attendance" (p. 352). Schur now interrupts his own narrative with the more horrific description of Freud's serious postsurgical condition that Ernest Jones arrived at after questioning Deutsch, Freud, and Anna Freud:

> The ward sister sent the two ladies home at lunch time, when visitors were not allowed, and assured them the patient [Freud] would be all right. When they returned an hour or two later they learned that he had had an attack of profuse bleeding, and to get help had rung the bell, which was, however, out of order; he himself could neither speak nor call out. The friendly dwarf, however, had rushed for help, and after some difficulty the bleeding was stopped; perhaps his action saved Freud's life. Anna then refused to leave again and spent the night sitting by her father's side. He was weak from loss of blood, was half-drugged from the medicines, and was in great pain. During the night she and the nurse became alarmed at his condition and sent for the house surgeon, who, however, refused to get out of bed. The next morning Hajek demonstrated the case to a crowd of students, and later in the day Freud was allowed to go home [Jones, 1957, pp. 90–91].

Schur does not mince words in his criticism of Hajek. As both a student and a practicing internist, he had witnessed several of Hajek's operations and attests to what he claims was "generally known" at the time—that Hajek was " a somewhat mediocre surgeon" and "certainly was not qualified to operate on a malignancy involving the resection of the maxilla" (1972, pp. 351, 351n). And, in point of fact, Hajek's treatment of Freud was sadly deficient on all counts. Sharon Romm, whose monographic study of Freud's cancer ably brings together all the available medical evidence on Freud's treatment, provides a dismaying catalog of Hajek's surgical and ethical shortcomings: he performed an incomplete operation, may not even have excised a portion of the primary lesion, made no allowance for scar contracture, denied to Freud that the biopsied tissue was malignant, made no admission that the lesion extended far beyond the biopsied area, and provided no aftercare beyond referral for radiation treatment (1983a, pp. 7–8, 17, 34). "In the least pitifully inadequate and at worst negligently deficient" (p. 9)—this is Romm's verdict on Hajek's treatment of Freud. But surgical incompetence cannot account for Hajek's dubious medical ethics, and Schur deems this aspect of his behavior "difficult to explain":

> Jones has rightly characterized it [Hajek's behavior] as 'cavalier.' That he satisfied himself with a local excision which, as he must have known, could not have arrested the spread of the malignancy, can be explained only by the assumption that he had given up the case as hopeless, and was therefore just going through the motions of taking palliative measures. That Hajek performed the not-so-small excision on an ambulatory basis and then left Freud without proper medical and nursing care after his hemorrhage would have been inexcusable in any case, even if the patient had not been someone who had achieved world fame and was, moreover, a friend of his brother-in-law's [1972, p. 354].

There can be no defense of Hajek in the matter of Freud's surgical treatment and aftercare, and we are left with the puzzle of why Freud initially turned to him. Presumably, he had been recommended, or at least mentioned, by one of Freud's attending physicians of the time, either Steiner or Deutsch. The only explanation is obvious and less than satisfying: Hajek was the type of scholarly clinician with whom Freud could identify; whatever his surgical limitations, he was eminently well credentialed and admired as an enthusiastic teacher (Romm, 1983a, p. 6). The assistant of Johann Schnitzler, head of the Vienna General Policlinic's Department of Laryngology from 1872 until his death in 1893, Hajek had coedited Schnitzler's *Clinical Atlas of Laryngology* for posthumous publication in 1895 and proceeded to ascend the rungs of the department's clinical ladder. Despite the early opposition of Leopold von Shrötter, chief of the University Polyclinic, he completed specialty training and became chief of the university's Rhinologic Hospital. From here, he contributed abundantly to the clinical literature, with over 150 clinical papers and several textbooks on rhinological anatomy, pathology, and treatment applications. Moreover, his early description of the anatomy of the accessory nasal sinuses led to a bona fide clinical discovery, the delimitation of "Hajek's triad" (mucosal dryness, septal deviation, and infection) as a cause of perforation of the nasal septum . By 1919, Hajek had become titular full professor and head of the department (Lesky, 1976, pp. 377–378).

Freud, whose ability to evaluate surgical technique appears to have been vanishingly small, presumably equated Hajek's scholarly attainments in otorhinolaryngology with surgical competence within the oral cavity.[5] As early as the spring of 1898, when Freud was enmeshed in his medicosurgical dependency on Wilhelm Fliess, he conveyed an appreciation of Hajek as a surgeon of choice. When Freud's daughter Mathilde developed throat symptoms, he awaited Fliess's diagnostic evaluation, allowing that Fliess might well recommend the necessary throat operation, "which Hajek can carry out here" (FFlL, p. 313). A quarter century later, whatever his personal misgivings about entrusting his oral cavity to a personal acquaintance, Freud apparently thought well of Hajek as surgeon. Nor did he evince radical disillusionment in the aftermath of Hajek's abysmal performance. After five months of postsurgical pain and the onset of trismus,[6] on the eve of a second, more radical operation at the hands of Hans Pichler, Freud informed Jones that he was still awaiting "the final

---

[5] The analogy between the grounds of Freud's (mis)estimation of Hajek and Fliess is self-evident. In the case of Fliess, too, Freud's appreciation of intellectual attainments — in this case, feats of numerological ingenuity and seeming insights into human bisexuality — gave Fliess a priori credibility as a medical adviser and surgical consultant.

[6] Trismus, significant difficulty opening the jaws, can be due to pain or mechanical obstruction; in Freud's case, the onset of trismus signified that his neoplasm had "deeply infiltrated the underlying tissue" (Romm, 1983a, p. 35).

judgment of the man [Hajek] who operated on me" (FJC, p. 527).

Of course, those around Freud were by then in full knowledge of a verdict that left no room for the play of clinical judgment. The pathology report of Freud's excised specimen confirmed the diagnosis of malignant epithelioma, and in the weeks following the operation, Hajek sent him to Guido Holzknecht at the *Allgemeines Krankenhaus* for two X-ray treatments.[7]

Hajek's specious reassurances had no effect on Freud, who, we may reasonably surmise, fully grasped the onerous nature of his "dear neoplasm" (Freud to Deutsch, in Schur, 1972, p. 357) shortly after the procedure. And the nature of Freud's "recovery" in the months following Hajek's excision provided little grounds for optimism. By the summer of 1923, the suffering attendant to his x-ray treatment was compounded by progressively worse trismus, or pain opening his mouth. When Felix Deutsch allowed Freud his August vacation in Italy, it was only on condition that he consult another surgeon immediately on his return. If Freud managed to retain any illusion at all about his condition in the wake of Hajek's local procedure, it was shattered during the holiday itself, when he experienced a massive oral hemorrhage during a nighttime train ride from Verona to Rome (Romm, 1983a, p. 11).

Still, Deutsch withheld from Freud the laboratory confirmation of malignancy prior to the August holiday, nor did he enlighten him during a visit in Lavarone during the latter part of the month. Deutsch did take the occasion of this visit to apprise the assembled members of Freud's Committee — Abraham, Eitingon, Ferenczi, Jones, Rank, and Sachs — of the true nature of Freud's condition, and he proceeded to make arrangements for a second operation by Hans Pichler at the conclusion of Freud's summer holiday.

Schur, who otherwise has little good to say about Deutsch's medical management of Freud, applauds the belated referral

---

[7] Romm (1983a, pp. 47–52) provides a brief, illuminating overview of X-ray therapy at the time Freud received treatment. She observes that "Freud probably received much less radiation than today's accepted curative dose" (p. 48).

to Pichler, whom he deems "the ideal choice for Freud's case" (1972, p. 361). We are indebted to Romm (1983a, pp. 11–16; 1983b; Romm and Luce, 1984) for a useful portrait of him that attests to the wisdom of Deutsch's referral and confirms Schur's judgment. I draw on her studies in the following brief portrait.

The son of a highly regarded Viennese dentist who served the Austrian court, Hans Pichler received medical training in Vienna, Freibourg, and Prague. Following completion of his training in 1900, he remained in Vienna, where he began surgical training under Anton von Eiselsberg, one of Billroth's most gifted assistants (Lesky, 1976, p. 453). Pichler had to forego a career in general surgery when, during training under Eiselsberg, he developed eczema from repeated application of the antiseptic carbol spray then used as a disinfectant prior to surgery. He thereupon shifted both the locale and professional focus of his studies and enrolled in Northwestern University's School of Dentistry in 1902. Quickly overcoming an initial sense of dislocation, Pichler distinguished himself in his dental training and received his dental degree after a year of study.[8] On his return to Vienna, he began a successful dental practice that would span 30 years. As full professor at the University of Vienna, he would direct the university's Dental Institute, where he taught general dentistry as well as oral surgery and played a key role in instituting the curriculum covered in the qualifying examinations of Austrian dentists. During the war years, Pichler headed the university hospital's newly established department of oral surgery, where he operated on scores of severely injured soldiers, employing "heroic procedures" with "excellent results" (Schur, 1972, p. 361). Lesky (1976, p. 453) dubs him the founder of Viennese oral surgery.

Pichler's scientific achievements spanned various aspects of his specialty and attested to his conviction that dentistry was a medical specialty requiring a general medical education. The author of 125 technical papers, he contributed especially to

---

[8] While studying dentistry in Chicago, Pichler worked with G. V. Black, "the first proponent of the principle of 'preventive extension,' the expansion of a cavity during its preparation for a filling as a preventative measure against further decay of the tooth" (Romm, 1983a, pp. 12–13).

the topics of jaw surgery and preventive dentistry, but also addressed prosthetic treatment following jaw resection, treatment of trigeminal neuralgia, and the management of facial clefts. In addition to translating Black's classic textbook of dentistry into German, Pichler brought together his clinical contributions and vast clinical experience in a three-volume work, *Mund und Kieferchirurgie* (Surgery of the Mouth and Jaws) (Pichler and Trauner, 1948).

On his return from summer holiday in September 1923, Freud accepted the arrangements made on his behalf with apparent equanimity, and, following his initial consultation with Pichler, advised Max Eitingon of his forthcoming ordeal with the optimistic reassurance conveyed by his new surgeon: "the operation will be performed by Professor Pichler, the greatest expert in these matters, who is also preparing the prosthesis that will be needed afterward. He promises that within 4–5 weeks I shall be able to eat and talk satisfactorily, so that for the time being I have postponed the beginning of my practice until November" (Freud to Eitingon, in Schur, 1972, p. 361).

Between Hajek's local excision in April 1923 and Pichler's radical resection of his upper jaw the following September, Freud's devastating losses of the postwar years culminated in the death of his beloved grandson Heinz (Heinele), the second child of his daughter Sophie Freud Halberstadt. Sophie herself had earlier succumbed to fulminant influenza pneumonia in June of 1920, just a few days after the death of Freud's beloved friend and benefactor, Anton von Freund. Two years later, in August of 1922, Freud was again "deeply shaken," this time by the death of his sister Rosa's daughter Caecilie Graf, his "best niece, a dear girl of 23, who took Veronal last week while alone at Vienna" (FJC, p. 499).

But it was the death of Freud's four-and-a-half-year-old Heinele, a victim of the miliary tuberculosis (or tubercular meningitis) then rampant in Vienna, that proved Freud's most grievous loss. Six days before Heinele's death on June 19, 1923, while the child lay comatose without any possibility of recovery, Freud confessed his anguish to two close Hungarian friends, Kata and Lajos Levy, in an oft-quoted passage: "I find this loss very hard to bear. I don't think I have ever experienced such grief; perhaps my own sickness contributes to the shock. I work out of sheer necessity; fundamentally everything has lost its meaning for me" [quoted in Schur, 1972, p. 358]. In the aftermath of Heinele's death, Freud owned up to suffering "the first depression in my life" (Freud to Ferenczi, in Schur, 1972, p. 359), and when Ludwig Binswanger's eight-year-old son subsequently also succumbed to tubercular meningitis in 1926, Freud, in heartfelt testimony to his comprehension of Binswanger's loss, recurred to the enduring impact of his grandson's death three years earlier:

> He [Heinele] was far advanced intellectually, so much so that the consulting specialist based his diagnosis on this fact when the nature of the disease was still uncertain. To me this child had taken the place of all my children and other grandchildren, and since then, since Heinele's death, I don't care for my grandchildren any more, but find no joy in life either. This is also the secret of my indifference — it was called courage — toward the danger to my own life [Freud to Binswanger, 15 October 1926, in Schur, 1972, p. 360].

On October 4, 1923, less than four months after the death of Heinele, Freud underwent the first of three successive surgical interventions performed by Hans Pichler. The initial operation, which was preparatory to the radical resection, consisted of removal of Freud's submaxillary salivary gland and surrounding lymph nodes along with the ligation (i.e., tying off) of the external carotid artery, the blood vessel that supplies blood to the head and face (Romm, 1983a, pp. 23–24).

The first of two resections followed eight days later, on October 12. The operation, Schur tells us, "consist[ed] of a resection of the major part of the right maxilla, a considerable part of the mandible, the right soft palate, and the buccal (cheek) and lingual (tongue) mucous membranes. Finally, [Pichler] replaced with skin grafts those parts of the removed mucous membranes which could not be sutured, and put the prosthesis in place" (1972, pp. 362–363; see Romm [1983a, pp. 25–27] for a more detailed account of the actual surgery). The skin grafts, taken from Freud's upper left arm and wrapped around an obturator — a piece of malleable dental compound that is pressed into a wound cavity before the compound hardens at room temperature—provided a lining for the raw surface of the surgically created cavity and of Freud's dissected cheek. Pichler then packed the remaining portion of the cavity with iodoform gauze, still the surgical packing agent of choice.

A month later, on November 7, Pichler, on examining Freud's oral cavity, observed a necrotic tag of tissue and small ulcer in the area of the pterygoid process; tissue biopsy revealed residual malignancy, and Pichler thereupon persuaded Freud to submit to further resection on the very day he received the pathology report. The third operation, which removed additional soft tissue and bone from Freud's hard palate and pterygoid process, took place on November 12 (Romm, 1983a, p. 30; Schur, 1972, p. 363).

Schur is lavish in his praise of Pichler, whose boldness was matched by attention to detail and superb operative technique. "Only a *homo surgicus*," he notes, "could have performed this type of surgery at that time." And the surgery proved "entirely successful," as Freud "did not die of a recurrence or a metastasis of the original cancer" (1972, p. 363). But, as Schur is quick to add, the operations of October and November 1923 represented only a surgical beginning. For Freud, unable to overcome his addiction to cigars, continued smoking, and the cigar smoke "caused a constant irritation of the [surgical] area and provided the stimulus for the formation of new leukoplakias. It soon became evident that these had a tendency to grow and proliferate" (p. 364). And so it was that, beginning in 1926, the "endless torture" occasioned by Freud's succession of imperfect prostheses was compounded by "an endless cycle of leukoplakia, proliferation, precancerous lesions." Let us quote Schur in full by way of briefly summarizing the surgical sequelae to the operations of 1923—sequelae that remained a part of Freud's life until his death in 1939:

> Each of them [leukoplakia] had to be treated surgically, by excision, electrocoagulation, or a combination of both. This happened more than 30 times. Only in 1936 was one of these lesions again malignant, and only in 1939 was such a lesion so situated that it could no longer be reached surgically. Frequently the attempt was made to cover the operative site with skin grafts. For the most part local anesthesia was used. The procedure

often lasted over an hour, but only more extensive surgery was done in a hospital. After each intervention the prosthesis had to remain in place for several days; cleaning was possible only by irrigation. The first insertions and removals were usually a special ordeal, and generally could be done only by Pichler himself [1972, p. 364].

Given the lifelong ordeal inaugurated by the multiple oral surgeries of 1923, is it surprising that the surgical metaphor should continue its retreat, that it should become little more than a metaphoric undercurrent in the didactic and clinical writings of the period? And the surgical metaphor is not only reduced to an undercurrent; it is transformed in its semantic *thrust* as well. From earlier metaphoric allusions to surgical penetration and excision, we proceed to a new emphasis on the refinement of the analytic instrument and the skill requisite to its employment. In "The Resistances to Psychoanalysis," written in September 1924, the month of his initial examination by Pichler, Freud addressed neither the surgical requirements of the analytic field nor the surgical nature of the psychoanalytic method. Rather his emphasis was now on the *delicacy* of the analytic procedure. One cannot practice psychoanalysis, he enjoined, "without having acquired a specific and decidedly delicate technique" (1925a, p. 222).

If we turn to Freud's consideration of transference in his "Autobiographical Study" of 1924, we find yet another instance of the new concern with instrumental precision. It occurs in the context of one of Freud's occasional conflations of military and surgical analogies. Via the analysand's reexperience of his transference onto the analyst, Freud noted, "the transference is changed from *the strongest weapon* of the resistance into *the best instrument* of the analytic treatment." But it is an instrument that placed great technical demands on the analytic operator, for "its handling remains the most difficult as well as the most important part of the technique of analysis" (1925b, p. 43).

Consider finally Freud's chapter on psychoanalysis commissioned by *Encyclopedia Britannica* for a collection entitled "These Eventful Years: The Twentieth Century in the Making, as Told by Many of Its Makers." Freud composed his essay in the fall of 1923, during the intervals between his operations (FJC, p. 557). Republished as "A Short Account of Psycho-

Analysis" five years later, the piece avoids entirely the surgical analogies of the papers on technique and introductory lectures. There is but a single allusion to surgical thinking, and this in the context of a brief review of the historical development of psychoanalysis. Writing in the third person, Freud recorded the dissolution of the partnership with Breuer that followed the publication of the *Studies on Hysteria*, at which point, Freud the author observed, "Freud devoted himself to the further *perfection of the instrument* left over to him by his elder collaborator" (1924, p. 195, emphasis added). It is not difficult to see beneath the image of instrumental perfection the image of Hans Pichler, the surgeon whose operative boldness was informed by surgical refinement, meticulous attention to detail, and painstaking preparations.[9] Indeed, even Pichler's personality provided a model of deportment for what Freud had once advocated for the analytic operator, his clinical style a template for how Freud once viewed the employment of the analytic instrument. As Romm observes, Pichler

> was a man who was able to care for his patient [Freud] with
> perfect detachment. Without visible emotion he performed the
> unpleasant, often extremely painful maneuvers that became
> absolutely necessary to prolong Freud's life. And beneath the
> mild, controlled manner was the most exacting physician,
> attentive to every detail. Nothing escaped his observation, and
> nothing was too insignificant for his attentive appraisal. His
> sense of self-discipline was apparent in every aspect of his life
> and his 16-year relationship with Freud [1983a, p. 12].

Perfect detachment, emotional invisibility, imperturbability in the face of the pain induced by his procedure, and scrupulous attentiveness to every observational detail, however insignificant in appearance — can we imagine a more compelling portrait of the *analytic* operator as Freud had long envisioned him?

Between the fall of 1923, when Freud endured Pichler's major resection, and 1926, when the recurring leukoplakias

---

[9] "Pichler was, fortunately, an 'obsessive' man in the best, sublimated sense of the word. Throughout the 15 years that he treated Freud, he kept notes on every single visit and surgical intervention." Prior to his first operation on Freud, Pichler "made complex preparations, including several different models for the prosthesis of both the maxilla and mandible to allow for whatever surgery might be required" (Schur, 1972, p. 362).

led to a new operative regimen, Freud's closest followers followed his medical status with an urgency born of devotion. Their generous expressions of concern were always positive and occasionally tended toward the euphoric. Ernest Jones, still recovering from his own abdominal surgery of May 1923, and, by the fall, suffering as well from "the most severe influenza imaginable" (FJC, p. 526), congratulated Freud in a letter of October 23, 1923 on "the brilliant success of the operation, the excellent prognosis, and—last but not least—that you have borne the painful situation so courageously." Never one to shy away from a clinical judgment outside the realm of psychological medicine, Jones let Freud know that "personally I felt confident about the surgical aspect of the case, but I feared that the weeks after the operation would be very distressing. The reports seem to indicate that—unpleasant as it must have been—this was less so than in many cases, probably because the disease had not extended far" (FJC, p. 529).

Even Karl Abraham, whose tactful circumspection led him to acknowledge Freud's "local" operation with Hajek with a "promise beforehand that this letter will not say anything about your health" (FAL, p. 339), gave way to celebration in the aftermath of the first radical operation with Pichler. "This is indeed a day of joy," he wrote Freud on October 16, 1923,

> and now that I know there is every cause for optimism, I want to congratulate you and your family with all my heart. I do not tend toward pessimism as you know, and I was therefore able during the anxious days to hold on to the impression of undiminished vitality which I had so recently observed in you. And the confidence I felt did not deceive me. But I breathe more freely again now that I know my hope has become a reality. From the reports it appears that you are not suffering too much from the direct consequences of the operation. All of us who are devoted to you may permit ourselves to enjoy the great gift which fate has granted us [FAL, p. 341].

Less restrained still was Lou Andreas-Salomé, whose litany of professional and economic woes in the postwar years gave way to jubilation that Freud had weathered his surgical ordeal. In November 1923, she wrote of "the almost continuous joy I feel in knowing that you are out of torment and danger—despite the fact that you no doubt still have to endure much pain and discomfort every day. That is bad enough, but nevertheless the joy predominates. This is the really important thing for all of us and one of which we are continuously aware" (FAnSL, p. 129).

For Freud, of course, the pain and discomfort was quite bad enough; even worse, however, was the fear of recurrence, the "really important thing" for him in the months immediately following the radical resections. On November 17, 1923, a mere 10 days after Pichler's second resection, Freud addressed his anxieties on this score by submitting to yet another surgical intervention, a Steinach procedure, probably performed by Victor Gregor Blum, a fashionable Viennese urologist whose practice included Austrians of noble rank (Romm, 1983a, pp. 83–84). The Steinach procedure, brainchild of one Eugen Steinach, a professor of physiology at Vienna University best known for his bizarre surgical efforts to remedy the "problem" of homosexuality,[10] was what we today term vasectomy—a simple ligating, or tying off, of the vas deferens, the duct that carries sperm from the testicle to the seminal vesicle. Steinach theorized that the interstitial cells of the testicles produced secretions able to ward off the aging process and combat illness; ligation of the vas deferens, so he held, would stimulate the interstitial cells to produce still more of their special youth-retaining substances. Since cancer was commonly associated with the aging process, the operation, so its proponents hoped, might halt and even reverse the disease process (Romm, 1983a, p. 73).

The procedure, first performed on a human subject in November 1921, was urged on Freud by his analytic follower Paul Federn, who was himself persuaded of its rejuvenating and curative properties by the Viennese internist Rudolph von Urban, a coworker of Steinach's and admirer of Freud's (Jones,

---

[10] Proceeding on the assumption that homosexuality was a variant of a biological hermaphroditism, Steinach surgically removed one of the "hermaphroditic testes" of a homosexual patient and replaced it with the undescended testes of a "normal" male. See Magee and Miller (1997, p. 72).

1957, p. 99; Romm, 1983a, pp. 80–82). Freud was not alone in succumbing to this bit of specious pseudoscience. The Steinach procedure was greatly in vogue in the 1920s; it received testimonials not only from surgeons and urologists throughout the world but from notable personalities, like the poet William Butler Yeats, who had had the procedure and were well satisfied with the results.

In Freud's case, events conspired to make the decision easier than it might otherwise have been. For one thing, he took quite seriously Steinach's surgical experiments on homosexuals, lauding the surgery for effecting "remarkable transformations" of inversion far beyond what psychoanalysis could hope to accomplish (Freud, 1920b, p. 171). Further, his own radiologist, the well-respected Guido Holzknect, was Steinach's collaborator in developing the procedure and propounding its rationale. Finally, Freud gave way only after personally approaching von Urban and hearing glowing first-hand reports from patients who had submitted to the procedure. It is unclear whether Freud imputed any benefits to the procedure in later years (Jones, 1957, p. 99; Gay, 1988, p. 426). More to the point is the fact of his willingness to undergo it: in the cruel year of 1923, Freud was apparently willing to pursue any means of remediation, however fanciful, offered by the surgical science of his time and place.

"A Refractory Piece of Equipment"
⁂

In the matter of his health, as in so many other ways, Freud strived to maintain a sense of reserve consistent with what his reason told him. Following his operations, he accepted his disciples' good wishes with grace and confirmed their general understanding of his recovery but refused to yield to their heady prognostic optimism. He was grateful for the occasional follower who refrained from querying him about his condition (FPL, p. 91), but such disciples were few and far between. He himself remained a realist for whom "recovery" from radical cancer surgery signified the most temporary of reprieves. When, on November 8, 1923, Georg Groddeck, arguably the most eccentric and certainly the most therapeutically optimistic of his followers, wrote him of his knowledge of the operation, assuring him that his thoughts and best wishes were "with you whom I love so much," Freud replied with a candor that lacked any trace of the sentimental. "About myself I can say that I am ill," he replied to Groddeck less than two weeks after Pichler's second resection of his jaw. "You seem to know the details. I know of course that it is the beginning of the end. However, one cannot know whether it will develop steadily or at intervals. But there has to be an end, and that does not mean that there will not be further developments" (FGL, p. 84).

This note of uncertainly hemmed in by fatalism is sounded repeatedly in Freud's letters to those closest to him. The attitude is evident even at the time of the botched ambulatory procedure of April 1923, when Freud took Hajek's favorable prognosis to "mean(s) no more than a slight lessening of the uncertainty that is bound to hover over the years to come" (FAnSL, p. 104). And it only intensified following Pichler's radical interventions six months later. "I am by no means out of trouble or released from treatment," he wrote Abraham at the beginning of 1924, "but I resumed my analytic work on the 2nd and hope to be able to manage" (FAL, p. 344). In May, he was more explicit to Karl Abraham about the pessimism—even depression—that colored his by now undeniable recovery. There is, as well, one of Freud's rare admissions that the chronic pain subsequent to Pichler's interventions could not be entirely surmounted, and that its life-shaping impact was an intensification of Freud's preoccupation with his mortality. "Though apparently on the way to recovery," he wrote,

> there is deep inside me a pessimistic belief in the closeness of the end of my life, nourished by the never-ceasing petty torments and discomforts of the scar, a kind of senile depression centered on the conflict between irrational pleasure in life and intelligent resignation. Accompanying this there is a need for rest and a disinclination to human contacts, neither of which are satisfied, because I cannot avoid working for six or seven hours a day [FAL, p. 360].

Teamed with Freud's "new and much reduced level of life and work" (FAL, p. 359) was a new and uncharacteristic dependency on a personal physician—Hans Pichler, the surgeon whose ongoing adjustments of the prosthesis represented Freud's only hope of relief and a fuller resumption of professional activity. Freud was of course admiring of Pichler's skill and composure, but neither Pichler's adjustments to the original prosthesis nor his construction of two new appliances in 1924 were adequate to Pichler's own goals for prosthetic replacement: complete restoration of the normal functions of speaking and eating with a sufficient degree of comfort.

Three decades earlier, the New York prosthodontist Kassan Gibson had achieved these very goals with the two prostheses he designed for President Grover Cleveland—to the utter delight of his distinguished patient. The first prosthesis, as noted earlier, enabled Cleveland to address Congress a mere three weeks after surgery without any discernible physical or speech impairment. Of the improved second prosthesis, delivered in October 1893, the President was frankly jubilant. "I hasten to announce that you have scored another dental victory," he gratefully wrote Dr. Gibson shortly after receiving the appliance. And he expatiated as follows:

> The new plate came last night. I looked at it quite askance — in point of fact with disfavor. I put it in this morning. It is now about 11 o'clock at night. I have worn it all day with the utmost ease and comfort without a shred of packing of any kind. I took it out to cleanse it after breakfast and lunch, but found very little on or behind it that needed attention. My wife says that my voice and articulation are much better than they had been for a number of days [in Aziz, 1995, p. 1090].

Freud, whose large and elaborate appliance had to make good a deficit far greater than Cleveland's,[1] would never approximate — never even approach — this happy outcome. In the aftermath of the two resections of 1924, Freud's speech was significantly compromised, whereas eating "became a strictly private activity." To smoke his beloved cigars, moreover, Freud had to prop his jaws open with a clothes peg (Romm, 1983a, p. 71). The bothersome sense of pressure in his ears and increased nasal secretions were constant accompaniments to his permanent functional impairment. It comes as no surprise, then, that for Freud the prosthesis was a constant reminder of "a life under sentence" — an idea far less tolerable to him than the "foul realities" of cancer and surgery (FAnSL, p. 135).

In reviewing the correspondence of 1924, we see how Freud's ambivalence about his dependency on Pichler became tantamount to ambivalence about the prosthetic device itself: both represented unremitting sources of pain, both compromised his freedom of movement, yet both enabled him to sidestep, for a time, the abyss of utter dysfunction and death that, so he believed, lay around the corner. In May of 1924, Freud was quite explicit in linking his uncertainty about

---

[1] Cleveland's prosthesis simply had to fit the President's maxilla in order to cover the defect in the roof of the President's mouth. Freud's far bulkier apparatus, on the other hand, had to make good Pichler's partial resection of the maxilla and simultaneous removal of a sizable inner wedge of the mandible, or lower jaw (including its upward extension, the coronoid process), and surrounding tissue (see Romm, 1983a, pp. 20ff.).

Pichler's positive prognosis to his dissatisfaction with the prosthesis. "It is not six months since my last operation," he confided to Lou Andreas-Salomé,

> and the attitude of my surgeon, who allows me to travel far afield in summer, ought to lull me into something like security—so far as such a feeling is admissible, considering the *di doman non c'e certezza* [no one is sure of the morrow] which affects us all. But it has no effect on me; perhaps partly because the extent to which the prosthesis has restored both functions of the mouth is a very modest one. In the beginning it promised to be much more successful, but the promise has not been fulfilled [FAnSL, p. 135].

A letter to Abraham of July 4, 1924 restates in a more perfunctory manner the close proximity of these complementary dimensions of Freud's postsurgical malaise. Freud informs Abraham that he has changed his vacation plans in order to remain within a day of Vienna:

> I have too clearly recognized my dependence on my doctor's consulting room to put such a distance between him and me . . . I have recently been having *ups and downs*, according to whether the prosthesis, the nose, or the ear chose to torment me more or less. I hope we shall now find a *modus vivendi* with each other [FAL, p. 364].

But the modus vivendi could not be effected, not by Pichler's skill and not by Freud's remarkable forbearance and strength of will. For how could Freud be one with a prosthesis that restored his oral functioning so partially and only at the price of chronic pain? Indeed, how do people generally learn to integrate into their sense of self those mechanical aids that imperfectly restore functioning from without and, as such, remain ameliorative intruders, ego-alien helpmates to the end? This aspect of the psychological sequelae to oral and maxillofacial surgery continues to elicit commentary in our own time (Strauss, 1989). Freud, for his part, reflected deeply on the matter in a letter to Lou Andreas-Salomé of August 11, 1924, where his ongoing attempts to make peace with the prosthesis finally give way to a military metaphor, as Freud realized he was literally waging war with the prosthesis in a fateful struggle for minimally acceptable oral functioning:

> I am writing to you from the deep contentment of a boundless inactivity, interspersed with the unpleasant sensations of a small-scale war waged with a refractory piece of equipment. Reflecting on the fine but not entirely acceptable sentences in which you discussed the relationship of man to his body, I ask myself what you would say to the analogous relationship to a substitute such as this, which tries to be and yet cannot be the self. This is a problem which arises even in the case of spectacles, false teeth and wigs, but not so insistent as in the case of a prosthesis. At the moment, in view of the ten months in which I have been free from relapses, I catch myself adjusting to the idea of a reprieve, not without a suspicion, however, that 'Nature' tends to lull us into a sense of security, before administering the *coup de grâce*—which of course on the other hand is one of her ways of being merciful [FAnSL, p. 137].

When, a month later, Freud suggests that his sense of self *has* fused with the prosthesis, it is now in an entirely negative sense, as if the latter's ultimate resistance to final adjustment— its obdurate unadjustability—has become the mechanical sign of the former's own ultimate uncurability. "I, that is to say, my prosthesis, is again under treatment to adapt it to changed conditions," he wrote Abraham (FAL, p. 369). But the changing contours of Freud's oral landscape outpaced his surgeon's mechanical ministrations time and again, so that the ego-sustaining ego-alien device remained refractory, an instigator of oral warfare without truce to the end of his days. Adjustment after adjustment, prosthesis after prosthesis, an end was never in sight.

In late November of 1924, Freud was reportedly experiencing "bad trouble" with a new prosthesis designed by Pichler. His "two new preoccupations" had become "the Rank affair and the prosthesis affair," he quipped to Lou Andreas-Salomé. By the former, Freud had in mind the deviant theorizing of his pupil and secretary Otto Rank, who had taken his new theory of primal birth trauma and the revised treatment methods accompanying it to America, where he received, to Freud's dismay, a cordial welcome.[2] But his disappointment in Rank paled alongside his daily battle with the prosthesis. "You would be surprised if you knew how much more concerned I am about the prosthesis than about Rank," Freud wrote Lou Salomé. "Perhaps you would see in this a proof of the increase of narcissism in old age. In any case I have adjusted myself inwardly to Rank, which I have not yet done with the prosthesis, although it is a more external matter" (FAnSL, p. 143).

By the spring of 1925, Freud seemed to have all but given up entirely on a modus vivendi among the organ systems implicated in his oral pathology, and with this relinquishment came an admission of frustration with the surgeon whose unremitting quest for the "good" prosthesis had come to signify therapeutic failure. Even before the recurrence of leukoplakias in 1926, surgical skill had virtually become the "sign" of Freud's pain and oral dysfunction. Thus to Groddeck: "I am not very well locally. My masochism as object of treatment is almost used up, it is time for me to be independent of the doctor" (FGL, p. 92).

Independence of a sort—a brief reprieve from Pichler's ministrations—came only in 1928, when Freud's prosthetic woes were compounded by newly arising problems with his Pichler-designed appliances: springs that kept cutting into Freud's cheek and breaking. It was at this juncture that Freud abandoned Pichler for Hermann Schroeder, director of the Dental Institute of the University of Berlin, whom he consulted from comfortable lodgings at Ernst Simmel's Schloss Tegel Sanitarium, which he visited in September 1928 and then again in March and September, 1929 (Molnar, 1992, p. 81). Between November 23, 1929 and October 3, 1930, Freud did not consult the estimable Pichler at all.

---

[2] Even here, Freud's illness supervened. Here is how he explained Rank's recent behavior to Salomé: "He [Rank] felt his livelihood to be threatened by my illness and its dangers, looked round for a place of refuge, and hit upon the idea of making his appearance in America. It is really a case of the rat leaving the sinking ship" (FAnSL, p. 143).

But Schroeder's work, as modified and adjusted by his assistant Trebitsch, proved no more satisfactory than Pichler's, so that Freud's problems with Pichler were, in the final analysis, merely transferred onto the person of another oral surgeon. By the late spring of 1930, as Freud impatiently awaited Schroeder's final effort at a prosthesis, he had become as cynically dispirited as he had been in 1924. "Of course it [Schroeder's new prosthesis] will be a masterpiece and one cannot yet foretell in what manner it will spoil my life," he complained to his wife Martha in early June. "What is difficult to bear," he added, "is dependence upon a person [i.e., Schroeder] one can't actually get hold of. I cannot expect that the new prosthesis will grant me independence" (quoted in Molnar, 1992, p. 76).

Newly persuaded that Pichler's prosthodontic limitations were no greater than those of his colleagues, Freud returned to him the following October, when Max Schur detected a new and suspicious growth that required surgical attention (Molnar, 1992, pp. 84–85). It was at this time that Pichler began operative management of the first of many "precancerous proliferations of the epithelium" in Freud's mouth. The first procedure of October 14 — as if to undo the effects of Freud's trial of Berlin dentistry — included excising the exposed scar tissue that resulted from Schroeder's treatment earlier in the year.

Freud, by now fully resigned to lifelong dependency on oral surgeons, apparently preferred dependency on the loyal and gracious Pichler to dependency on anyone else. Endlessly available to Freud and affecting a professional calm and an observational acuity consonant with Freud's own ideal of "psychoanalytic neutrality," Pichler was the one surgeon whom Freud could "actually get hold of" and continue to hold on to for his remaining years. But Pichler was not a surgical god, and we take nothing from him in observing how Freud's gratitude to him, particular from 1929 on, went hand in hand with a more profound understanding of the life-compromising limits of "successful" surgery. For Pichler's surgical aftercare, certainly commendable and even heroic in the context of existing knowledge and available prosthetic technologies, could not make good the promise of his surgical interventions; it could not, that is, enable his patient to achieve a degree of *reliable* pain management teamed with oral functioning that was *invariant* at a satisfactory, if not fully satisfying, level.[3] Nor could the surgeons who subsequently tried their hands at an improved prosthesis do any better than Pichler.[4]

With maxillectomy patients in general, it has been observed, it is precisely the functional adequacy of the obturator prosthesis that determines the quality of life patients may subsequently reclaim. And among the dimensions of obturator functioning linked to postsurgical psychosocial adjustment and subjective sense of well-being, restoration of speech and eating are of paramount importance (Kornblith et al., 1996). But it is precisely in these core areas of functioning that Freud's successive prostheses were uniformly disappointing, since none of them was adequate to the conjoint requirements of speech and food intake. A year after the surgery, I suggest, Freud's professed hopefulness that the prosthesis would ultimately yield to

---

[3] Thus Schur: ". . . the extensive surgery made a really satisfactory prosthesis impossible, and the loss of the greater part of the buccal mucous membrane could not be made good completely by grafting. The result was a life of endless torture. Eating, smoking, talking could be carried on only with great effort and pain. If the prosthesis was just right for proper occlusion and separation between the oral and nasal cavities, this resulted in sores, pressure upon the mandibular joint, and often intolerable pain. If some of the prosthesis was removed, speech, eating, and smoking became much more difficult. This was really existing between Scylla and Charybdis" (1972, p. 364). Revealingly, Schur confines to a footnote his single reservation about Pichler's surgical aftercare of Freud: "Concerning the prosthesis, I must add that while Pichler was a superb surgeon and an excellent physician, his art as a dental technician may not have been quite the equal of his surgical skill. In later years, two other specialists were asked to try their hand at creating a prosthesis. Perhaps, given an opportunity to be in constant attendance, they could have produced a more efficient and less troublesome instrument" (p. 364n).

[4] In addition to Hermann Schroeder, there was Varaztad Kazanjian, a Harvard-trained dentist and plastic surgeon, who, through the good offices of Ruth Mack Brunswick and Marie Bonaparte, journeyed to Vienna in 1931 where, using Pichler's office, he designed three new prostheses for Freud (Romm, 1983a, pp. 91–92, 99–102; Molnar, 1992, pp. 102–104). Freud's response to Kazanjian's work, like his response to Schroeder's, was one of initial hopefulness followed by great disappointment. The three rubber appliances designed by Kazanjian were smaller and lighter than Pichler's, but were too soft for Freud to smoke with; further, he bit his tongue while using them. Pichler spent several months modifying these prostheses, but without notable success (Molnar, 1992, p. 104).

Pichler's painful and painstaking manipulations and thereby enable him to speak and eat in some manner commensurate with his presurgical self—this hopefulness had taken on the quality of the *pro forma*. It tended, that is, to be a postscript to more pointed admissions of the misery attendant to his "new and much reduced level of life and work," as in this missive to Abraham of October 17, 1924:

> I am still alive, as you see, but I have no desire to lecture, and shall be able to think of traveling again only if Pichler succeeds in making a good and stable foundation for my prosthesis, which so far is not the case. My condition, that is to say, my capacity to speak and chew, is still so variable that there is ample room for the optimism of all the Casimiros [FAL, p. 371].

A letter to Jones several weeks earlier had given voice to this optimism—or to as much optimism, we may say, as Freud's fatalism could allow. The self-assessment here is artfully, even painfully, even-handed. Freud was "much better than [he] had reason to expect," which is only to say that he was finding his surgically effected reprieve to be lengthy enough and his restored oral functioning satisfactory enough to permit a slightly circuitous path to death, a path perhaps permitting the "further developments" he had mentioned to Groddeck a year earlier:

> My health is much better than I had reason to expect. It is now 10 1/2 months since my last operation and no sign of a relapse. The exertions of Pichler have succeeded at last in a fargoing restoration of the two damaged functions of speaking and eating. My general condition is pretty satisfactory. Yet, I am no more what I was. I am subject to feel fatigued in the evening, one of my ears is damaged in a permanent way. I will be obliged to resign the leadership of the Vienna Group at the election next month [FJC, p. 552].

"The Surgeons Very Nearly
Killed Him"

Nineteen twenty three, Freud's surgical *annus horribilis*, was only slightly better for the redoubtable Ernest Jones. In May, he underwent major abdominal surgery, duly reported to Freud with wry analytic humor,[1] and his recuperation was compromised by what he modestly termed "the most severe influenza imaginable" (FJC, p. 526). The year also saw recurrent episodes of the rheumatism that had plagued him in the past (Brome, 1983, p. 143). Near the end of 1923, Joan Riviere too returned to London for major surgery, and it fell to Jones to advise Freud of the "excellent recovery" of Jones's former analysand who, by this time, had become his strong-willed rival in managing the affairs of the International Psycho-Analytical Press (FJC, pp. 537, 538; Brome, 1983, pp. 135–137).

A year later, Jones resumed his role as medicosurgical Hermes, informing Freud that his wife, Katherine, had "sustained a Pott's injury to the ankle" and, further, "had to go through the experience of having her tonsils dissected out." "The operation passed off smoothly," he continued, "but she is still having a miserable time from the pain and discomfort involved" (FJC, p. 566).

---

[1] "An abdominal operation is not altogether uninstructive and brings home to one some aspects of life which one does not ordinarily realize fully. But it is a disagreeable experience, none the less" (FJC, p. 523). Freud's reply maintained the light tone of Jones's revelation: "I am deeply disappointed that you should be ill too thinking it a prerogative of my age and condition. But I expect you will soon have recovered strength and be the former man again or become a still better one" (p. 527).

Three weeks later, at the beginning of February 1925, Jones was finally able to report an upswing in his medical fortunes. His wife had at last recovered from her tonsillectomy, and he "from my perforative otitis (the second within a month)" (FJC, p. 567). In reply, Freud demurred from the optimistic assessment of his own condition that Jones had received from Max Eitingon, but was willing to "readily admit that, apart from the continuing dissatisfaction with my prosthesis, I cannot complain about my health" (p. 568).

And then, nine months later, Jones conveyed medical information that, as events would show, was far more portentous in character. Karl Abraham, he wrote Freud, "is in hospital facing the possibility of a gall-bladder operation" (FJC, p. 583). What Jones neglected to mention—but Freud knew full well— was the disquieting medical context of this impending surgical event. For Abraham was a sick man and had been a sick man since the end of the Great War. Near the end of his term of service, he contracted a severe case of dysentery from which he never fully recovered. He suffered recurrent attacks thereafter, the final one in the spring of 1924. Superimposed on his compromised resistance was the tragic chain of events that ultimately led to his death on Christmas Day, 1925.

Among the analysts, it was widely, if incorrectly, believed that Abraham, while lecturing in Holland, had swallowed a fishbone that lodged in a bronchus and gave rise to septic bronchial pneumonia (Jones, 1957, p. 112). The acute infection never entirely cleared and, so the analysts believed, led to chronic bronchiectasis, a stretching of the bronchus due to obstruction and infection that produces severe bronchial symptoms. At the Bad Homburg Psychoanalytic Congress of early September 1925, Abraham, the presiding president of the International Association, was in attendance, but the gravity of his condition was apparent to all. He struggled to control his chronic cough with morphia and left the Congress utterly debilitated by the press of events. "I found it a very great strain and I shall need several days to get my breathing right again," he wrote Freud when the Congress had ended. As if his admission of near physical collapse were not sufficiently disquieting to Freud, Abraham outlined the course of treatment he was then envisioning: "I shall in any case have to undergo some treatment for my nose and throat from Fliess. If this letter were not already unduly long, I would tell you how my illness has most strikingly confirmed all Fliess's views on periodicity" [FAL, p. 395).

And so we are back to Fliess, whose skills as clinician and diagnostician—and perhaps as surgeon as well—had elicited Abraham's deep admiration in the prewar years. Abraham, we recall, had been drawn to the Fliessian theory of periodicity back in 1911, an interest that intensified following an initial meeting with Fliess that left him with the impression of "a penetrating and original thinker" (FAL, p. 48). We have scant documentation of Abraham's contact with Fliess from 1911 until the period of his fatal illness,[2] but Hilda Abraham's (1974) unfinished biography of her father leaves no doubt that the relationship remained altogether admiring.

Did Freud collude in Abraham's final turn to Fliess in 1925? Not consciously, to be sure. And yet, their correspondence of the previous year includes an exchange that may well have fanned Abraham's revived interest in Fliessian periodicity. Near the end of April 1924, Abraham had written Freud of a project that could not be launched in his remaining months: an investigation of the significance of the number seven in myths and customs (FAL, p. 365n). Four months later, when Abraham was already dying, Freud sought to sustain Abraham's numero-logical interest by putting at his disposal an idea gleaned from his historical reading, namely, that the number seven was taboo and had originated during a period when men counted in sixes. Freud even indulged in some quasi-Fliessian speculations about this preastronomical "system of sixes" before ending on a cautionary note with an unmistakable allusion to Fliess or, more specifically, to the treacherous shoals in the ocean of Fliessian numerological possibility: "The craziest things can be done with numbers, so be careful" (p. 365).

---

[2] On November 2, 1917, Abraham mentioned to Freud that he had "recently received a very interesting paper by Fliess; it contains brilliant new observations about a pituitary syndrome. Would you be interested? If so, I could send it to you." Freud replied nine days later as follows: "I have heard about Fliess's book; things are too uncertain to send it to me, unless you have two copies I shall try to hunt up a copy here" (FAL, pp. 260, 261).

In a reply written immediately on receipt of the letter, Abraham ignored this final proviso and responded to Freud as a fellow explorer of uncharted numerological seas. He warmly thanked Freud for his "stimulating ideas," and expressed pleasure that Freud "immediately took up the problem of the number seven and made it yours." "The idea about the system of the sixes is very interesting and undoubtedly an important contribution," Abraham continued. "Your communication encourages me to report to you as soon as I have any new findings" (FAL, pp. 366, 367).

Back in his native Berlin less than two weeks after the Homburg Congress, Abraham immediately placed himself under Fliess's care. Fliess's ministrations had no effect on Abraham's quickening deterioration, but the nose surgeon and master of periodicity continued to inspire confidence nonetheless. Was a transference in play? We have only Hilda Abraham's suggestive aside that her father maintained his high estimation of Fliess during the final months of his life, "when the need for a helpful, omnipotent father interfered at times with his critical judgment" (H. Abraham, 1974, p. 49).

To Freud, Abraham was all too forthright about Fliess, who had become his doctor, his friend, and even his confidant. "You may be interested to hear that Fliess, who heard about your illness two years ago, has repeatedly asked after your health with the warmest interest," he wrote Freud in mid-October. And then, as if pouring salt on Freud's residual wounds in the matter of Fliess, Abraham added: "As far as I am concerned, I must repeat here once again that I owe him the utmost gratitude" (FAL, p. 397). When, in the days that followed, Abraham's bronchial symptoms were complicated by a painful and swollen liver, the patient himself erroneously diagnosed gall bladder trouble and insisted on surgery. But even here, in a surgical turn away from the nose and throat, the influence of Fliess was clear, for the operation, which only hastened Abraham's demise, was performed on a day deemed auspicious by Fliess's numerological calculations.

In retrospect, the futility of Fliessian nasal/throat interventions and gall bladder surgery alike is all too clear, for Abraham, we now know, was stricken with a lung cancer that ran its course in the six months leading up to his death (Jones, 1957, p. 116).

This was unknown in his final weeks and months. The analysts, led by Jones, held to the story of the swallowed fish bone, followed by bronchial pneumonia and then persisting bronchiectasis. To this sequence, the gall bladder surgery was added as a surgical coup de grâce. In the obituary Jones prepared for the *International Journal of Psycho-Analysis* in the weeks following Abraham's death, he wrote that Abraham appeared better following an extended convalescence after the Homburg Congress. But the period of recuperation was short-lived, for Abraham's "condition got worse, obscure complications set in, and in November he had to enter a hospital. A fortnight later he underwent a serious operation which did not have the hoped-for effect. He gradually sank, and finally succumbed on Christmas Day, 1925" (Jones, 1926, p. 19).

What was the "hoped-for effect" of Abraham's operation supposed to be? We can only guess at the mental gymnastics by which Abraham, no doubt sustained by Fliess, linked worsening pulmonary symptoms to his gall bladder. And what of the operation itself? Did Abraham's surgeons botch a routine gall bladder removal? Did they cause damage incidental to gall bladder removal? Or, more likely, was it simply the shock of major surgery at this advanced stage of lung cancer that hastened Abraham's demise? The extant record is silent on these issues; we know only that there was an operation and that Abraham was manifestly the worse for it.

Helpless witnesses to Abraham's precipitous decline, Jones, Freud, and the circle of analytic colleagues had no choice but to place their trust in the surgeons who attended him. "Abraham's illness has us all holding our breath," wrote Jones, after learning that Abraham had undergone the gallbladder surgery in the second week of December. Felix Deutsch, the analyst-internist on whom Freud had relied in pursuing his own surgical course of action in 1923, was hastily dispatched to Berlin as the analysts' emissary. "He will probably bring us as much enlightenment as is at all available now," Jones informed Freud. But the enlightenment from Berlin was far from heartening. Deutsch duly reported on Abraham's "gloomy prospect" following the operation, a judgment rendered more definitive a day or two later by Hanns Sachs. *Abrahams Zustand hoffnungslos* — Abraham's condition is hopeless — Sachs telegrammed Jones a week before Abraham died (FJC, pp. 585, 587).

Jones was quick to offer a definitive judgment on the surgical episode, though here as elsewhere it is difficult to distinguish between his posturing and his actual medical knowledge of the events in question. He was extremely close to Abraham, personally and professionally, and he struggled alongside Freud to comprehend the reality of his friend's impending death. If Abraham was indeed dying from the complications of bronchiectasis, then the medical management of his case had to be questioned, not least the final recourse to surgery. "It is evident that the surgeons made a bad mistake and very nearly killed him," he wrote Freud six days before Abraham's death. And then, true to form, he added: "I only wish I could have some say on the medical questions involved, but there is already such a multiplicity of advice that I had to renounce this desire" (FJC, p. 589).

"Neither Medicines Nor Instruments"

∝⊗∾

Six months before the onset of his terminal illness, at the beginning of December 1924, Abraham began a letter to Freud with perfunctory thanks for Freud's most recent letter: "All your news interested me greatly, particularly the expert opinion you were asked to give" (FAL, p. 375). The expert opinion in question, solicited by an Austrian medical personage of unknown identity, involved the question of lay analysis, the acceptability, that is, of nonphysicians employing the analytic procedure and thereby practicing clinical psychoanalysis.

This issue of lay practitioners, knotty to everyone but Freud, only reached public attention in the years following the Great War, when the several lay analysts who had been working with children and adolescents prior to the war, most notably Hermine Hug-Hellmuth in Vienna and Oskar Pfister in Zurich, were joined by a number of colleagues. Even before the war's end, Melanie Klein had launched her career by assisting her own analyst, Ferenczi, in his Budapest Clinic. Klein followed the cautious example of her nonmedical forbears by limiting her clinical work to children, as did Otto Rank, who began practicing in Vienna shortly after the war. He was joined soon thereafter by Siegfried Bernfeld and Theodor Reik, and then in 1923 by Freud's daughter Anna. She, in turn, was followed by August Aichhorn, Ernst Kris, Robert Waelder, and others. By the time Austrian authorities were alerted to this trouble-some—so it seemed to them—situation, lay analysis had also gained a foothold in London, where J.C. Flugel, Barbara Low, Joan Riviere, and Ella Sharpe were in clinical practice, to be joined before long by James and Alix Strachey (Jones, 1957, p. 291).

154

Freud's affirmative reply to the question put to him by a medical functionary came as no surprise; his commitment to the integrity of psychoanalysis as a free-standing discipline— both the methodological integrity of the procedure it employed and the epistemic integrity of the knowledge gained thereby— were by then matters of record. Despite the fact that a number of Freud's early adherents and closest associates came from the ranks of neurology and psychiatry, Freud by 1924 was through courting psychiatry. Psychiatric interest in the analytic contribution to the war neuroses, a welcome surprise to Freud during the later years of the war, did not prove a harbinger of things to come. Official psychiatry continued to view analysis warily, skeptically, and, often enough, derisively. Near the end of 1919, when Siegfried Bernfeld, a school teacher turned analyst, proposed an organization of lay persons interested in psychoanalysis to be loosely affiliated with the Vienna Psychoanalytic Society, Freud was so enthusiastic that he donated to the project the sum of 11,000 kronen ($2,200) he had just received from the fund established by his late friend and benefactor, Anton von Freund (Jones, 1957, pp. 290–291).

Freud's enthusiasm for lay analysis was not shared by many. And not surprisingly, those colleagues who demurred from Freud's defense of nonmedical practitioners were precisely those for whom surgical analogizing remained a congenial enterprise. This is true especially of Freud's American followers, whose popularizing accounts of the time readily invoked surgery in setting forth the properly medical character of psychoanalytic practice. Isador Coriat, for one, wrote in 1917 that "for an untrained person to use psychoanalysis is as much to be deprecated as it is for someone to use radium who is ignorant of the physics of radioactivity or as dangerous as to attempt a surgical operation without a knowledge of anatomy" (p. 22). Three years later, Joseph Ralph of California entitled his brief synopsis of the psychoanalytic method "Psychical Surgery."[1] And a year later, in his *Fundamental Conceptions of Psychoanalysis* (1921), A. A. Brill followed suit. As the Freudian

---

[1] "... a popular and brief, but clear and correct, account of the aim, practice and theory of the psychoanalytic method," was Ernest Jones's (1920) judgment of Ralph's self-published brochure.

"somewhat responsible" for the introduction of analysis into America, he felt obliged to clarify that "whereas psychoanalysis is as wonderful a discovery in mental science as, let us, say, the X-ray in surgery, it can be utilized only be persons who have been trained in anatomy and pathology" (quoted in Gay, 1988, pp. 497–498).

Several months after Freud delivered his "expert opinion" to the contrary, at the beginning of 1925, Viennese municipal authorities, apparently alerted to the presence of lay analysts in Vienna by Wilhelm Stekel, accused Theodor Reik, one of Freud's younger lay followers, of "unauthorized medical practice." Reik staunchly defended himself during the ensuing weeks of expert testimony and legal wrangling; nor did he wilt when the Vienna Municipal Council prohibited him from practicing psychoanalysis as of February 24, 1925. Rather, "he consulted a lawyer, enlisted Freud's support, appealed the verdict, and for some time continued to practice" (Gay, 1988, p. 490).[2] But the matter did not end there. The following spring, an American patient who had been sent to Reik by Freud himself, one Newton Murphy, sued Reik for quackery after a presumably unsatisfactory analytic experience.

It was at this juncture that Freud composed his famous polemic, *The Question of Lay Analysis* (1926a), a modest tract that would play a central role in the struggle of nonmedical analysts for collegial acceptance and public recognition for the next six decades (Wallerstein, 1998). The defense of Reik, who had long been a beneficiary of Freud's paternal guidance and financial support, was the occasion of this writing, but the terms in which Freud cast his defense of lay analysis far transcended the legal predicament of a single, highly gifted lay follower. As Peter Gay rightly observes, "Freud fought for Reik as though he were fighting for himself" (1988, p. 490).

---

[2] Freud's support took the form, among other things, of a biting letter of protest on Reik's behalf to Professor Julius Tandler, an anatomist and head of the (Public) Health Department at Vienna University. Freud viewed the Council's injunction against Reik "as an unjustified encroachment in favor of the medical profession and to the detriment of patients and science" (FL, pp. 359–360).

Freud's spirited defense of the disciplinary integrity of psycho-analysis has an intriguing subtext: it is the retreat from surgery and surgical analogizing. We have reviewed the events of 1925 that likely imparted this surgical edge to Freud's ruminations about the relationship of medicine and analysis. I refer to his disappointment with the succession of prosthetic devices, designed and modified by Hans Pichler, which were intended to restore oral functioning in the aftermath of the radical surgeries of 1923.

By the spring of 1925, we recall, Freud's initial optimism had given way to resignation over the impossibility of his surgeon's ever devising a good prosthesis, a prosthesis that would let him write and chew and smoke with manageable levels of discomfort. During the very months when he came to grips with the true magnitude of his permanent oral deficit and the human limitations of the surgeon whose life-saving inter-ventions had created it, he beheld the accelerating deterioration of Karl Abraham, whose misdiagnosed lung cancer was equally resistant to the laryngological ministrations of Fliess and the gall bladder surgery that, at Abraham's insistence, was under-taken days before his death at the end of 1925. "It is evident the surgeons made a bad mistake and very nearly killed him," Jones had intoned at the time.

But surgeons and surgery would not go away. The months immediately following Abraham's death witnessed the onset of Freud's final, prolonged surgical ordeal: the recurrence of precancerous lesions, the leukoplakias, that required excision and electrocautery treatment by Pichler. We do well to recall Max Schur's demoralizing tally of these interventions: Freud would submit to local operations over 30 times between 1926 and his death in 1939. To the continuing round of oral examinations, cauterizations, and biopsies were added Pichler's ongoing adjustments to the prosthesis.

So 1926 was not a year destined to endear the medical profession to Freud. His failure to gain ground in the intractable "battle with the prostheses" led Pichler to construct a fourth device; the fit was better, but by the fall Freud complained of indistinct speech when he used it (Romma, 1983, pp. 90–91). The cycle of examinations, cauterizations, and biopsies instituted in 1925, accompanied by virtually constant oral pain, continued into the new year. And there is more: 1926 also began with an intensification of the sinus discharge and flulike symptoms that plagued Freud for the rest of his life. Teamed with these long-standing symptoms were new and vehement complaints about the sensitivity of his teeth, which resulted in a series of root canal treatments (pp. 88–89). And then, in February, Freud experienced angina pectoris following some slight exertion; his cardiac symptoms, similar to those of the 1890s, were sufficient to lead his cardiologist, Ludwig Braun, to induce him temporarily to give up smoking and to spend several weeks recuperating at the Cottage Sanitarium on the outskirts of Vienna (p. 90).

With these anlagen in mind, we turn to *The Question of Lay Analysis*, a work that Freud himself was content to describe as "shallow stuff with some cutting remarks, which because of my bad mood at present are rather bitter" (Freud to Ferenczi, 6 July 1926, in Jones, 1957, p. 292). "The bad mood in question," Ernest Jones informs us, "came from his being more than usually plagued by his prosthesis so that he was even unable to speak" (p. 292). We glean the extent of Freud's pain during this period by an admission to Havelock Ellis, an epistolary professional acquaintance of years' standing but hardly a confidant. Commiserating with Ellis, who had recently developed serious medical problems of his own, Freud could not refrain from a sobering admission: "As for myself I am of course reminded every hour of the mutilation caused by the operation on my jaw," and this despite the fact that "after almost three years a relapse is not expected to occur" (FL, p. 371). Small wonder, given the oral pain and severely compromised functioning subsequent to his multiple surgeries, that Freud wrote Ferenczi of his "cutting" remarks and that the central metaphor of *The Question of Lay Analysis* was oral, to wit, Freud's fear lest psychoanalysis be "swallowed up by medicine" (1926a, p. 244).

The price of such "swallowing" would be devastating, Freud explains, since analysis as a therapeutic procedure bears so little relation to medicine. Yes, he grants, analytic training "intersects" with medical training, but only in a single, circumscribed sphere: that of differentiating psychogenic from somatogenic causes of neurosis (1926a, p. 241). With respect to the core subject matter of a medical education, however, medicine is of little consequence to the analyst; it "neither helps him directly to understand a neurosis and to cure it nor does it contribute to a sharpening of those intellectual capacities on which his occupation makes the greatest demands" (p. 244). And by way of exemplifying the irrelevance of medical training to the type of understanding he has in mind, Freud provides a brief but suggestive list of biomedical particulars, all useless to the analytic endeavor: "a knowledge of the anatomy of the tarsal bones, of the constitution of the carbohydrates, of the course of the cranial nerves, a grasp of all that medicine has brought to light on bacillary exciting causes of disease and the means of combating them, on serum reactions *and on neoplasms*" (p. 244, emphasis added).

The last of these particulars puts us on guard. Two years earlier, convalescing in southern Italy after his "local" surgical ordeal with Hajek, Freud had written Felix Deutsch knowingly of his "dear neoplasm"; it was an ironic shorthand conveying understanding and acceptance of his condition, even before the pathology report confirming malignancy had been passed on to him (Schur, 1972, p. 357). Now, in the wake of Pichler's two radical resections and his resignation to prosthetic torture, Freud pondered anew the nature of his psychoanalytic procedure, especially its relation to matters medical, among them the diagnosis and surgical treatment of neoplasms.

Are we at the point of idle psychobiographical speculation? Perhaps not. It is intriguing that in dismissing the analogy between analysis and "other medical specialties" Freud invariably recurs to the surgical specialties, specifically to general surgery, ophthalmology, and laryngology. At first, the radical disjunction between these surgical disciplines and analysis appears superficial, since it concerns only the institutional context of, and opportunities for, training. "For surgery, ophthalmology, and so on, the medical school itself offers an opportunity for further education," he writes, whereas analytic training institutes are few in number and without authority (Freud, 1926a, p. 232). And then there are the different consequences of incompetence in analysis and in the surgical specialties:

If [an untrained physician] tried to undertake eye-operations
without sufficient preparation, the failure of his cataract
extractions and iridectomies [surgical removal of part of the
iris] and the absence of patients would soon bring his hazardous
enterprise to an end. The practice of analysis is comparatively
safe for him. The public is spoilt by the average successful
outcome of eye-operations and expects cure from the surgeon.
But if a 'nerve-specialist' fails to restore his patients no one is
surprised [p. 232].

Freud offered these several comparisons by way of high-
lighting the unique nature of analytic training. Well and good.
There are well-trained lay analysts just as there are analytically
untrained physicians practicing analysis; it is the latter, moreover, encouraged by the minimal risks attendant to therapeutic
failure, who pose the greater risk of analytic quackery. But the
demoralizing prospect of untrained physicians appropriating
the analytic mantle with professional impunity only underscores
the reality of what analysts do: *they talk.* And so, Freud writes,
"Honesty compels me to admit that the activity of an untrained
analyst does less harm to his patients than that of an unskilled
surgeon" (1926a, p. 233). But if analytic failure is both far less
demonstrable and far less consequential than surgical failure,
how can a law against "lay analysis" be "significantly pro-
hibitive"? After all, Freud continues, "The course of an analysis
is most inconspicuous, it employs neither medicines nor
instruments and consists only in talking and an exchange of
information; it will not be easy to prove that a layman is
practicing 'analysis,' if he asserts that he is merely giving
encouragement and explanations" (p. 236).

True, the analyst can still learn something from the
comportment of the skilled surgeon. He can derive from the
surgical model the "skill, patience, calm, and self-abnegation"
needed to cope with the demands of the transference (1926a,
p. 227). And like the skilled surgeon, like the gifted Hans
Pichler, he must master a "delicate technique," which in the
realm of talking therapy pertains to "the art of interpretation,
of fighting resistances, and of handling the transference"
(p. 228). But is the analytic procedure thereby *surgical*, a
disciplined penetration to, and dissection of, the unconscious,
all in the context of a surgically uncontaminated, suggestion-

free environment? Here, in the realm of method and its deployment, there is discernible movement away from the surgical
metaphor. It is not tantamount to a radical re-visioning of the
psychoanalytic procedure, but it is a clear shift in emphasis.
The cautionary provisos of the papers on technique and the
introductory lectures have been supplanted by the realization
that the analyst's work, his restorative talk, is not the stuff of
surgical penetration and excision. As Freud notes early in *The
Question of Lay Analysis*:

> We try to *restore* the ego, free it from its restrictions, and to *give
> it back* the command over the id which it has lost owing to its
> early repressions. It is for this one purpose that we carry out
> analysis, our whole technique is directed to this aim. We have
> to seek out the repressions which have been set up and to *urge*
> the ego to correct them with our help and to deal with conflicts
> better than by an attempt at flight [1926a, p. 205, emphasis
> added].

In *Inhibitions, Symptoms, and Anxiety*, published the same
year as *The Question of Lay Analysis*, the gentler, nonsurgical
take on psychoanalytic procedure is joined to a new theory of
the ego and its role in anxiety. Freud now moves away even
from the use of surgery as a template of curative possibilities.
Six years earlier, in "Lines of Advance in Psychoanalytic
Therapy" (1919a), psychoanalysis was deemed capable of "the
life-saving help offered by surgery" (p. 167). Now, in 1926, the
very search for "single ultimate causes" is no longer an analytic
prerogative, the administration of life-saving interventions no
longer an analytic possibility. Analysis must cede to medicine
both the investigatory mentality and the interventionist
modalities that animate this search. In *Inhibitions, Symptoms,
and Anxiety*, Otto Rank's proposal of primal birth trauma as
the universal cause of neurosis spurred Freud to the following
cautionary appraisal, but the larger context of Freud's remarks
is the biomedical world from which analysis is now eman-
cipating itself:

> It is to be feared that our need to find a single, tangible 'ultimate
> cause' of neurotic illness will remain unsatisfied. The ideal
> solution, which *medical men* no doubt still yearn for, would be

to discover some bacillus which could be isolated and bred in a pure culture and which, when injected into anyone, would invariably produce the same illness; or, to put it rather less extravagantly, to demonstrate the existence of certain chemical substances the administration of which would bring about or cure particular neuroses. But the probability of a solution of this kind seems slight [1926b, p. 153, emphasis added].

Where do these realities of the neurotic condition leave the analyst and his analytic method? No longer on a mission of surgical cure, analytic therapy has become a matter of verbal remediation. It is a matter, Freud tells us, of appraising the danger situations of everyday life and appealing to an ego whose natural restorative properties lie in ready:

> When, in analysis, we have given the ego assistance which is able to put it in a position to lift its repressions, it recovers its power over the repressed id and can allow the instinctual impulses to run their course as though the old situations of danger no longer existed. What we can do in this way tallies with what can be achieved in other fields of medicine; for as a rule our therapy must be content with bringing about more quickly, more reliably and with less expenditure of energy than would otherwise be the case the good result which in favorable circumstances would have occurred of itself [1926b, p. 154].

We are a far cry here from the surgical injunctions of the papers on technique written more than a decade earlier. If the analyst's gently restorative ministrations invite a medical analogy, it is no longer to be found in the modern surgeon's art. We are rather in the realm of internal medicine, of cautious clinical fact-finding and nonheroic therapeutics guided by the physician's patient willingness to let nature itself bring about "the good result." Or better still, we are back in the realm of premodern surgery, of simple wound management bolstered by faith in God. For Freud in 1926, Hippocrates's baleful aphorism—"Diseases which are not cured by medicines are cured by iron; those which are not cured by iron are cured by fire; those not cured by fire are incurable"—has seemingly given way to Ambroise Paré's self-effacing maxim: "I dressed him and God healed him." We recall that Freud quoted this very maxim in his "Recommendations to Physicians Practicing Psycho-analysis" (1912), where it figured in his justification of the analyst's emotional coldness, his resolve to put aside "all his feelings, even his human sympathy" in undertaking the analytic operation. Now, in 1926, the maxim can be read in a different way—a way more consonant with the historical Paré, the provincial barber-surgeon from the city of Laval who could read neither Hippocrates in Greek nor even Galen in Latin trans-lation, and for whom surgical coldness was less at issue than therapeutic humility underwritten by religious faith.[3] "As a surgeon," Paré tells us, "I can do *no more* than dress his wounds; God *alone* is capable of cure." And the same can be said for the psychoanalyst, who seeks to facilitate "the good result" consonant with the ego's naturally restorative powers—and the luck of circumstance.

Not surprisingly, those who took issue with Freud's spirited defense of lay analysis had recourse to surgical analogies and surgical contingencies in their advocacy of medical analysis. C. P. Oberndorf, a New York analyst who participated in the *International Journal of Psycho-Analysis*'s lengthy consideration of the issue in 1927, began his missive with a curiously surgical rendering of Freud's antipathy to medicine: "Professor Freud's endorsement of nonmedical analysis is comparable to the premature incision of an ugly-looking subcutaneous inflam-mation which has not yet come to a head, and which perhaps might after a period of irritation have vanished without surgical interference" (1927, p. 201).

Ernest Jones, for his part, felt constrained to counter the "cavalier fashion" in which Freud had dismissed the role of physical diagnosis in psychoanalytic practice with his own avowal of the role of medical knowledge in the treatment situation. Here is the illustration he adduced, to which, he added, "most medical analysts could doubtless supply similar ones":

---

[3] Paré's was the faith of a French Protestant (or Huguenot), despite his outward conformity to the dominant Catholicism of sixteenth-century France. Indeed, his life may well have been endangered at the Massacre of St. Bartholomew of 1572 (Keynes, 1952, pp. xvii–xviii).

A patient, a man in his thirties, mentioned that he had pain in the neighborhood of the anus when going to sleep. He himself wanted to explain the pain as a paresthesia, of the kind so common in this region, probably aroused by our current discussion of his anal-erotic complex. Various features, however, in the distribution, quality and occurrence of the pain stirred elements of my medical knowledge, and I urged him to consult a surgeon at once. An early carcinoma of the rectum in an unusually favorable state was found, and a formidable operation performed without delay. That was more than ten years ago and the patient, well and happy, is now engaged in an active professional life [1927, p. 193].

Jones, via this surgical example, was calling attention to what other discussants likewise attributed to medical training: the development of a "sharpened clinical susceptibility," a "clinical sense" that translated into "the development of a sense of danger, an alertness for signals often of a very minute sort" (Glover, 1927, pp. 217, 218; cf. Horney, 1927, p. 257). The importance of this "sense" in psychoanalytic work went hand in hand with an emergent psychosomatic sensibility, a conviction "that the boundary line which separates a functionally conditioned disorder from an organic one is uncertain," so that the analyst "sees again and again that chronic pathological mental states can lead gradually to truly organic changes" (Alexander, 1927, p. 226).

Of course, the wavy boundary line between the psychic and somatic lent equal weight to the complementary claim: just as psychoanalysts should have "a complete medical training," so "the medical man should have a psychoanalytical training." The two claims, according to Franz Alexander, were at least equally justified:

If the analyst of today has often to call in the physician when dealing with intercurrent organic diseases, or when making his diagnosis, then the same holds good, or at least ought to hold good, of the physician, i.e., he should, perhaps more frequently than in the other case, consult the psychoanalyst, whether the latter is a layman or not [1927, p. 227].

Indeed, Alexander continued, the analyst's "psychical auscultation-technique is in no wise inferior to the physical technique of the doctor, either in scientific thoroughness or in effectiveness" (p. 227). And, in point of fact, at the present time, "psychoanalysis needs medicine less than medicine psychoanalysis." Medicine should embrace analysts "not on the ground of our medical qualification—to that we owe very little in our healing of psychoneurotics—but on the ground of our psychoanalytic therapeutic achievements." Only by insisting on this type of acceptance would analysts effect far-reaching changes in the medical curriculum, changes whereby "a knowledge of the structure and function of the psychical apparatus shall be as fundamental and as indispensable a part of the medical training of the future as knowledge of the anatomy and physiology of the body." And so Alexander concluded, "Psychoanalysis can never be merged into medicine as a special subject, as a branch of therapeutics: it can only enter it in its entirety as a half of equal importance. The science of personality and the knowledge of the body will stand side by side as two parts of the whole, equal in value and complementary to one another" (1927, p. 229).

In this verdict, if nowhere else, the proponents and opponents of lay analysis shared common ground. No one in 1927 believed that analysis should be, or could be, absorbed into the family of medical specialties. Within the boundaries of this understanding, the discussants of course diverged—they diverged not only on the relevance of preparatory medical training to analytic practice but on the normative and epistemic relationship of psychoanalytic knowledge to medical understanding. The proponents of lay analysis believed that analysis stood apart from medicine because it transcended medical apperception; in the words of the German lay analyst Carl Müller-Braunschweig, analysis diverged from medicine in its "breadth of scientific content." Unlike the clinician grounded in natural science and medicine, that is, the clinical analyst, who dealt "with the *whole* of man, and not merely with his body," was led in a different direction. He was obliged to "get to know the human being, not in any partial way, but in the largest possible number of those aspects and relations in which all the other sciences endeavor to comprehend him" (1927, p. 237, emphasis in original). This "getting to know" the human animal in the experiential fullness of his being had always been a supremely psychological task. "The analyst is above all a psychologist," intoned Theodor Reik, "whatever else he may be, physician, teacher, jurist, pastor. To whatever spheres he may apply his methods, his points of view and his interests remain always and preeminently psychological. If it is not so, he has no right to call himself a psychoanalyst." And this question of professional identity was not one of idle oneupsmanship. On the contrary, Reik held, "it touches on the question of the future fate of psychoanalysis: analysis will exist as an essential part of psychology or not at all" (p. 241).

The proponents of medical analysis, for all their concern with the role of a medically inculcated clinical "sense" in diagnosing and managing intercurrent organic illness, hardly demurred from this judgment.[4] How could it be otherwise? The fact, then and now, is that "psychoanalysis is not part of the practice of medicine in the sense of ordinary medical treatment. The modern physician, engrossed with an infinity of technical remedies at the sick bed, has no comprehension of the mental life of his patients" (Nunberg, 1927, p. 247). The physicians, while acknowledging this regrettable state of affairs, held to a different prognostic course. Rather than setting analysis *to the side* of medicine in the manner of Reik and the psychologists, they stressed the way in which it *absorbed* medicine and was therefore called upon to deepen and eventually transform it.[5]

---

[4] I say "hardly" because there is a single notable exception to the claim. I refer to Wilhelm Reich, whose defense of medical analysis, following from his idiosyncratic interests of the time, stressed the compatibility of analysis with "organic medicine" and hearkened to Freud's remark "that the time would come when the organic basis of psychoanalysis would be established" (Reich, 1927, p. 253).

[5] Hermann Nunberg and Ernst Simmel were even more forceful than Franz Alexander in underscoring this transformative potential. According to Nunberg, "It is therefore more necessary that all physicians should undergo psychoanalytical training before they so much as approach the sick than that nonmedical analysts should first study medicine" (1927, p. 248). Likewise Simmel, whose sense of transformation was more enveloping still: "As a universal science of 'depth-psychology' psychoanalysis is called upon in ever-increasing measure to provide a new basis for every department of science which is in any way at all concerned with the study of humanity. This holds good for pedagogy, art, theology and sociology, no less than for the science of medicine as a whole" (1927a, p. 260). Such claims, tendentiously exaggerated in the discussions of 1927, achieved more temperate expression two decades later when analysts adduced the historical anlagen of the psychosomatic viewpoint. See, for example, Alexander (1950, p. 33).

But all the discussants of 1927, with the lone exception of Wilhelm Reich, embraced the distinctively *transmedical* character of both the psychoanalytic method and the holistic findings to which it gave rise.

In the decade following publication of *The Question of Lay Analysis*, this belief in analysis as a transmedical gateway to understanding capable of reordering all the healing arts would blossom beyond Freud's own modest expectations. The discussion of lay analysis in the pages of the *International Journal of Psycho-Analysis* in 1927 is a watershed in the development of this notion but marks neither its inception nor its coming to fruition. We must now consider the trajectory of this conception, which, in both its theoretical and polemical aspects, marks the final dethronement of the surgical model that played so curious a role in the early development of psychoanalytic technique.

"Not Primarily Operative Interferences"

∞

T he nettlesome question of lay analysis elicited a variety of viewpoints on the relevance of medical training to the psychoanalytic endeavor. As we have seen, many of the medical contributors to the 1927 symposium in the *International Journal of Psycho-Analysis* took issue with Freud's disparagement of medicine. On the contrary, they insisted that medical training cultivated a scientific mind set and a clinical sensibility consistent with the requirements of analytic work. There was, of course, the matter of recognizing, referring, and consulting with respect to intercurrent illnesses that might complicate the patient's symptomatic picture. But aside from the matter of medical knowledge, there was the general attitude engendered by medical training. Where Freud took this attitude to be a decided negative, others, such as Karen Horney, took it as a positive. "In contradistinction to theoretical schools of study," she observed, "medicine has the advantage that its object of study is the same as that of the analyst, i.e., the living human being and particularly the suffering human being" (1927, p. 257). The one-sided preoccupation with the organic that was the legacy of a medical education was regrettable, to be sure, but bound to be "more than compensated for" by subsequent analytic training. Perhaps most important, Horney held, medical study provided "an education in dealing with sick people, and a feeling of responsibility toward them, and above all a will to heal" (p. 258).

Plausible claims, to be sure, and food for thought among medical and lay analysts alike. But these and a host of similar arguments advanced in 1927 have nothing to do with the nature of psychoanalysis itself. To argue for the advantages of medical education as preliminary to psychoanalytic training is very different from arguing that psychoanalysis per se is medical. To adopt the latter viewpoint would be to posit, as a derivative claim, that the employment of the psychoanalytic method is a medicosurgical undertaking, analogous to the procedures employed by other medical specialists. It is precisely this latter claim, which might well have been made a decade earlier, that was conspicuously absent by 1927.

To be sure, the absence of this claim in the aftermath of *The Question of Lay Analysis* does not bespeak a complete meeting of minds. Freud, in particular, construed the demedicalizing enterprise in a manner that set him apart from his colleagues. His turn away from medicosurgical models, as I have argued, was partly a response to his own surgical travail and the unremitting pain occasioned by the series of prostheses; as such, it was an aspect of his strategy for *temporizing* the therapeutic claims of analysis.

This strategy, as we have seem, was already discernible in *The Question of Lay Analysis* and *Inhibitions, Symptoms, and Anxiety*, the pivotal publications of 1926. But it came to fruition in the various discussions of psychoanalytic technique written in the final decade of his life. By the time of the *New Introductory Lectures* of 1932, Freud was constrained to acknowledge that "the therapeutic effectiveness of psychoanalysis remains cramped by a number of weighty and scarcely assailable factors" (1933, p. 154). Even apart from these factors—by which Freud meant "psychical rigidity" and the form of the illness "with all that that covers in the way of deeper determinants"—the curative potential of analysis was drastically limited. There were, among other things, the inordinate time required for lasting psychic change, the difficulties of analyzing entrenched character pathology, and the sobering realization that "severely handicapped people" required "analytic supervision" and intermittent treatment throughout their lives. With respect to such realities, Freud again makes a passing nod to the internist's patient ministrations over and against the surgeon's operative interventions. The forces arrayed against psychological change may make the analyst feel impotent, and his "therapeutic ambition may feel unsatisfied by such results." But still, Freud continues, "we have learned from the example of tuberculosis and lupus that success can only be obtained when the treatment has been adapted to the characteristics of the illness" (p. 156).

In "Analysis Terminable and Interminable" (1937a), there is the oft-noted deepening of Freud's therapeutic pessimism; it takes the form of a further retreat from even the modest therapeutics of the internist. The analytic effort "to replace repressions that are insecure by reliable ego-syntonic controls," we now learn, can be achieved only partially, and this because "portions of the old mechanisms remain untouched by the work of analysis" (p. 229). Freud next offers a new and more onerous catalogue of "weighty and scarcely assailable factors" inveighing against therapeutic change, and these factors now concern the instinctual sources of the patient's resistance to recovery. "If the strength of the instinct is excessive," Freud intones, "the mature ego, supported by analysis, fails in its task, just as the helpless ego failed formerly. Its control over instinct is improved, but it remains imperfect because the transformation in the defensive mechanisms is only incomplete" (p. 230). In endeavoring to account for the narrow parameters within which therapeutic movement typically occurs, Freud fleetingly returns to a surgical nomenclature, but now, ironically, as part of the effort to *distance* analysis from the model of surgical efficacy. Analysts should not be surprised at their failures, he cautions, "since the power of the instruments with which analysis operates is not unlimited but restricted, and the final upshot always depends on the relative strength of the psychical agencies which are struggling with one another" (p. 230).

"Analysis Terminable and Interminable" thereupon culminates in the same modest injunction as *Inhibitions, Symptoms, and Anxiety* a decade earlier: "The business of the analysis is to secure the best possible psychological conditions for the functions of the ego; with that it has discharged its task" (p. 250). Freud's remaining technical writings further characterize, in a consistently nonsurgical and nonmedical way, the realistic constraints on these "best possible psychological conditions." In "Constructions in Analysis" (1937b), the epistemic peculiarities of psychoanalytic reconstruction and, by implication, of the analyst's authority in general, occupy the foreground. From analytic experience, Freud writes, we learn "that no damage is done if, for once in a way, we make a mistake and offer the patient a wrong construction as the probable historical truth" (p. 261). Unlike the surgeon, that is, the analyst must rest content with exploratory verbal probings, satisfied with the knowledge that the analytic process, once set in motion, will be self-correcting and modestly ameliorative. Still, there can be no presumption of operative boldness or surgical precision in the implementation of analytic technique: "We do not pretend that an individual construction is anything more than a conjecture which awaits examination, confirmation, or rejection. We claim no authority for it, we require no direct agreement from the patient, nor do we argue with him if at first he denies it" (p. 265).

The *Outline of Psychoanalysis* (1938), Freud's final reprise on his science and its prospects, caps the retreat from medicosurgical analogizing, since here it is not merely the curative efficacy of technique that is questioned but the very therapeutic presumption that informs the use of the procedure. The analyst's "pact" with the analysand's "weakened ego," we now learn, conveys nothing of the surgeon's promise of operative remedy; it is not even akin to the conventional alliance of physician and patient. But for the intrusion of transference, Freud informs us, the patient would see the analyst in "the light of reality," which is to say, "as a helper and adviser who, moreover, is remunerated for the trouble he takes and who would himself be content with some such role as that of a guide on a difficult mountain climb" (p. 174). The role of helper, adviser, and guide initially obliges the analyst to encourage the patient simply to collaborate in the analytic endeavor (p. 177). But this type of "intellectual work," of course, is only preliminary to actual analytic engagement. And the latter, to our surprise, now embraces a virtually pastoral dimension, since to overcome resistance, the patient's ego "must be constantly encouraged and soothed if it is not to fail us" (p. 178). It follows from these procedural obligations that the analyst's job of "restor[ing] order in the ego" can be equated with several overlapping roles, none of which is medical:

We serve the patient in various functions, as an authority and a substitute for his parents, as a teacher and educator; and we have done the best for him if, as analysts, we raise the mental processes in his ego to a normal level, transform what has become unconscious and repressed into preconscious material and thus return it once more to the possession of his ego [p. 181].

The analyst as helper, adviser, guide, and soother, whose therapeutic leverage derives from the borrowed authority of parents, teachers, and educators—there is little here of medical diagnosis and treatment, not even the passive ministrations of the internist who brings scientific understanding and prognostic accuracy to bear on degenerative disease processes he cannot hope to alter. The surgical model of the papers on technique is no longer in retreat; it has been effectively vanquished by curative improbabilities wed to the psychobiology of instinctual life.

What then of Freud's followers, particularly those close colleagues who, judging from their experiences during the war years and, in certain instances, their own health-related preoccupations in the years thereafter, seemed poised to accompany him in the retreat from medicosurgical analogizing? We have already considered Ferenczi as a noteworthy exception; his commitment to analytic midwifery carried the surgical metaphor in a new obstetrical guise into the decade of the 1920s. But what of Abraham, Simmel, and Jones? Here the matter is more complicated; their writings seem to provide a sentient echo to Freud's, but the echo is in a different key and therefore paradoxical. To be sure, Abraham, Jones, and Simmel followed Freud in a newfound disinclination to medicalize the psychoanalytic method. But where did this refusal take them? As we shall see, their sense of the nonmedical character of the psychoanalytic procedure did not mimic Freud's. It did not, that is, mire them in a Freudian quicksand of therapeutic equivocation and prognostic fatalism. Rather, it opened to a garden of emergent clinical possibility informed by very different assumptions about the curative potential of psychoanalytic insight and its relationship to doctoring of the conventional sort.

In March of 1925, as Freud composed *The Question of Lay Analysis* and shortly before the onset of his own terminal lung cancer, Karl Abraham lectured on "Psychoanalysis and Gynecology" to the Berlin Gynecological Association. No more an operating room surgeon at a German military hospital, Abraham now apprised members of a surgical specialty of the special importance to them of the analytic method. For Abraham, the theoretical findings of analysis were self-evidently important to his gynecological colleagues; how else could they appreciate the frequency with which psychological symptoms appeared in conjunction with organic symptoms, or "as plausible-looking substitutes for them." In either case, he held, "true understanding of such pathological processes is only possible on the basis of psychoanalytical observation" (1925, p. 95).

But what were gynecologists to do with the gift of psycho-analytic insight? In many instances, Abraham averred, gyneco-logical symptoms pointed to a need for "radical treatment by a psychological specialist" (p. 95), so that the gynecologist's best course of action was simply to refer the patient. The analytic method, after all, was far from the interests, skills, and tem-perament of surgeons. And how many gynecologists were prepared to master a technique that was countersurgical in both its grounds and its implementation?

> Both psychological theory and psychoanalytical technique require a separate course of study. The ability of a physician to use this method largely depends upon the extent of his interest in psychological processes. A keen interest in organic disease, in gynecological technique and particularly in surgical procedures is but rarely to be found in combination with an inclination for the thorough investigation of the patient's psychic life. There are different types of medical temperaments: the surgeon's rapid intervention appeals to some, the tentative and patient attitude of the psychologist to others. Even where both types of inclination and ability are found combined in one physician, however, it would be impracticable for him to do justice to two such contrasting tasks. In psychoanalytical practice each patient is treated over a period of time in daily sessions lasting an hour. Such a routine of work, involving a

regular timetable filling up the whole day, is incompatible, for instance, with surgical practice [p. 95].

In 1926, Ernst Simmel, whose introduction to psychoanalysis, we have seen, came by way of a hypnotic-cathartic approach to the war neuroses, came of age methodologically with an intriguing study of "The 'Doctor-Game', Illness and the Profession of Medicine." Here, as with Abraham, the reversal is complete: It is no longer surgery that captures an essential aspect of analytic intervention; rather it is the analytic method that lends resonance to the medical and even the surgical calling. Simmel's paper does not merely address the anlagen of these callings, namely, the child's "doctor games" and "surgeon games" in which, so he holds, we discern "the outlines of the profession in later life" (p. 479). Simmel is concerned as well with the oedipal concomitants of the choice of profession, with the reason, for example, that specialists tend to fall victim to the particular disease which they treat, or with the defensive measures they adopt to contain their destructive impulses toward patients.

And there is finally, and more provocatively still, Simmel's effort to deconstruct the very fact of physical pain, to render it less an index of organic dysfunction than an analogue of anxiety defending against psychoeconomic disequilibrium. Between the war years and 1926, we plainly see, Simmel had completed his psychoanalytic conversion, the task set for him by Freud and Abraham. Now under the sway of the theory of life and death instincts propounded by Freud in *Beyond the Pleasure Principle* (1920a), he envisioned "every morbid process" to which the body is subject as promising a more accelerated pathway to the final relief from tension, death. Diseased organs signal the impending demise of Eros; they threaten the organism with "the deleterious consequences of the abrupt subsidence of libido." Hence, physical pain and mental anxiety both "are in general the alarm signals which summon the physician to the sufferer's assistance" (Simmel, 1926, p. 482). And what is the nature of this "assistance" the physician is called on to provide? For Simmel, analysis opens the door to fresh curative methods for addressing organic disease, and these methods lead us far from the model of surgical intervention:

But liberation from organic pain, such, for instance, as announces the presence of a morbid inflammation of [sic] the susceptibility to bacterial infection, requires of the physician of the body not primarily operative interferences but courage to adopt a new technique, comparable to that achieved by analysis through the methods formulated by Freud. In every case the physician must take into account the libidinal constitution of his patients. He must inform himself of the cause of the peculiar erotogenic demand of the organ which is attacked by disease (i.e., which is pressing to live at a more rapid pace), and he must try to assist the adjustment of the economy of the narcissistic libido [1926, p. 483].

We see that Simmel is not merely testifying to what a colleague would shortly thereafter term the psychiatrist's "rubbing shoulders with the general medical profession" (Johnson, 1928, p. 247). Nor is he urging on his colleagues, as he would the following year, "a systematic psychotherapy of organic diseases, on lines in accordance with psychoanalytical theory" (Simmel, 1927b, p. 72). Nor is he simply affirming, in the manner of Freud, the self-sufficiency of analytic technique as a counterpoise to conventional medicosurgical methods. Rather, he is imbuing a specifically analytic mode of intervention with such epistemic rightness and curative power as to operate outside the domain of analysis proper. As such, analytic technique now militates against "operative interferences" — even, we are told, in operative specialties. The analyst, it seems, has little if anything to learn from the surgeon; rather, he is the master of a countersurgical technique of such potency as to have a cautionary, even propaedeutic, significance for the surgeon himself.

Three years later, in 1929, Anita Muhl, writing in the *Psychoanalytic Review* about "Problems in General Medicine from the Emotional Standpoint," implicitly endorsed Simmel's verdict with a telling example:

At this point I wish to cite an amusing case of an eastern psychiatrist. A very famous surgeon sent a young woman who was suffering with toxic thyroid to him with the request that he get rid of some of her fears so she could be operated on, her pulse being so rapid that surgery could not be considered. The

psychiatrist analyzed the girl and at the end of three months
sent her back to the surgeon minus fears and minus her goiter!
The famous surgeon bewailed the loss of his patient but
expressed happiness over the outcome of the case [pp. 392–
393].

Thus did Simmel instantiate in 1926 the very dictum he
would lay down in 1927 in his consideration of lay analysis:
that analysis, a "universal science of 'depth psychology,'"
provided a new basis "for the science of medicine as a whole"
(1927a, p. 260). Thanks to psychoanalysis, he would proclaim,
"an epoch in medicine is drawing visibly to a close." The epoch
in question was one "in which the attention of students was
directed only to 'anatomical, physical or chemical facts that
could be objectively established,' and in which 'the problem
of existence was brought within his horizon only in so far as it
was explained by the action of forces which were also demonstrable in the inorganic world' " (p. 263). Now, under the impetus of psychoanalytic science, a new medical age was
dawning. The first Congress of Medical Psychotherapeutists,
which Simmel attended in 1926, was a harbinger of the changes
to come. There, he reported in 1927, one beheld

> a unanimous conviction that every disease, no matter whether
> the outstanding symptoms were psychical or somatic, was
> ultimately the manifestation of an inadequacy in the total
> personality, and had to be therapeutically conceived as such.
> That this idea, so new to medicine, was to a very large extent
> the result of the spread of psychoanalytical knowledge is clearly
> shown by the fact that almost every investigator who took part
> in the work of the Congress dealt exhaustively with the relation
> of psychoanalysis to his own subject [1927a, p. 264].

As to Ernest Jones, psychoanalytic propagandist par excellence, we have seen the strong medicosurgical component of
his professional identity surface repeatedly over the years. From
his medical management of Loe Kann's kidney attacks in 1914–
1915, to his medicosurgical ministrations to Morfydd Owen
following what would be her fatal appendicitis of 1918, to
his authoritative pronouncements on Karl Abraham's condition
in 1925, Jones emerges as the most resolutely doctorly of
the early analysts. Yet, Jones's writings throughout the 1920s

and 30s, no less than Freud's, bear witness to a move away from medicine and surgery as templates of psychoanalytic intervention.

In Jones's case, like Simmel's, the move is tantamount to an explanatory reversal, since Jones, rather than yielding pride of place to medicosurgical models, now forged links among analysis, psychiatry, and clinical medicine by underscoring the cautionary significance of the unconscious in all manner of therapeutics. At an address given at the opening exercises of Columbia University's Institute of Psychiatry in December 1929, the role of somatic factors in psychiatric illness was reduced to their impact on the ego's capacity to perform its regulatory tasks. In this manner, mental morbidity itself was subordinated to psychoanalytic insight; it represented "in the organic just as in the psychogenic cases—the triumph of the imperfectly controlled unconscious impulses." Disorders like dementia paralytica and alcoholic psychosis were not to be explained "as a direct result of the toxins concerned." Rather "they are expressions of individual conflicts which can no longer be coped with by an ego weakened by the cerebral poisoning" (1930, p. 376).

Several years later, Jones broadened this view of organic pathology to clinical medicine writ large. It was no longer medicosurgical models that provided methodological anchorage for psychoanalysis. Now it was psychoanalysis that came to the aid of physicians and surgeons, and this by offering the medical profession just what it lacked: "both understanding of these disorders and the power of dealing with them." The problem, as Jones saw it, was that the medical profession "is as yet only very imperfectly aware of its lack" (1934, p. 342).

In exemplifying how psychoanalysis rescued medicine from its clinical myopia, Jones again rested his case on the unconscious. Now, however, he appealed not only to the unconscious valence of the disease process but also to the unconscious impact of medicosurgical interventions aimed at reversing it. Surgery, no less than accidental injury, was a genre of bodily mutilation that fell within the analyst's explanatory domain:

> The unconscious apprehends any affliction of the body, notably accidents and surgical operations, but also simple diseases, as assaults the ultimate aim of which is mutilation. And the essence

of the mutilation is damage to an erotic organ, most typically castration or destruction of the womb. These irrational fears are again connected with infantile guilt" [1934, p. 348].

In 1938, discoursing on "The Unconscious Mind and Medical Practice," Jones's tone was as confident as ever, his claims more expansive still. What had been offered a decade earlier as a psychoanalytic attitude about the significance of organic pathology had evolved into the germ of a theory of physical illness and the contrasting pathways to its remediation. Jones began with the bold assertion that the unconscious "invariably interprets every physical illness as a personal attack, which it colors with a projection of its own aggressivity," and then adduced the following:

> The unconscious then conceives of help in coping with the invasion in one of two ways: the doctor is either to offer something good that will neutralize the malevolent foreign body or to display a violence greater than this. We are familiar with these two broad types of treatment, psychologically regarded, and perhaps also with corresponding types of doctor. The one is illustrated by a soothing cough medicine or a gentle manipulative massage, the other by most medicines or by surgical operations [1938, pp. 362–363].

Psychoanalysis alone, it would seem, was capable of illuminating the unconscious reverberations of surgical intervention. But its superordinacy did not end here. Equally important for the surgeon, analysis provided enlightenment about the patient's attitude toward, even need for, the scalpel. Anticipating Karl Menninger's examination of polysurgical addiction that same year (1934), Jones called attention to a particularly troublesome category of surgical patient: "Every surgeon, whether he recognizes them or not, must encounter many cases where the patient is secretly bent on having some operation or other under various more or less plausible pretexts, and it may happen that the situation happily coincides with some repressed trend of sadism in his own nature" (1934, pp. 348–349).

It was a short step from explanatory inferences about the patient's attitude toward surgery to analytic focus on the unconscious mind of the physician and surgeon. Only the latter's unconscious resistance, after all, could explain the medical neglect of psychology: "It is that, just as their patients, physicians too are human beings" (1938, p. 356). Thus, the next topic of analytic elucidation would be the physician's own "situation" and, most of all, "the subtle and extensive interaction" of the situations of patient and doctor, respectively (p. 357). Jones was content to leave this topic to others, but not before opining that the doctor's unconscious mind "may interfere with his clinical judgment in making diagnoses and deciding on treatment." Indeed, he himself was persuaded "that the potential skill of most doctors is considerably reduced by such aberrant activity" (p. 364).

The retreat from surgical analogizing begun by Freud and endorsed latterly by Abraham, Simmel, and Jones enlisted other theorists throughout the 1930s, perhaps none more colorful than the American psychiatrist Karl Menninger. With the publication of *The Human Mind* in 1930, Menninger achieved a celebrity that extended far beyond his native Kansas. There, with his father, Charles, and younger brother, Will, he had established an outpatient psychiatric clinic and inpatient sanitarium that, by the summer of 1928, occupied a single integrated campus on the outskirts of Topeka—this the birth of the illustrious Menninger Clinic.

Menninger's advocacy of the "new psychiatry," the psychodynamic psychiatry he had learned from Smith Ely Jelliffe during his residency at Boston Psychopathic Hospital in 1918–1919, initially incorporated only the most superficial exposure to psychoanalysis; it was not until 1931 that his schedule permitted a year of episodic personal analysis with Franz Alexander at the Chicago Institute for Psychoanalysis (L. J. Friedman, 1990, p. 59). But this late and abbreviated experience of analysis did not prevent Menninger from becoming a psychoanalytic spokesman of the first rank, one whose authority in America approached that of Ernest Jones on the continent. And, like Jones, he mimicked Freud's retreat from surgical analogizing by juxtaposing the insights of psychoanalytic psychiatry with those of medicine and surgery.

In a series of papers that were propagandistic in tone and optimistic to the point of mild euphoria, Menninger elevated psychiatry—by which he meant always and only psychoanalytic psychiatry—to the rank of "Cinderella" specialty, a specialty that had absorbed and thereby transcended the explanatory perspectives of medicine and surgery.[1] It was not merely a matter of training the psychoanalytic searchlight on medicosurgical terrain, of exploring, for example, the unconscious motives underlying the surgeon's behavior in operating or the patient's behavior in submitting to surgery (K. Menninger, 1934). Such interpretive exercises were entirely conventional by the 1930s, though Menninger delivered his judgments with a finality and a rhetorical flourish that could be unsettling.[2]

But Menninger went further still: he enshrined psycho-analytic psychiatry to the point that it reframed, and potentially even supplanted, the surgical sense that surgeons brought to surgical problems. The surgical attitude, that is, with its coolness, detachment, and narrowed clinical focus, was ill-equipped to unravel the unconscious motives shaping ostensibly surgical problems. The surgeon was in effect blinded by the manifest content of pathophysiological dysfunction; a

---

[1] " . . . it is not necessary to explain why psychiatry, the Cinderella, left the kitchen and married the prince. The fact is that she has done so. If you doubt this, reflect upon the fact that in several medical schools more time is devoted today to the teaching of psychiatry than to the teaching of surgery, that more hospital beds are filled with psychiatric patients tonight than are filled with all the medical and surgical and tuberculous and orthopedic and all other cases combined, that the state of New York spends many thousand times as much upon the care of psychiatric cases as upon the care or prevention of medical and surgical diseases of all other types" (K. Menninger, 1938, pp. 185–186).

[2] "Certainly there is nothing in the practice of medicine so barbarous and so fraught with psychological danger as the prevalent custom of taking a child into a strange white room, surrounding him with white-garbed strangers, exhibiting queer paraphernalia and glittering knives and at the height of his consternation pressing an ether cone over his face and telling him to breathe deeply. The anxiety stimulated by such horrors is probably never surpassed in the child's subsequent life. Also the way in which surgery is proposed to children and the reasons advanced for it by the surgeon frequently betray the surgeon's own neurotic motives. Within a month I have observed the incident of a surgeon telling his own son that unless he behaved better in school he would take him to the hospital and cut his insides out. If such a surgeon would tell his own child this, one can only imagine what his surgical work really means to him and what he would tell patients" (K. Menninger, 1934, pp. 173–174).

psychoanalytic naïf, he remained oblivious to the variegated ways in which neurotic demands commanded organic compliance. If, for example, a hysterical patient required "a surgical manipulation" to gratify unconscious needs, "the means will not fail him to bring about a condition which even the most conscientious surgeon will be inclined to regard as indicative, if not imperative, of surgical interference" (1934, p. 176). Indeed, in cases of unconsciously motivated demands for repeated surgical intervention—in cases, that is, of actual addiction to polysurgery—the surgeon was usually not at fault. His was the guileless complicity of the analytically unschooled. The procedures demanded by such patients, after all "cannot always be labeled unnecessary operations because such patients are very often able to make the particular operation appear to be imperative" (p. 176).[3]

Wise the surgeon, then, who deferred to the psychoanalytic psychiatrist. For it was the latter's conceptual armamentarium, with its notions of repetition compulsion, castration anxiety and castration wish, father transference, and primary and secondary gain, that provided the more penetrating vantage point from which to weigh the operative possibilities in ostensibly surgical cases. In the words of William Menninger, who, after World War II, joined his brother in the propagandizing campaign of the 1950s, psychiatry was "in a very real sense, 'comprehensive medicine'"; it was the "relatively new specialty" able to "make comprehensible medical observations which formerly had been incomprehensible." Only when the principles underlying the diagnosis and treatment of mental illness were "accepted and applied by all physicians and adapted to their special situations," the younger Menninger enjoined, would the medical profession advance to "a more effective and

---

[3] Of course, polysurgical addiction did not arise in the 1930s. Edward Shorter (1992, pp. 86–94) documents the emergence of the "desire for surgery," which he interprets as a particular psychosomatic symptom, in the late nineteenth century. More controversial is Shorter's specific thesis that addiction to surgery is a characteristically American phenomenon that arose "as a sequel of half a century of medically suggesting the population into the belief that vague, nonspecific physical symptoms were the consequences of reflex phenomena from peripheral organs" (p. 91).

scientific brand of medical practice" (W. Menninger, 1953, pp. 171, 173).

But the subordination of medicosurgical treatment planning to psychiatric assessment did not end with the hortatory insistence that the psychiatrist was uniquely equipped "to provide helpful information regarding the emotional factors in illness to the internist, surgeon, and to all other medical specialists" (W. Menninger, 1953, p. 171). Beginning in the late 1920s, the psychoanalytic literature reveals an even more ambitious project of co-optation: the breaking down of the very distinction between functional or psychogenic disorders and organic pathology. This task presupposed no uniformity of psychoanalytic outlook; it was pursued from different theoretical directions and at varying levels of abstraction.

We have already touched on Ernest Jones's (1938) contribution to the project: the construal of physical illness as personal attack, with the physician enlisted as ally in subduing a "malevolent foreign body" engaged in aggressive assault. But Jones was preceded by Simmel and others. Strategies of co-optation ranged from Cavendish Moxon's (1928) argument that "universal, unconscious mother attachment," qua Otto Rank, was an inevitable intensifier—even a constituent—of organic pathology, to Franz Alexander's appropriation of Freud's tension reduction model to reframe organic disease as "morphological tissue changes under the influence of the chronic functional disturbance" (1936, p. 554; cf. 1950, pp. 43–44). Karl Menninger, like Simmel before him and Jones after him, looked to Freud's metabiological life and death instincts in formulating a plan of medicosurgical deconstruction. The death instinct, he began, points us to a new appreciation of mankind's self-destructive impulses. Ordinarily, the self-destructive impulses are held in abeyance. But sick people, on the other hand,

> may be conceived of as persons in whom the battle has erupted so that they are trying to destroy themselves and at the same time fighting against it, imploring aid in this from the doctor. Such an hypothesis might be applied to such immediate and sudden self-destruction as is represented by suicide, or to more gradual and diffuse self-destruction such as neurotic invalidism. Perhaps such a thing as tuberculosis in which the individual

seems to yield, sometimes all too willingly, to the invasion of an available assailant, and even the more localized or focalized diseases of the body may be thought of as further illustrations. Such an extension of the theory to organic disease was not made definitely by Freud and we are not yet in any position to support it with convincing evidence; it is, however, a logical conclusion from the theory that if there is a self-destructive impulse with the strength which Freud has postulated and which much clinical evidence supports, then we should not be surprised to find that it had an active part in the production of physical as well as psychological disease [1936, pp. 7–8].

In the propagandizing of the Menningers, we discern a trend that masks an important paradox in American psychoanalysis commencing in the 1930s. At the same time as leading American analysts staunchly repudiated Freud's defense of lay analysis, they articulated a defense of medical analysis that was, in its own way, nonmedical — or, better, transmedical — in character. Rather than subordinating their claim to medical specialty status to the modus operandi of other medicosurgical specialties, that is, the analysts assumed a superordinate status via their privileged access to the unconscious dimensions of organic pathology. As medical specialists, the analysts, glibly conflated with psychiatrists sympathetic to analysis, became something other, indeed something more, than physician-surgeons. At their most grandiose, they rose above medicine, laying claim to ordering principles, even transcendental insights, that reframed the very meaning of disease and suffering; more characteristically, they claimed the status of primus inter pares, of physicians whose insights, vouchsafed by a method sui generis, greatly enriched the medicosurgical viewpoint. As such, they were uniquely situated to arbitrate among physicians and surgeons in the conventional realms of etiology, diagnosis, and treatment planning.

Needless to say, the same transdisciplinary wisdom that enabled the psychoanalytic psychiatrist to advise his colleagues on ostensibly medicosurgical problems rendered him — and him alone — adequate to the infinite complexity of psychiatric problems. "Whatever the case may be in general medicine about which we have our ideas if not a large experience," Karl Menninger lectured a journalist in June of 1936,

> the fact is that psychiatry involves an extremely complicated
> and broad view not only of medical science but of psychology,
> sociology, and general culture. It is a little extreme, but perhaps
> fairly illustrative, to say that one cannot properly understand
> psychiatric cases unless he is familiar with an extremely wide
> range of subjects from English literature and the history of
> music to political developments in medieval Europe and the
> nature of action currents in the heart. So far as I know, no
> other branch of medicine requires such an extensive scope as a
> part of the professional accouterment [Faulker and Pruitt, 1988,
> p. 210].

Extensive indeed. And yet there is something disingenuous about Menninger's cataloguing of the prerequisites of psychiatric *virtu*. All but one of his disciplinary exemplars fall outside of medicine; he conjures up a vision of the psychiatrist as imposing savant, a veritable repository of high culture and broad learning. But when it came to the social and professional status of the psychiatrist, such wide-ranging scholarly "accouterments" counted for little. Menninger did not wish the psychoanalytic psychiatrist to be enshrined as a recondite university professor. Rather, he sought the identity—and acclaim—of a medical specialist among specialists, a surgeon among surgeons. "You might say, 'the Menninger Clinic which is for psychiatry what the Mayo Clinic is for surgery'"—this was his editorial advice to a journalist researching an article on the Clinic's Southard School in the summer of 1939.

More than a year later, Menninger offered congenial praise to Lewellys Barker, a Johns Hopkins internist who had published an introductory work on the role of psychotherapy in medical practice. Menninger heartily endorsed a well-regarded clinician's effort to convey to colleagues his realization "that your success with your patients did not depend entirely upon the physical and chemical measures which you instituted to combat their illnesses." But he could not refrain from addressing certain of Barker's demurrers about psychoanalysis proper. Yes, he acknowledged, "the high-priest attitude of some psychoanalysts is just as irritating as the former high-priest attitude of some surgeons was." But Barker was asked to remember that "psychoanalysis is still a very young technique; surgery in its early days certainly made many equally serious mistakes. Psychoanalysis is still further handicapped by the fact that the training is much more difficult than surgery; it requires more intelligence, more time and more money" (Faulkner and Pruitt, 1988, p. 337).

Consonant with the avowal of analytic superiority to mundane medicosurgical methods was the emergence of that new analytic prerogative: psychodynamic scrutiny of the motivational grounds for entering surgery and other medical specialties. As early as 1930, we find analytic ruminations about the anthropological and psychological origins of surgery (Schmideberg, 1930, pp. 409ff.), and by the early 1950s we find the physician's choice of specialty brought fully within analytic purview, including the inhibitions and symptoms related to the choice of surgery as a profession (Glauber, 1953). It was again Karl Menninger who rose to the fore in conveying a sense of analytic *mastery* of the psychodynamic meaning of becoming a physician and thence of the various medicosurgical styles of intervention. From general speculations about the unconscious factors entering into the choice of medicine as a profession (K. Menninger, 1957a), he proceeded to more focal observations on the fons et origo of each of the medical specialties. Of surgeons, he observed:

> It is no reflection upon the surgeons to say that a connection exists between fantasies of mutilation and the skilled, tender handling of body tissues by the trained operator. It does not follow that surgeons are more sadistic than other people, or more driven by blind impulses toward cruelty; in fact, just the opposite may be true. The chances are that surgeons have less unconscious guilt about their sadistic proclivities than most people and hence do not need to repress them, but use them constructively. They can sublimate sadistic impulses in a closely related but enormously more approved form of behavior. That this form appeals to the public is obvious in the dramatic interest which attaches to the surgical operation, in the romantic interest which (so often) attaches to the surgeon. He becomes the great life saver, the performer of miracles, the very incarnation of curative science [1957b, p. 102].

With Menninger, it seems, we have circled back to the late nineteenth-century ideal of the heroic surgeon, the operator who boldly sallies forth where therapists fear to tread. But the ideal has been undermined by psychodynamic insight and is no more what it was. Deconstructed and robbed of mystique, it is now offered up psychoanalytically, by doctors of the mind who dare to understand what surgeons fear to know.

"A Panic Application of Magic"
⊂⊗⊃

There is a gruesome irony in the foregoing developments, for the very period during which Simmel, Jones, Menninger, and others attested to the analytic transcendence of medico-surgical methods witnessed general psychiatry's tragically surgical turn in pursuit of the "great and desperate cures" of which Elliot Valenstein (1986) has written. It was in the fall of 1935, the year after Jones lectured to the Paddington Medical Society on "Psychoanalysis and Modern Medicine" and Menninger published his influential study of polysurgical addiction, that Egas Moniz, a Portuguese neurologist whose pioneering work on cerebral angiography failed to win him a coveted Nobel Prize, devised and performed what he termed "prefrontal leucotomy" on a series of schizophrenics. Within a year, this genre of "psychosurgery," a term of Moniz's invention, was being performed on mental patients in half a dozen other countries and, shortly thereafter, throughout the world (Valenstein, 1986, pp. 62ff.). By the fall of 1936, the operation had been taken up by Walter Freeman and James Winston Watts of George Washington University. After the employment of Moniz's procedure in a single case of agitated depression, the two rechristened Moniz's "prefrontal leucotomy" as "prefrontal lobotomy"[1] and immediately became its outspoken proponents

---

[1] Moniz's procedure employed a leucotome—a surgical instrument with a wire loop that could be extended and rotated after it was positioned at the target site—to cut or crush nerve fibers in the frontal lobes of the brain; "leucotomy" derived from the Greek *leuco*, meaning "white matter," and referred, in the case of this procedure, to nerve fibers. After their initial case in 1936, Freeman and Watts became convinced that the procedure destroyed nerve-cell bodies as well as nerve fibers and proposed the more radical term "lobotomy" to describe it (Valenstein, 1986, pp. 62, 106–107, 142–143; see also the illustrations in Valenstein, 1973, pp. 278–280).

and proselytizers. Following the publication of Freeman and Watts's influential *Psychosurgery* in 1942, prefrontal lobotomy became an enormously popular, if scientifically specious and clinically questionable, treatment for intractable psychiatric disorders.[2]

In America, the lure of an invasive somatic psychiatry, of a literally surgical psychiatry, did not have to await the advent of prefrontal lobotomy. As early as 1919, Henry A. Cotton, of New Jersey's Trenton State Hospital, created a minor stir with his theory of septic psychosis. Convinced that "focal infections" underlay the entire panoply of mental disorders, Cotton converted his state hospital into a surgical mill, where all patients underwent routine "defocalization" of allegedly infected tissue. Cotton's operative regime began with routine extraction of teeth and removal of tonsils, but these operations, so he held, failed to eradicate all the "septic foci" dwelling within. So defocalizing interventions went on to include "electrical coadulation of the cervix" and frequently proceeded to surgery of the abdominal cavity (laparotomy) and actual removal of bowel (cholectomy).

Cotton's bizarre mission of surgicalization—positively medieval in the urgency with which it sought to exorcise bacterial demons lurking within—was premised on a very real contempt for talking therapy, which refused to subordinate psychic status to physical condition. "Treat the physical condition and the patient will recover from the secondary mental disorders"— this the proud slogan of Cotton and his staff (Grob, 1985, p. 118). To which philosophy the American analyst William

---

[2] Valenstein (1973, pp. 294-335) provides a fair-minded evaluation of the clinical results of prefrontal psychosurgery, including both first-generation lobotomy and second-generation refinements of the procedure. For an illuminating overview of somatic treatments throughout psychiatric history, an account contemporary with, and responsive to, the advent of radical somatic therapies in the 1930s, see Diethelm (1939). Tourney (1969) is representative of psychiatric accounts that, in the manner of Whig history, laud the radical somatic therapies (here dubbed the "physical therapies") for providing "tremendous impetus" to the development of modern biological psychiatry. Grob's (1983, pp. 291–308) more measured historical review stresses the personal and institutional imperatives that aided and abetted recourse to somatic treatments in the United States. Romano (1990) provides an interesting personal account of the rise and fall of somatic therapies and psychosurgery in American psychiatry.

Alanson White, then superintendent of St. Elizabeth's Hospital in Washington, commented with due sobriety:

> I do not know what the degree of relationship is that exists between focal infection as a causative factory of insanity, but I do believe that Cotton and Reed[3] are both infected with red ants. . . . The world has been overflowing for the last few years with lots of damn fool theories, and I think it important for the welfare of humanity that some of us doctors at least retain what little sense we have and try to keep our feet on the ground [in Grob, 1985, pp. 109–110].

That psychiatry should be reduced to "an adjunct or the handmaiden of the gastroenterologist, the genito-urinary surgeon and the dentist" while "man's crowning glory, his mind, receive no further consideration"—this, lamented White, was "most profoundly unfortunate for psychiatry" (in Grob, 1985, p. 115). Rather less dismissive was the analytic reaction to the three radical somatic therapies—all involving the induce-ment of shock—introduced more than a decade later: insulin-coma therapy (1933), metrazol-convulsion therapy (1935), and electroconvulsive shock (1938).[4]

Insulin-coma therapy in particular was taken seriously by a number of analytically knowledgeable observers in the 30s. It was the brainchild of Manfred Joshua Sakel, a Polish neuro-physiologist and psychiatrist who, following medical studies at the University of Vienna from 1919 to 1925, proceeded to Berlin, where he began psychiatric practice in an institution dedicated to the treatment of patients in drug withdrawal (Fink, 1984). Following contemporary reports of the metabolic effects of insulin, Sakel administered the drug to induce weight gain and attenuate motility, excitement, and insomnia during opiate withdrawal. Occasionally, he found, the insulin doses induced coma, albeit with negligible impact on morphine dependence.

---

[3] Dr. Charles A. L. Reed of Cincinnati, who subscribed to Cotton's theory of focal infections and was deemed by White to be even more extreme and hence dangerous than Cotton.

[4] The following summary of each of the three principal types of shock therapy draws on Kalinowsky and Hoch (1946), Fink (1984), Bollorino et al. (1995), and Sabbatini (1997/98).

In the case of a single drug-addicted schizophrenic, however, Sakel made the surprising observation that insulin-induced coma reduced anxiety and excitement; with repeated doses of insulin, the patient's overall mental condition improved still further. Sakel thereupon began regularly to employ insulin-induced coma in the management of schizophrenics and, following his return to Vienna in 1933, publicized his findings within the medical community. By 1937 insulin-induced coma and convulsions, eventually known throughout Europe as "Sakel's therapy," had become a treatment of choice at mental institutions worldwide.

In the same year (1933) that Sakel began publicizing his findings about insulin-induced convulsions, the Hungarian neuropathologist Ladislas Meduna came across two brief clinical reports from 1929 in which his colleagues J. Nyirö and A. Jablonsky reported a marked diminution in the frequency of seizures among epileptics who developed schizophrenic symptoms. Meduna, taken with the authors' conclusion of a basic antagonism between schizophrenia and epilepsy, proceeded to the complementary inference: perhaps the onset of epilepsy would attenuate the symptoms of schizophrenia. Neuropathic examination of brain tissue of deceased schizophrenics, on the one hand, and epileptics who had died in the midst of seizures (in status epilepticus), on the other, bolstered his surmise. Whereas ablated tissue sections of schizophrenic brains showed a virtual absence of glia cells, sections of epileptic brains revealed a wild proliferation of these same cells (glial hyperplasia). Perhaps, Meduna reasoned, the absence of glial cells was causally implicated in schizophrenia, and the induction of epilepticlike seizures in schizophrenic patients would stimulate glial production and thereby improve their mental functioning. In November 1933, he began to experiment with various substances—strychnine, thebaine, nikethamide, caffeine, absinthe—capable of inducing epileptic attacks; two months later, he was persuaded that intramuscular camphor in oil was the least toxic seizure-producing agent.

Meduna proceeded to induce seizures in 26 psychotic patients, first with camphor and, beginning in 1934, with the more reliable pentylentetrazol, a central nervous system stimulant marketed as metrazol or cardiazol. One of the early analeptics, metrazol stimulated the respiratory and vasomotor centers in the medulla if that area of the brain had been previously depressed by drugs. It thus found a medical application in the treatment of barbiturate poisoning (Beckman, 1958, pp. 269–275). In this context, metrazol's tendency to produce convulsions was an unwanted side effect and a principal source of opposition to the drug (p. 270). For Meduna, of course, it was precisely the side effect that suggested a therapeutic result in the treatment of psychotics. And initial publication of his clinical experiments in January 1935 contained promising findings: full recovery in 10 patients, significant improvement in three, and no change at all in 13. Meduna's colleagues at the University of Budapest reacted critically to his research, but colleagues outside of Hungary were immediately appreciative. By 1936, visitors from Europe, Asia, and America were coming to Hungary to learn first-hand about metrazol therapy.

Among the colleagues appreciative of Meduna's discovery were the Italian researcher Ugo Cerletti and his coworkers, N. Accornero and Lucio Bini. At the first international conference devoted to the "modern treatment of schizophrenia," which took place in Münsingen, Switzerland in 1937, they described their own variable experiences with metrazol, and Bini further reported on attempts to induce seizures with electrical stimuli in dogs. As early as 1931, Cerletti, then a neurologist specializing in the histopathology of epilepsy, had employed electroshock to induce reliable seizures in dogs and other animals. But he remained highly skeptical about substituting electricity for metrazol in human subjects until a visit in 1935 to a Roman slaughterhouse, where butchers were using the building's electric current to anesthetize pigs prior to slaughter, suggested its feasibility.[5] He proceeded to persuade

---

[5] Cerletti observed how the pigs reacted to 70–80 volts of alternating current with general clonic shock, after which they fell to the ground unconscious, at which point their throats were slit; they bled to death before regaining consciousness. Cerletti thereupon obtained permission to conduct his own experiments at the slaughterhouse. Using the same large electric pincers as the butchers, he applied current through various dimensions of pig heads and, being otherwise disinclined to slit the pigs' throats, he was able to confirm what Bini had discovered in dogs: that animals could withstand 70–125 volts of current, even for several seconds, without apparent injury. Perhaps, he reasoned, humans too could tolerate strong electric current.

two of his colleagues, Lucio Bini and Lothar Kalinowsky, to help him develop an apparatus that would deliver brief electric shocks to human beings, and he supported their continuing animal research involving electricity.

A year later, in April 1938, Cerletti and his colleagues found the first human subject for their shock-inducing apparatus: a 39-year-old vagrant wandering the streets of Rome. Mentally disorganized, delusional, and speaking only in neologisms, he was admitted to the neurology department of Rome University (of which Cerletti was chairman) and was administered an electrically induced seizure through the frontal parietal area with a current of 80 volts for 1/5 second. The patient immediately began to speak coherently, if only to plead against receiving a second dose of electric shock. Two months later, following 11 complete and nine incomplete applications of shock, he was discharged as cured. A month earlier, in May 1938, Bini and Cerletti's initial reports on Bini's animal research and its potential applicability to schizophrenics reached both Italian (Cerletti and Bini, 1938) and American (Bini, 1938) readerships. In 1939, their colleague Kalinowsky toured Europe and the United States to promote the new Cerletti-Bini method of inducing shock, and researchers were shortly thereafter reporting spectacular results from the use of electroshock therapy (ECT) with patients with affective disorders, especially severe, treatment-resistant depression. By 1942, Byron Stewart, a former staff member of the Menninger Clinic, would laud ECT as the state of the art in shock therapy. Safer than insulin coma treatment, it likewise overcame the greatest obstacle to inducing shock through metrazol: the practically universal fear and anxiety reaction that followed administration of the drug.[6]

For the European theorists dedicated to analysis and intent on elaborating what was fast becoming its transmedical mode of therapeutic action, the turn to aggressive somatic interven-

---

[6] Specifically, Stewart was referring to fear "due to the aura and painful anxiety sensations of the latent period which occurs between the injection of the drug and loss of consciousness. In some cases the latent period may be prolonged 30 to 60 seconds. During this time the patient complains of sensations of pain, of impending death, or complete annihilation, one or all of which arouse such an opposition in the patient that the treatment sometimes must be abandoned or forcibly applied" (1942, p. 23).

tions elicited scarcely a murmur. The murmur, such as it was, amounted to analytically informed endorsements, varyingly circumscribed, of shock therapy. In 1940, the German analyst Isidor Silbermann, recently relocated in Britain with the assistance of Ernest Jones, offered an ego-psychological rendering of the shock experience as a regressive dissolution of the psychotic ego followed by beneficent psychological rebirth. Three years later, the London analyst A. Cyril Wilson, overcoming a basic mistrust of violent methods of treatment, owned up that in certain cases shock therapy resulted in "a shortening of the psychotic attack" (1943, p. 59). Further, in an ego-psychological formulation that followed Schilder (1939) and Silbermann (1940), he suggested that the patient's superego accepted shock therapy "as a form of punishment for incestuous sadistic phantasies, but less severe than that expected, and so suspense and guilt are lessened; the individual is more able to forgive himself for his forbidden phantasies" (p. 60).

Three years later, the Italian psychiatrist-analyst Joachim Flescher likewise formulated the therapeutic action of shock therapy in terms of the psychology of aggression, but he had scant need for the new language of ego psychology. In a presentation at the National Congress of the Italian Society of Psychiatry in the fall of 1946, he reverted to a defense of shock therapy in terms of the psychoeconomics of instinctual life pure and simple. The "induced convulsive seizures" of electric shock treatment, he held, "owe their efficacy to the discharge of destructive energies, whose quantitative ratio towards the libidinous ones (in their psychoanalytical sense) is altered in the latter's favor" (1950, p. 228). Indeed, the special effectiveness of electric shock in cases of depression followed from the particular need for motoric aggressive discharge among depressives, in whom "the subject's exalted aggressiveness is released in a centripetal direction (self-accusation, micromania) to reach its climax in suicidal tendencies" (p. 277).

Among these commentators, Wilson anticipated his countryman D. W. Winnicott in chiding psychiatrists who employed shock treatment for failing to recognize and utilize the transference relationship that invariably arose in the course of treatment. But among the Europeans, Winnicott, a British pediatrician and psychoanalyst, stood alone in appropriating the transmedical mantle to spur his colleagues to analytic consideration of the new shock therapies, especially the range of meanings, conscious and unconscious, attendant to their employment (1944). Alas, Winnicott would remain a voice in the wilderness; European analysts tended to be indifferent to the whole matter. Not so the Americans, whose analytic identities always fell back on their professional status as medical men, as psychiatrists. They could ill afford to ignore an invasive procedure that, according to its proponents, was emblematic of scientific medical psychiatry. And so the American analysts spoke out one way or the other, and often equivocally.

William Alanson White, true to his analytic convictions, remained skeptical of all the somatic therapies. But others were duly impressed. Shortly after arriving in Vienna in 1934 to undertake a training analysis with Freud, the psychiatrist Joseph Wortis visited Sakel's clinic and wrote his colleagues at New York's Bellevue Hospital that the use of insulin-coma was among the most remarkable therapies he had ever beheld (Valenstein, 1986, p. 47). Back in the States, the analyst Smith Ely Jelliffe not only endorsed insulin-coma treatment, but even offered a convoluted explanation of its action in terms of Freud's theory of metabiological life and death instincts (pp. 54–55). Adolf Meyer demurred from Jelliffe's "highly interpretative" explanation, but remained sufficiently impressed with Sakel's procedure to introduce insulin treatment at the Phipps Clinic of the Johns Hopkins School of Medicine. Even A. A. Brill, a standard bearer of Freudian orthodoxy and erstwhile critic of somatic therapies throughout the 30s, felt that Sakel's results were promising enough to oblige psychiatrists at least to try out the procedure (p. 56).[7]

---

[7] Even when the results of shock therapy fell short of therapeutic expectations, American analysts seemed reluctant to distance themselves from the procedure on the basis of psychoanalytic principles. Writing in the *Psychoanalytic Quarterly* in 1948, the New York analysts John Frosch and David Impastato cataloged a series of therapeutic failures in which the virtual "dissolution of the ego" induced by shock treatment was not followed by successful ego reintegration. Still, they held to the possibility of amelioration through the "partial integration" that elicited primitive defensive structures: "Through the establishment of regressive defenses, the ego is given, so to speak, a breathing spell, to build up its strength anew, to

Only at The Menninger Clinic, where both insulin and metrazol were employed as treatment adjuncts by the fall of 1937, was American receptiveness to the new somatic therapies dampened by a preexisting commitment to psychodynamic principles. To be sure, there was a willingness, in the spirit of Jelliffe and Brill, to try out the new approaches and even to achieve expertise in treatment preparation and aftercare (Erickson and Ramsey, 1938). But the willingness was tempered by a resolutely psychoanalytic skepticism about the ultimate efficacy of psychomotor insults on long-term psychodynamic functioning. In his initial report on the use of metrazol with 26 sanitarium patients, of whom 22 were diagnosed with schizophrenia and four with depression, William Menninger, true to his psychoanalytic lineage, framed the therapeutic issue in a manner fully consonant with the less than impressive results he proceeded to report:

> Our understanding of the nature of the illnesses classed as schizophrenia would not permit us to regard convulsions as being a specific cure: they may momentarily break a vicious cycle in the patient's psychomotor adjustment, but we cannot assume that they change the emotional conflicts nor prepare the patient to face any more adequately the reality problems in his particular environment [1937, p. 130].

With respect to the minority of schizophrenics who evinced improvement after treatment, Menninger was at pains to explain outcome as the product of "milieu and psychotherapy *in addition to* the metrazol" (p. 138, emphasis in original). This was the Menninger Clinic, after all, where psychotherapy invariably supplemented whatever other methods were employed. Indeed, in 14 of the 26 patients treated with metrazol—including the four depressives who showed marked improvement—a "special

---

achieve later a higher level of integration, and to attack the conflicts with renewed vigor. This usually leads to a sharper delineation of the ego boundaries, the abandoning of the more primitive defenses, and the establishment of defenses at a higher level, reproducing the previous [the pre-shock therapy] clinical picture. In some instances this may carry even further to a still higher and a more successful level of defense, resulting in seeming improvement" (1948, pp. 237–238).

effort was made to help the patient through psychotherapy," so that, unsurprisingly, the greatest postmetrazol improvement was obtained in patients "who were most able to profit from this help." It followed for Menninger that "a major advantage of the use of metrazol is that it tends to make the patient more accessible, and thus permits psychotherapy to take place which otherwise could not occur" (p. 139).

Subsequent experience with metrazol at the sanitarium only strengthened Menninger's conviction on this score (W. Menninger, 1940, p. 103). He was seconded in this judgment by his Menninger colleague Martin Grotjahn, whose "psychiatric observations" on metrazol treatment added, by way of explanation of the emergent accessibility to psychotherapy, that "the convulsion-shock of the metrazol convulsion enables the narcissistic schizophrenic patient to make some kind of transference." Analysts working in other institutional settings, such as Bernard Glueck, made this same claim, and far more forcefully than the Menninger staff psychiatrists.[8] For Grotjahn, even "feeble" movement toward a therapeutic relationship provided some warrant for metrazol treatment, and he concluded his report with a measured optimism that William Menninger could not muster:

> The psychiatrist whose goal is to establish a friendship between the patient and his physician regards such a new-gained relation of the patient to reality as a first step towards a new readjustment. If metrazol treatment of schizophrenic patients does not accomplish more than a first stimulation in this direction, then everyone who knows the difficulties in the therapeutic approach to this narcissistic psychosis will be satisfied that some progress has been made [1938, p. 149].

It was in the context of this cautious receptiveness to somatic intervention as a treatment option — at least among institution-

---

[8] Glueck made precisely the same claim for insulin coma therapy that Grotjahn made for metrazol, albeit in much stronger language: "What is technically termed a transference capacity is, at times, released in a most convincing and dramatic manner very soon after the introduction of the insulin therapy, rendering patients who had hitherto been utterly inaccessible to any psychological influence, quite approachable and capable of benefiting from the various services which the hospital offers" [1937, pp. 171–172].

alized patients—that prefrontal lobotomy was introduced in 1936. And the analytic reaction to this most invasive of all procedures was no less equivocal than the reaction to the several shock therapies.[9] Once more the European analysts, with the notable exception of Winnicott, took little note, while the various Americans went their respective ways. Karl Menninger, whose advocacy of psychoanalytic psychiatry, I have argued, was an aspect of the broad retreat from surgical analogizing during the 30s, was ecumenical enough to greet the advent of lobotomy with open-minded interest. When, in September 1936, he learned that the mother-in-law of a local physician was among Walter Freeman's first series of patients at George Washington University, he wrote the pioneer lobotomist a friendly professional inquiry:

---

[9] Following a presentation of this chapter to the section on psychiatric history of the department of psychiatry, Cornell University Medical College (October 7, 1998), some of my colleagues suggested that the American psychoanalysts cited in my chapter, which is to say those analysts who published qualified defenses of lobotomy in the literature, are not representative of analysts of the time, to whom psychosurgery was anathema. As a historian working with the published record, I can do no more than record this demurrer. To my best knowledge, the sources I cite represent virtually all that American psychoanalysts had to say in print about psychosurgery in the two decades following its development. If there is an "oral tradition" tending toward outright analytic repudiation of lobotomy, it gains no expression in the published record of which I am aware—excepting only the writings of H. S. Sullivan and D. W. Winnicott, which I discuss. There were no doubt rank-and-file neurologists and neurosurgeons who were equally unhappy. The point is that, among psychoanalysts, whatever collective uneasiness existed gained little if any expression in the life of the profession and is therefore a weak basis for contesting the position that emerges from the written record. The handful of articles and presentations in which American analysts spoke up on lobotomy—with equivocation and qualified acceptance—elicited no disclaimers in the form of discussions, commentaries, replies, or "letters to the editor." Nor am I aware of any official reports or position papers by the American Psychoanalytic Association or other psychoanalytic organizations on psychosurgery that would lead us to view the published accounts as unrepresentative of what analysts in general believed, or at least could live with, in the domain of psychosurgery. American psychoanalysts, whatever their private feelings about lobotomy, hardly mobilized the profession to go on record with warnings about the psychosurgical variant of what Judge David Bazelon (1974) later termed "the perils of wizardry." The Topeka psychoanalyst Jan Frank (1950, p. 35) no doubt had it right in pointing to the very dearth of analytic contributions to psychosurgery as the most salient aspect of the analytic "response."

Of course, I was glad to tell him [the local physician] how well we knew you and how highly we regarded you. He said that you had contemplated an interesting brain operation for the relief of what I took to be an agitated depression. Since then he has called and told me that visitors have found her much improved immediately following the operation. Naturally, I am extremely interested in this and would appreciate it very much if you would have time to write me a little more in detail about the theory and practice of this new treatment [Faulkner and Pruitt, 1988, p. 223].

Freeman replied to Menninger in a similarly cordial professional manner (p. 224), and there the exchange ended. Menninger's polemics, which, as we have seen, were already subjecting the motivation of surgical patient and operator alike to psychoanalytic deconstruction, steered clear of psychosurgery.[10] Among the Americans, only A. A. Brill in 1938 and Harry Stack Sullivan five years later managed to muster true analytic indignation at the butchery of cortical white matter. For Sullivan, who had begun his medical career as an industrial surgeon in the steel mills outside Chicago, lobotomy, no less than the shock-inducing interventions that preceded it, was a method of "partial decortication," and

when the 'treatment' of victims of severe mental disorder by diffuse decortication and destruction of some of their human abilities is sanctioned on the grounds of social expediency, and all other methods of therapy are discarded as impractically difficult if not wholly absurd, one may well be concerned for psychiatry and its place in the security-giving aspects of the social order itself [1943, p. 229].

Sullivan, for his part, embodies an unusual variant of the American psychoanalytic sensibility. Throughout the 1920s, he

---

[10] Menninger was, however, appropriated by at least one outspoken critic of lobotomy. An unsigned editorial to the *Medical Record* in 1940, in calling the attention of "these mutilating surgeons to the Hippocratic oath," recommended that lobotomizing aspirants for neurosurgical honors "read and digest Karl Menninger's remarks on polysurgical castration devices, not those of strictly phallic significance but those that maim and destroy the creative functions of a nonmutilated body" (cited in Valenstein, 1973, p. 295).

built a clinical reputation on the basis of therapeutic work with hospitalized schizophrenics, whom he championed with uncharacteristic fervor. At Maryland's Sheppard and Enoch Pratt Hospital, where Sullivan developed his theory of interpersonal psychiatry, he was famously possessive about *his* schizophrenics and brooked no inference from colleagues with different treatment approaches. It is unsurprising, then, that in the decades thereafter "the convulsive, anoxic, and psycho-surgical methods were anathema to him" (Rioch, 1985, p. 145).

Among Sullivan's European compatriots, such indignation was matched only by that of Winnicott, whose background in clinical pediatrics and sensitivity to indoctrinating authority figures in the lives of children were no more typical among the analysts than was Sullivan's devotion to psychotherapy with hospitalized schizophrenics.[11] Beginning in 1943, he dispatched periodic missives to the editors of the *British Medical Journal* and the *Lancet*, decrying all the radical somatic interventions but reserving special opprobrium for the proponents of psycho-surgery. By the end of 1945, he was calling for speedy enactment of a new habeas corpus, a "habeas cerebrum," all the while admonishing his colleagues that "surgical interference with the brain in mental disorders is absolutely never justified" (in Rodman, 1987, p. 7). Two years later, in 1947, leucotomy was deemed "the worst honest error in the history of medical practice"; it amounted to a social appeal to medical science to authorize "a panic application of magic" (p. 537). In 1949, it had become "the worst possible trend in medical practice," a surgical procedure "on the borderline between science and superstition" (pp. 543, 547).

In point of fact, Winnicott's rhetoric did not do justice to his sober consideration of psychosurgery and the radical shock therapies in general. He went beyond even Sullivan in his sensitivity to the social and institutional contexts that tended to the employment of all the somatic interventions. Insofar as the radical somatic interventions lessened the "immense frustration" attendant to work with institutionalized populations and provided "new hope" to doctors and nurses, they improved

---

[11] Winnicott spent the war years setting up evacuation hostels for homeless British children in the county of Oxford (Phillips, 1988, pp. 62ff.).

staff morale and staff performance alike. And there were derivative benefits as well. With respect to shock therapy, for example, Winnicott readily allowed that

> the high degree of skill and knowledge required for proper control of, for instance, insulin therapy, brings to the mental hospital medical men and women who have knowledge and skill in biochemistry and other subjects and this must all tend to awaken or keep alive a spirit of scientific enquiry which I think was generally lacking in mental hospitals a few decades ago [1944, p. 530].

As to psychosurgery, Winnicott granted that "leucotomy does make some very difficult patients less difficult, and relieves some acute sufferers from prolonged suffering" (1949, p. 543). Indeed, if the surgery could be limited to "very ill patients, then no harm has been done, and to some there has been benefit" (p. 545). But, alas, this was not—indeed this *could* not—be the case, for "a treatment cannot exist in a circumscribed way like this." Rather, "it soon becomes applied to less severe cases. Theories arise and (in the case of leucotomy) the possibility of treatment gives power and direction in the mental hospital to the neurosurgeon, whose skill is in surgery of the brain and who is not trained to be a student of human nature" (p. 544).

It was at this point in his consideration of psychosurgery that Winnicott's analytic identity rose to the fore. His claims, keyed as they were to leucotomy and the shock therapies, were less expansive than Karl Menninger's, but his assumptions about the explanatory weight of psychoanalytic science and the attendant responsibilities of psychoanalytic practitioners were no less profound and deeply felt. "The neurosurgeon," he held, "who starts off with a readiness to see insanity as a collection of separate illnesses, with brain-tissue changes, is not easily persuaded that his patients are still human beings." Being human, for Winnicott, meant living with symptoms and resistances grounded in "the unconscious struggle of the person to find himself"; simply to bypass resistance via leucotomy was to risk "the final loss of the individuality of the person concerned." Before all other disciplines, psychoanalysis illuminated the existential centrality of this unconscious struggle to the *condi-*

tion humaine. The leucotomizing neurosurgeon, for all his technical skill, had no warrant even to participate in the discussion. He was "an unqualified practitioner from the point of view of the psychologist" (1947, p. 537).

Nor could the surgeon acquire psychoanalytic knowledge in the manner of conventional medicosurgical know-how. In fact, Winnicott held, "it would be easier for a really first-rate psychologist to learn to be a neurosurgeon than for the latter to learn to be a psychologist, simply because psychology can only be learned over a period of time in which the learner has to grow to meet the emotional demands that psychology puts on himself." As if to make the point plainer still, to make the disjunction between surgical and psychological mindsets as radical as it possibly could be, Winnicott appended an unequivocal endorsement of the traditional psychoanalytic credo, namely, "that the psychology of the unconscious can only be taught to people if they are themselves being analyzed or if they have had previous successful analysis" (1949, p. 545).

And so Winnicott pitted psychoanalysis, which pointed psychiatry to "the study of human nature and of mental health as a matter of maturity of emotional development of the individual," against the dark forces of psychosurgery. To the extent that surgical interference with the physical brain jeopardized identity, it rendered specious the surgeon's simplistic criteria of clinical improvement: "If I behave still better because I have had a leucotomy I am not making a better contribution, because it is not me behaving" (1949, pp. 546, 547). Indeed, for Winnicott, the surgeon's clinical rationalization of the procedure masked a gigantic oxymoron. Since brain tissue was by and large "the somatic (or physical) prerequisite for the existence of the psyche," the notion that mutilation of healthy brain tissue could provide "treatment" for psychic disorders was preposterous; it amounted to trying to remediate psychic disorders through a procedure "which attacks the psyche itself, by disturbing its physical basis" (1951, p. 551).

In their psychoanalytically grounded skepticism about psychosurgery, Brill, White, Sullivan, and Winnicott were lone voices in the wilderness. Winnicott's attentiveness to the social context and psychological significance of psychosurgery—and especially to the ethical dimension of so permanent an intervention—elicited little response within the German, Austrian, or even British psychoanalytic communities. When we turn to the American psychoanalytic mainstream, on the other hand, we encounter far less indignation than equivocation. Smith Ely Jelliffe (1938) reacted far more typically than Harry Stack Sullivan did. He argued less against lobotomy than for refining it in accord with psychoanalytic theory—or at least his own idiosyncratic rendering of it. What was needed, he held, was a more precise surgical intervention, one that only severed fibers connecting the frontal lobe to the brain's "anal sensory perceptions area."

At a panel on lobotomy at the 1941 meeting of the American Medical Association, Roy Grinker, the well-known Chicago analyst, was openly critical of lobotomy but stopped short of dismissing it outright. Grinker questioned whether the alleged improvement of lobotomized patients was actually a transference effect; the patients, after all, were the beneficiaries of enthusiastic surgeons and solicitous nurses.[12] He was also quick to adduce the serious cognitive defects that resulted from the surgery, possibly including delayed effects arising years later. Still, Grinker held, "I think there is no question that the operation has a usefulness," and he allowed for further experiments— "since I think this is still an experiment"—on "older patients, perhaps people who have no chance whatever except to continue in state hospitals" (quoted in Valenstein, 1986, p. 186). According to Valenstein, Grinker's measured remarks are representative of the type of criticism offered by American analysts: "They usually were skeptical, but ended on some middle ground, recommending a limited use of lobotomy—only on patients in whom all other less 'heroic' measures had been completely exhausted" (pp. 184–185).

In a presentation before the American Psychoanalytic Association in 1949, Jan Frank, then director of the Topeka Institute for Psychoanalysis, berated his colleagues for failing

---

[12] This is not exactly the point that Wilson (1943) made two years later. He suggested, rather, that the transference arose during the course of shock therapy and had to be worked with therapeutically in the aftermath of shock therapy in order to consolidate its beneficial effect and prevent relapse.

to demarcate this middle ground. The very dearth of analytic contributions to lobotomy was itself "an overreaction to the subject in the analytic literature." Furthermore, Frank was constrained to raise an analytic eyebrow at this state of affairs, given that "lobotomy significantly interferes with psychic activity causing thereby a quantitative shift of instinctual impulsivity and changes in its psychic representations, and since it alters certain facets of ego functioning" (1950, p. 35).

Frank was no fan of lobotomy and professed full understanding of the horror with which colleagues like Winnicott reacted to "the cavalierlike fashion in which psychosurgical enthusiasts mutilate healthy brains in patients with personality disorders." He was quick to cede that lobotomized patients were not at all analyzable, and he went on to catalog, in the analytic jargon of his day, the massive deficits attendant to psychosurgery. Among other things:

> The dependency cravings of the lobotomized have decidedly an archaic quality and have nothing to do with the true object relationship. Hand in hand with the rigidifying of the ego goes the loss of autoplasticity. They are unable to do creative work or to have religious or artistic experience. All those functions which involved internalization and symbolized elaboration are gravely impaired — processes which seem to occur in the twilighted precincts of the oneroid preconscious. The content of this mental dimension, however, is partly drained away by the operative injury of short-circuiting, and with it goes the above-mentioned rather important qualities of human existence [1950, p. 38].

Still, the "clarion call of psychoanalytic understanding" was no justification for his colleagues' refusal to confront the reality that lobotomy addressed. And what was this reality? Here Frank expatiated as follows:

> Despite the paramount importance of scientific work which issues from the ivory towers of the new psychoanalytic sanitaria, how can the department head of a university clinic or director of a state hospital apply these treatments practically, swamped as he is by a multitude of patients and at the same time hampered by lack of competent psychiatrists? But quite apart from these considerations, is the psychoanalytic clinician really able,

by psychotherapeutic or management devices alone, to help in *all* cases of schizophrenia, involutional melancholia, or even in cases of severe obsessionalism? . . . No responsible analyst-clinician will or can, a priori, condemn a procedure solely from the philosophical point of view. On the contrary, he might want to inquire whether the central-cerebral representations of instinctual impulses could not be modified in desperate cases by surgery [1950, p. 36, emphasis in original].

The middle ground enunciated by Frank lived on; indeed, it was sustained by purported "research findings" published as late as 1958, when Eugene B. Brody, writing in the prestigious *Journal of the American Psychoanalytic Association*, reported positively on therapeutic results subsequent to a "minimal lobotomy procedure" on 11 schizophrenic patients. Brody, a Yale psychiatrist whose entry to psychosurgery had been via observational research on the impact of prefrontal lobotomy on the dominance hierarchy in a group of six rhesus monkeys (Brody and Rosvold, 1952), conducted his research on schizophrenia under the auspices of the Department of Psychiatry of Yale University School of Medicine and with funding from the U. S. Veterans Administration. In a presentation at the midwinter meeting of the American Psychoanalytic Association in December 1956, he breezily conflated surgical changes in the "physiological apparatus" with the "energetics" of the Freudian psychic apparatus, and proceeded to evaluate the impact of lobotomy on schizophrenia at the level of hypothesized avenues of psychic energy discharge.

Specifically, Brody postulated a beneficent "leveling out of the variable cathectic charge," whereby the lobotomized schizophrenic ended up with "more avenues of energy discharge at his disposal than does the intact schizophrenic" (1958, pp. 485–487). This energic redistribution presumably gained expression in the ego's postsurgical ability "to relax its defenses and regress to infantile pleasure" along with the superego's increased awareness of aggressive impulses and greater tolerance of external aggressive discharge (p. 488).

Brody did not stop here, but went on to refract the energic or "cathectic" consequences of lobotomy under the rubric of what he and colleagues of the time understood as the "metapsychology of schizophrenia." To wit, following certain theoretical writings of the period, Brody construed schizophrenia as the product of a pathological superego that originated "in the introjection of a depriving, hostile mother." Lobotomy rendered the schizophrenic newly adaptive by facilitating this state of "oral unity" with a maternal figure, which, prior to surgery, had been defended against because it threatened the individual's sense of identity. By attenuating the defenses against this sense of merger, Brody held, lobotomy made it possible for the schizophrenic "more completely and comfortably to achieve such a state." In this way, it enabled him or her to become "a more successful schizophrenic" (1958, p. 497).

Brody's report of 1956, which was published two years later, is perhaps the pinnacle of the psychoanalytic accommodation of psychosurgery. It is a marvelous historical document as well. Beyond its specific relevance to the topic of psychosurgery, it encapsulates a central tension in the identity formation of American psychoanalysts during the postwar decades. Beneath the recourse to the abstractions of Freudian structural theory and metapsychology, that is, one discerns the resolutely utilitarian pragmatism that drove American psychoanalysis during this time. Unlike the Europeans, for whom medical and psychiatric training were at best useful preliminaries to the assumption of a psychoanalytic identity, the pragmatic Americans were, with few exceptions, content with the dual identity of psychiatrist *and* psychoanalyst. In the former role, they could ill afford to be dismissive of radical somatic interventions aimed at the population of chronically ill, institutionalized patients.[13] To dismiss these treatments out of

---

[13] As the analyst Jan Frank opined in 1949, "Is prolonged chemical restraint to be preferred to the desensitization of lobotomy in the intensely suffering, chronic involutionary melancholic who is sometimes refractory to anything which one can offer as treatment? Also should one let certain types of schizophrenics perish — patients who have for years suffered from lengthy periodical attack of most awesome panic combined with self-destructiveness?" (1950, p. 36). The eminent American psychiatrist John Romano, while designating psychosurgery "truly, a sad chapter in our history," has reminisced as follows: "One cannot overestimate the despair felt by psychiatrists, nurses, and families of patients in dealing day in and day out, at times for years, with patients who were assaultive, suicidal, homicidal, and overactive, conditions which at times led to exhaustion and death" (1990, p. 791).

hand was not only to forego participation in the psychiatric "progress" of their time; it was also to make themselves objects of their own interpretive searchlight, via the surmise that psychoanalytic antipathy to the radical therapies had its own unconscious determinants. As the New York psychiatrist-analysts John Millet and Eric Mosse observed in 1944:

> The question might well be raised whether the objections so often formulated by these [psychoanalytic] specialists may not have "unconscious" as well as rational grounds for their construction. If a patient can be restored to his former efficiency after three to four weeks of specialized electric treatment, the theory that such a patient needs a long period of deep psychotherapy would seem to be of dubious validity [p. 227].

And so the analysts devised their metapsychologically ingenious explanations of the effectiveness of shock therapy. Moreover, like Brody, they could be resourceful in invoking psychoanalytic theory even to provide a rationale for the ameliorative effects of surgical cutting. Finally, the Americans were willing to employ psychoanalysis to rationalize the clinical failures attendant to the radical somatic therapies; at the very least, they argued, such failures subserved an analytic research agenda.[14] Still, in their role as *analysts*, the Americans, led by the Menningers, radically dissociated the psychoanalytic procedure and the knowledge it elicited from medicosurgical treatment models. Indeed, the very disjunction between psycho-analysis and the rest of medicine—so I have argued—was the basis of what these psychoanalyst-psychiatrists saw as their privileged position within the medical profession, not to mention their popular recognition outside it.

In their ability to reconcile psychoanalytic theory with the "scientific" psychiatry of their day, the American analysts evinced an intellectual mobility and a professional adaptiveness

---

[14] Thus Frosch and Impastato concluded their interpretive review of clinical failures attendant to shock therapy by expressing the hope that they had "demonstrate[d] that through a study of shock treatment and its effects, one might obtain corroboration of many hitherto known factors about the levels of ego development and their relationship to the hierarchy of the mechanisms of defense" (1948, p. 238).

that stood them in good stead in the two decades following the end of World War II. This was the period of American analysis triumphant, when medical analysts achieved dominance within the psychiatric mainstream, shaping residency training programs and the content of psychiatric textbooks, spearheading efforts at psychiatric reform, and occupying positions of regional and national leadership within the profession. Further, it was the period that witnessed the flowering of psychosomatic medicine, when, owing to psychoanalytically guided recognition of the causal role of emotional factors in various functional disorders, "psychotherapy gained a legitimate entrance into medicine proper and could no longer be restricted exclusively to the field of psychiatry" (Alexander, 1950, p. 43). It is a story oft told—most recently and ably by Hale (1995, pp. 245–275)—and one that lies beyond our purview.[15]

I cannot conclude, however, without a final reprise on the surgical theme. From the outset, we have been guided by curiosity about the reality of surgery underlying Freud's surgical metaphor—the reality of surgery in his time, in his circle, and in his own life. This curiosity, in turn, opened to consideration of the early analysts' struggles with surgical models, surgical thinking, and medicosurgical identities. In bringing this study to a close, I wish to offer some reflections on the thematic counterpoint to these preoccupations. I refer to the evolution of modern surgical consciousness and the intriguing ways in which it has struggled with the psychoanalytic sensibility. In the broadening of surgical consciousness in the final quarter of our century, we behold a development that takes us far from the image of the heroic surgeon that influenced Freud and his followers but is perhaps no less relevant to the contemporary psychoanalyst's identity and sense of curative endeavor.

---

[15] On the birth of the psychosomatic orientation within mainstream psychoanalysis and its importation into the United States by Franz Alexander in the 1930s, see also Shorter (1992, pp. 258–261).

"One Is Partner, Sometimes Rival, to the Knife"

❧

As physicians acquired prestige in the late nineteenth century, the historian Edward Shorter has observed, "they rode on the coattails of the surgeons . . . public awe at the triumphs of surgery lent a reflected luster to the physician's image" (1985, p. 133). This public awe has been periodically rejuvenated by waves of surgical breakthrough in our own century, from the birth of thoracic surgery in the 1930s and 40s, to the advent of open-heart and blood vessel surgery in the 1950s, to the refinement of transplant surgery and microsurgery in the 1960s and 70s, and on through the dramatic surgical advances of our own time, among which the development of laser and computer-assisted operative technique must surely be mentioned.

Of course, physicians too are patients, and their private awe at the power wielded by *their* surgeons occasionally rises to the surface in self-reflections of illness, pain, and mortality. Psychiatrists and psychoanalysts are hardly exempt from this kind of surgical wonderment and in their more candid moments even wax eloquent in describing it. We encounter this sentiment in several of the candid reminiscences gathered in Pinner and Miller's intriguing collection of 1952, *When Doctors Are Patients*. Well before the surgical triumphs of our own time, we find, psychiatrists too labored under a burden of indebtedness to surgeons whose operative skill waved off a beckoning grim reaper. Here, for example, is Fredric Wertheim, a prominent New York psychiatrist of the 1940s, recounting the emergency surgery—a ligation of the right femoral vein—that followed a thrombophlebitis in his right leg with grave pulmonary sequelae:

> I remember only two factors which alleviated my general feeling of insecurity while on the operating table. One was the voice of the operating surgeon and one was the reassurance derived from definite contact.
>
> The surgeon's voice was deep, calm and authoritative. It was not raised at any time. One episode was characteristic of my mental state. I developed a very disagreeable pain in the right calf during the operative procedure. Somehow it seemed to me that this was due to my leg's 'falling asleep,' as it were in an awkward, hanging position from the knee down. . . . I remember that several times I moved the leg, seeking to ease its position — not exactly an appropriate behavior in the situation. I recall very distinctly the surgeon's voice saying quietly but definitely: 'Don't move your leg, Dr. Wertheim.' My emotional response to this remark is difficult to describe. From that moment on, it was unthinkable that I should move my leg, however it felt. The remark had such an authoritative effect on me that — pain or no pain, impulse or no impulse — the idea of moving my leg did not come up again [1952, p. 108].

In this same collection, Iago Galdston, another prominent New York psychiatrist-psychoanalyst of the time, offers up his own paean of praise in reminiscing about the convalescence that followed emergency surgery in his later years, when "a bolt from heaven laid low one who never before had need for surgery or hospital care." Out of the totality of his experiences, Galdston recounts,

> the residual appreciations were not for the skills witnessed, not for the science applied, not for the knowing and effective way in which an emergency threatening the life of one mortal was dealt with, but rather for the unique devotion of the surgeon and all of the associated personnel.
>
> Deep within was the feeling of identification, of having been absorbed by and merged with the being of the physician, so that his concerns and his doings were not with an external object, but rather with an entity for the while identified with his. One's soul was surging full with gratitude for that devotion,

even though there was present an ever so faint awareness that it was not devotion to the individual but rather to a function in which the particular mortal was the accidental and temporary recipient of benefits [1952, pp. 345–346].

Do Wertheim and Galdston simply give expression to common sentiments directed to those who proffer radical remedy in the face of life-threatening organic dysfunction? Or do their testimonies bespeak a diffidence — even awe — specific to those who minister to disordered minds with words rather than to diseased bodies with scalpels? Does the therapist, a full century after Freud, remain a surgeon manqué who looks to the surgeon proper as embodiment of the authoritative knowledgeability, the control, and the mastery so far removed from the messy ambiguities that inhere in psychotherapeutic work?[1]

In this study, we have focused principally on the example of Freud, whose self-proclaimed medicosurgical dependency on Wilhelm Fliess in the 1890s seemed to encompass these very elements of idealization and identification. Chroniclers of psychiatric and psychoanalytic reminiscences may well find testimonies of comparable import. Here I adduce two particulars from a more recent period that offer further food for thought. They suggest, inter alia, how a preoccupation with mind, as mediated by and through language, may reflect and even cultivate a certain apprehension — even at times a *misapprehension* — of physical pain and its remedies. In his contribution to *When Doctors Are Patients*, the distinguished analyst Martin Grotjahn, who thoughtfully considered the psychological impact of shock therapy in the 1930s, recalled his brief interlude of denial in the face of the searing pain of a kidney stone attack: "I preferred, however, to talk my way out of a physical sickness into the more humiliating but less

---

[1] For a brilliant, multifaceted examination of these "messy ambiguities," see Lawrence Friedman's *The Anatomy of Psychotherapy* (1988). Of special note, in the context of our concerns, is Friedman's acute examination of "the therapist as operator" as one of the "disambiguating roles" adopted by psychotherapists to cope with these ambiguities (pp. 472–505). For Friedman, the term "operator" conveys an operative or directive treatment approach that shades into manipulation. The implicitly surgical connotations of the term are not explored.

dangerous mental condition which I called 'anxiety state' "
(1952, p. 90). Grotjahn's admission opens to the question of
whether the psychoanalyst's training and professional identity
tend to perceptual confusion about the grounds and reality of
physical suffering, perhaps a heightening of dread in which
physical pain that is *only* physical pain approaches the uncanny.
Closer to our own time and more telling still, we have the
example of Jacques Lacan, who stubbornly refused what
promised to be curative surgery in 1980 following his self-
diagnosis of a local colon cancer: "He had always had a phobia
about surgery, and about physical illness in general, and
couldn't bear any intrusion on his person" (Roudinesco, 1993,
p. 403).

There is irony in such revelations, for the second half of the
twentieth century charts an evolving surgical consciousness
increasingly removed from the operative surety that accompanied the development of heroic surgery a century earlier. To
be sure, we discern little of this consciousness among surgeons
who trained in the early decades of the century. For men like
William Halsted, Harvey Cushing, John Benjamin Murphy,
Warren Cole, and Alton Ochsner, true heirs of the nineteenth
century, the "century of the surgeon" (Thorwald, 1956), the
instrumental power of surgery was unclouded by even the
faintest Freudian reverie. In this sense, the coming-of-age of
this generation of surgeons functions as an epilogue to the
nineteenth-century "triumph of surgery" (Thorwald, 1957).
Predictably, it provides us with personal narratives that are
psychologically unencumbered and professionally triumphant,
the true stuff of medical hagiography.

Of John Benjamin Murphy, who ranks alongside William
Halsted as one of the preeminent American surgeons from the
final years of the nineteenth century until his death in 1916,
there is a career ascent straight and true, rooted in a childhood
of Lincolnesque simplicity and resolve:

> To gain his elementary education, John walked eight miles
> round trip between home and a one-room school each day.
> After completing grammar school he attended high school in
> Appleton [Wisconsin] and worked part time in a drugstore to
> earn a little money. It was evident quite early that he had a

driving urge for knowledge and a stoical ability to work to obtain it. There was never any room for frivolity in his life [Schmitz and Oh, 1993, p. 1].

Of the young Warren Cole, destined for a career of distinction in surgery and surgical education at the University of Illinois, we read of his mother's untimely death following a kitchen-table hysterectomy in 1904, and of the "spur" it provided to the six-year-old Warren "to improve the lot of the surgical patient and help prevent death from operations" (Connaughton, 1991, pp. 9, 31). Of Alton Ochsner, the redoubtable "surgeon of the South," who made his indelible mark at Tulane University, we read of a swift ascent to surgical greatness adroitly engineered by the esteemed surgeon Albert John Ochsner, an older cousin who "became fond of Alton, to whom he referred as 'my nephew' " (Wilds and Harkey, 1990, pp. 18ff.).

For these and other surgeons trained in the early decades of the twentieth century, the ascent to surgical greatness assumes a simple narrative form with common features. There is the preliminary preceptorship with an obliging local physician who points the neophyte surgeon on his way. Then there is the journey to a medical school, often a distant one, with educational and clinical resources far beyond the aspirant's community of origin. Finally, there is the subsequent attachment to sympathetic and skilled mentors who introduce the initiate to the state of surgical art and the limitless promise of surgical science.[2] Proto-Freudian ruminations have no place in this

---

[2] The Harvard surgeon Francis D. Moore's recently published and absorbing account of his career (1995) comes as a final grand reprise on this genre of surgical memoir. Moore, who received his surgical training at Massachusetts General Hospital in the early 1940s, offers a saga of uninterrupted surgical maturation that meets the narrative requirements set forth above. There is the predictable reference to early encounters "with three remarkably able and appealing surgeons in Winnetka and Chicago" who provided young Moore with "a very attractive image of what it would be like to be a doctor" (pp. 19–21), followed by the journey to far-away Harvard for medical training in 1935, and then the period of mentorship under the gifted senior surgeons of the Massachusetts General Hospital surgical staff and apprenticeship with his fellow Midwesterner Leland McKittrick (pp. 79–86).

narrative trajectory, nor do they complicate the initiate's surgical calling once embraced. Neither Alton Ochsner's biographers—nor, from what they tell us, Ochsner himself—ponders the relationship between the man who was a humane and caring surgeon and the man who, as a father, was "the fastest belt in New Orleans," a father who "in a more permissive age," so one of his sons remarks, "might have been accused of child abuse" (Wilds and Harkey, 1990, p. 90).

We must look beyond these narratives to locate the birth of the self-reflective, even anxious, surgeon of our own time, the surgeon whose cutting is freighted with brooding awareness—an awareness not only of the uncertain outcome of surgical cutting but of the sheer unnaturalness of the surgical act. It is an existential burden largely unknown to Billroth, Kocher, and their early twentieth-century American disciples, conflict-free proponents, one and all, of radical surgery.

What is there of psychoanalysis in the modern surgeon's unhappy consciousness of the surgical enterprise? Even in the early decades of the century, good surgeons occasionally owned up to the psychological dimension of their calling. Not least among them is Arthur Hertzler, whose memoir of 1938, *The Horse and Buggy Doctor*, frames a surgical career in the American Midwest that bridges the contrasting surgical worlds of two centuries. Freud and the world of psychoanalysis could not be further from Hertzler, but his spacious review of a half century of surgical practice, including piquant reflections on the long lost art of "kitchen surgery," recurs to psychological common sense of a remarkably analytic character. All is aphorism here, but the aphorisms are telling, and they speak to us across intervening decades of diagnostic and operative advance. Of the need for interpretation and perspective in the taking of case histories: "Rouged lips sometimes tell the doctor more than the sounds that come out of them" (p. 203). Of patients who do not recover following successful operations: "The lesion operated on may have been only a part of the cause of the patient's complaint. If the patient is mad at Papa the most skillfully performed operation will not cure her complaints: that is to say, the lamentations will not cease" (p. 208). Of the unforeseen risk factors that make surgeons old before their time: "Surgeons of long experience, as I have known them, consciously or subconsciously long for the day when they shall do their last operation. The reason is that the disasters remain firmly implanted in the surgeon's memory" (p. 205).

Finally, Hertzler offers a characteristically rough-hewn but truthful reminder of the need to respect the defenses that sustain symptoms of long standing. He recurs to the case of "a maiden lady forty-six years of age" whose uterine tumor provided no anatomical basis for her refusal to walk a step for 18 years:

> The cause of the failure to walk, failure is the proper word—it was not a deliberate refusal—never was revealed. I did not inquire his name nor did I attempt to extract details as to the occurrence. To have done so likely would have excited consciously or unconsciously memories that likely would have defeated my purpose. It is said a good salesman knows when he has made a sale and pushes over the dotted line and hands over the pen. It is equally as important in the management of certain types of patient to know when one has learned enough. Such cases cannot be handled well in a clinic where all sorts of irrelevant things are entered into. Such cases are a one-man job. And if he is wise he will keep strictly his own council, reveal nothing to anyone. Even to such patients the local doctor may drop inadvertent remarks which may spoil all one's labor [pp. 241–242].

In the event, the maiden lady in question did walk following Hertzler's surgical removal of her tumor. Despite the fact that, on examination, the patient "could move her legs any way I directed," the surgeon authoritatively explained that her inability to walk was "due to the pressure on the nerves of that tumor and that its removal would relieve her of her difficulty." Hertzler operated, and following three weeks of postoperative convalescence he went into the patient's room "and abruptly announced that we were going for a walk. And we did and she has continued to walk since—lo, these many years" (p. 241). Thus, this shrewd and witting use of transference by a knowing operator of another era.

With Hertzler, we discern the outlines of a homespun psychological sensibility but not yet a psychoanalytically shaped consciousness that actively engages the surgical calling.[3] For this, we must turn to reflections more fully saturated with the Freudian ethos of our own time. Lawrence Shainberg's *Brain Surgeon: An Intimate View of His World* (1979) presents us with a neurosurgeon protagonist who wields Freud less like a scalpel than like a bludgeon in presenting the lineaments of career choice and the grounds of professional self-assurance. "Talk to my colleagues," he advises Shainberg, "and you'll find they were either interested in the neural sciences or attracted by surgery itself, the management of power, the all-or-nothing aspects of its decisions." He goes on, "For me it was the latter. All the powerful figures in my childhood were surgeons. It doesn't take any great psychoanalytic insight to see what neurosurgery offered. Shit, my personality is transparent. Do you know what I do when I'm on vacation? I get on my boat and go out fishing, looking to catch a fish twice my size" (p. 34).

The neurosurgeon in question, a 5'3" titan who readily owns up to "a little-man complex" that found "perfect consumma-tion" in the surgical calling (p. 33), undertook psychoanalysis as a surgical resident, when a "lifelong infatuation with women" driven, so he holds, by the same dynamic that led him to surgery, was at the point of destroying his marriage. "Luckily, I found a good doctor," he opines. "He helped me a lot. I didn't give up women—God, I couldn't do that!—but at least I got it under control" (p. 36).

---

[3] Of course, there are numerous reiterations of Hertzler's "homespun psychological sensibility" among surgeons of more recent times. The popular writings of the general surgeon William A. Nolen (1970, 1980), who received his training at New York's Bellevue Hospital in the 1950s, embody this same sensibility. Nolen's straightforward take on his doctoring, and especially on his surgical ministrations, is of a kind with Hertzler's. With Nolen, that is, we find ourselves in the presence of a traditional doctor whose training, experience, and credentials provide all the self-confidence he needs to go about his surgical business. To be sure, his writings evince compassion and sound psychological horsesense, but they do not open to reflection on the psychological dilemmas inhering in the surgical calling. (See, for example, Nolan's patronizing aside on the psychiatric division at Bellevue as it was perceived and used by the surgical house staff [1970, pp. 208–211].) The same omission characterizes the estimable memoir of the neurosurgeon Ben Carson (1990), for whom religious faith in the surgical calling forecloses any possibility of psychological rumination about the nature of that calling.

Given such self-satisfaction with this modest treatment outcome, it is not surprising that, for the surgeon in question, psychoanalytic insight is less about control in the guise of self-mastery than about interpersonal control teetering on the brink of archaic sexual triumph. "There aren't many times I leave the [operating] room without at least a quarter of an erection," he proudly announces: "Hell, why not? It's all totally primitive, isn't it? You're dealing with danger, blood, power, conquering the man or woman on the table. No wonder wives of patients fall in love with surgeons. Aren't we the male who conquers her male? I tell you, the man who says he isn't turned on by surgery is either a liar or a eunuch or both" (p. 88).

Surgery as the management of power is a leitmotiv in the coming-of-age saga of more than one contemporary surgeon. Often, issues of power and control revolve around the chief of the initiate's department or division, whose psychological *in*sensibility—and the emotional burdens to which it gives rise—forms a key aspect of the initiate's training experience. J. Kenyon Rainer's *First Do No Harm: Reflections on Becoming a Brain Surgeon* (1987) offers a characteristic portrait of one such chief, Richard T. Harkness, then Chairman of the Department of Neurosurgery at the University of Tennessee, where Rainer trained. Lacking even the rudimentary Freudian awareness of Shainberg's protagonist, Harkness takes on the cast of a surgical antihero; his "tirades, cursing, accusations, harangues, and blasts of ill temper" (p. 153) are not a call to reflection but a prerogative of power that the initiate, Rainer, must simply accommodate in his own picaresque journey to full-fledged surgeonhood. In *The Making of a Woman Surgeon* (1980), Elizabeth Morgan depicts an even more odious supervisor, a "Dr. Sharman," whom she came to know "for what he was—an adequate surgeon but a nasty man, a bad teacher and foul to his patients" (pp. 224–226, 244–246).

In *Gifted Hands* (1990), the neurosurgeon Ben Carson shies away from the seamy side of surgical training, but even Carson, who offers a Bunyanesque surgical journey guided by the hand of God, cannot ignore entirely the baser human realities attending a surgical coming-of-age. We discern it in his brief reprise on his "conflict" with a surgical chief resident, a racist who "couldn't seem to accept having a Black intern at Johns Hopkins" (pp. 126–127) and also in his passing acknowledgment of several general surgeons at Hopkins "who acted like the pompous, stereotyped surgeons" (p. 127). Small wonder that Carson "wanted out of that whole thing." He gained his release from the general surgery department after a year of internship and thence made his way, and brilliantly, in the Hopkins department of neurosurgery.

The coming-of-age sagas of women surgeons draw attention to other aspects of surgery as the management of power. There is the predictable sense in which women must struggle toward a surgical identity infused with male attributes. The plastic surgeon Elizabeth Morgan writes perceptively about the dilemma inherent in "being trained by good male surgeons to act like a good male surgeon" (1980, p. 154). For the transplant surgeon Rose-Marie Toussaint, it was the very remoteness of the possibility of pursuing a surgical career "as far as female students were concerned" that initially intrigued her and drew her to the specialty (1998, p. 210).

There is more to these ruminations than the challenge of overcoming sexism and gaining access to an all-male club, though the extraordinary demands of this challenge should never be underestimated.[4] More interestingly, the gender struggles of female surgeons in the making invariably involve the physical demands of surgery—another issue implicated in the surgeon's management of power. For Morgan, "Lack of physical strength is a woman's greatest disadvantage in surgery—not only in the O.R. but on the ward" (1980, p. 160). "Any woman is strong enough to do any surgery except surgery on the shoulder, hip and knee joints of an adult," she opines. "Then she needs two or three men to help her" (pp. 173–174). Morgan proffers her unwillingness to endorse the bodily dimension of surgical power as a sign of her own variant of surgical maturity: "As a woman I was not tempted to use physical strength to assert myself. The tempering influence of women was, I

---

[4] See, for example, Morgan (1980, pp. 134–135, 262) and, more recently, Frances K. Conley's harrowing *Walking Out on the Boys* (1998).

thought, a good change for surgery" (pp. 304–305). Rose-Marie Toussaint is more perceptive still in linking "the sheer physical stress of surgery" to the essential maleness that underwrites surgical authority:

> You'd go one-on-one with any man when it came to discussing the finer points of, say, percutaneous femoral vein cannulation or the most accurate method of accessing an abdominal aortic aneurysm. But when you had to compare your hands with one of theirs, measure your shoulders against theirs, your back, their backs, structure, body weight, muscle mass . . . yes, being male usually came with built-in, obvious advantages. You could not minimize these essentially male attributes as just so much brute force. Force, with luck and gentleness, with the best luck lovingly applied, has its place in surgery [1998, p. 280].

The autobiographies of Morgan and Toussaint offer valuable insights into the gender stereotypes and gender conflicts that are played out in the formation of a surgical identity. But these accounts, like those of Rainer and Carson, lack sustained psychological reflection about surgery per se; they are stories of professional triumph fueled by episodes of confession, exhortation, and occasional wonderment. To locate more halting trajectories of surgical maturation we must turn from the narratives of young surgeons in the making to the reminiscences of senior surgeons fully made, to surgeons, that is, willing and able to look back at careers that have reaped their harvest.

In his memoir of 1992, the pioneer liver transplant surgeon Thomas Starzl recalls groping for a surgical raison d'être amid a training regimen that entailed "caring for vast numbers of patients" (p. 53) in need of all manner of surgical intervention. In searching for a purpose beyond the achievement of surgical competence, he recalls, "something at a subconscious level seemed to point to the liver" (p. 54). But the force of this "subconscious" calling could not still inner demons that confounded Starzl's pathway of surgical advance. After a full nine years of surgical research and training, a period that gained him entry to the "legendary inner circle" of pioneer cardiac and vascular surgeons at Johns Hopkins, Starzl confesses to grave conflicts that belied his operative skills and led to the perception that the prolongation of his training served to avoid "the final agony of growing up and going into private practice."

> The truth was worse than anyone imagined. For the past six years, I had honed my surgical abilities. At the same time, I harbored anxieties which I was unable to discuss openly until more than three decades later, after I had stopped operating. I had an intense fear of failing the patients who had placed their health or life in my hands. Far from being relieved by each new layer of skill or experience, the anxieties grew worse. Even for simple operations, I would review books to be sure that no mistakes would be made or old lessons forgotten. Then, sick with apprehension, I would go to the operating room, almost unable to function until the case began [p. 59].

It is a short step from Starzl's admission of intense fear unrelieved by accretions of skill and experience to the existential broodings of the general surgeon Richard Selzer, whose writings give poignant expression to a contemporary surgical consciousness radically severed from its nineteenth-century scientistic moorings. For Selzer, as for Emerson, the poet alone is the true doctor, the one who "heals with his words, stanches the flow of blood, stills the rattling breath, applies poultices to the scalded flesh" (1976, p. 23). The surgeon, in his stolid reliance on mere technique, is but a "victim of vanity," the one who may know all the parts of the brain but nothing of the patient's dreams and memories (p. 28).

The surgeon's growth, in Selzer's poetic rendering, has little to do with the acquisition of surgical competence per se. Rather, the surgeon realizes his calling by learning to subordinate his "delicate art" to the poet's vision of tragedy, truth, and redemption. For Selzer, when all is said and done, the surgeon is a pilgrim, and his pilgrim's progress is a fateful journey that culminates in enlightenment far beyond the province of bodily repair. "Far away from the operating room," he writes, "the surgeon is taught that some deaths are undeniable, that this does not deny their meaning. To *perceive* tragedy is to wring from it beauty and truth. It is a thing beyond mere competence and technique or the handsomeness to precisely cut and stitch. Further, he learns that love can bloom in the stoniest desert, an intensive care unit, perhaps" (1976, p. 46).

Nor is Selzer alone in prescribing a program of humane *Bildung* that gives rise to the surgeon's compassion, the emotional accouterment of his doctorly calling. Contemporary surgeons are at pains to distance themselves from the emotional detachment imputed to heroic nineteenth-century operators. Sherwin Nuland, for one, enshrines Helen Taussig, the founder of pediatric cardiology, for a capacity for total empathic engagement that best exemplifies the bearing of "a Hippocratic healer" (1988, p. 443). For Nuland, it is the humane and caring Taussig, and not the virtuosic Alfred Blalock, the surgical colleague with whom she collaborated in devising the original "blue baby" operation in 1943,[5] who embodies a Weltanschauung adequate to all the medical specialties, surgery included. Indeed, pediatric cardiology per se, the very structure of which "is intertwined with the fabric of its patients' lives," is prescriptive of the compassion, the *lack* of distance between physician and patient, that should guide all the specialties. For Nuland, it is no less than "an exemplar for those who would be real doctors, whether they have been trained to be nephrologists, microvascular surgeons, interventional radiologists, or members of any other the other splinter-groups of modern healing" (p. 446).

Selzer, however, persistently declines this easy hortatory role in order to impress upon us what is problematic about surgery *as* a medical specialty. A single generation may separate Seltzer from Francis Moore, but there is a world of ontological disjunction between Seltzer's ruminations about the development of surgical compassion and Moore's brisk admonition that surgeons need "to develop skin of exactly the right thickness," followed by his summary declamation that this "middle ground of sensitivity is something that is either inborn or acquired from parents, probably in childhood. While it cannot be created, it can be strengthened by example" (1995, p. 70). Selzer would

---

[5] One of the first operations successfully addressing a type of congenital heart defect (the tetralogy of Fallot), the procedure, enshrined as the Blalock-Taussig shunt, shunted the circulation around the congenitally obstructed pulmonary artery, providing a bypass that increased blood flow to the lungs, giving these cyanotic children, these "blue babies," a new lease on life. Nuland (1988, pp. 430ff.) provides an engaging account of this chapter in surgical history.

have it otherwise. For him, the surgeon's capacity for compassion, no less than his ability to perceive operating-suite tragedy, is a gift of time; it comes only as the requirements of technique and art gradually give way to the enlargement of perception that sustains poetic self-reflection. As long as the surgeon operates only in the realm of surgery, of bodily repair, his empathy and compassion render him impotent; they are not his helpmates but his ruination: "The surgeon cannot weep. When he cuts the flesh, his own must not bleed. Here it is all work. Like an asthmatic hungering for air, longing to take just one deep breath, the surgeon struggles not to feel. It is suffocating to press the feeling out" (1974, p. 101).

To resist emotional suffocation while retaining an operative narrowing of consciousness undiluted by emotional distraction—this is the human challenge, hence the true challenge, of the surgical calling. "A surgeon does not slip from his mother's womb with compassion smeared upon him like the drippings of his birth," Selzer writes.

> It is much later that it comes. No easy shaft of grace this, but the cumulative murmuring of the numberless wounds he has dressed, the incisions he has made, all the sores and ulcers and cavities he has touched in order to heal. In the beginning it is barely audible, a whisper, as from many mouths. Slowly it gathers, rises from the streaming flesh until, at least, it is a pure *calling*—an exclusive sound, like the cry of certain solitary birds—telling that out of the resonance between the sick man and the one who tends him there may spring that profound courtesy that the religious call Love [1976, p. 46].

And what of technique itself, the "delicate art" that sustains a surgical calling even as the surgeon aspires to take technique for granted and thereby lay it to the side? Young surgeons tend to enshrine the delicate art; at most they are able to juxtapose it to elements of brutal invasion that run in parallel over the course of an operation.[6] Selzer, for his part, dissects the art

---

[6] ". . . the task of removing the diseased liver was also one of the most brutal and bloody experiences in a surgeon's life. At any stage disastrous or even lethal hemorrhage was a major threat. As brutal as part of the procedure was, a great portion of it required, by contrast, the most delicate and sophisticated technique" (Toussaint, 1998, p. 364).

itself and, in so doing, invokes images of troubled control and incomplete mastery that hearken back to premodern anxieties before the dark mysteries of surgical penetration. For Freud, outlining his vision of the mental apparatus in 1923, the seat of such troubled control and incomplete mastery was the ego itself. In its relation to the primitive instinctual energies of the id, he observed, the ego "is like a man on horseback, who has to hold in check the superior strength of the horse; with this difference, that the rider tries to do so with his own strength while the ego uses borrowed forces. The analogy may be carried a little further. Often a rider, if he is not to be parted from his horse, is obliged to guide it where it wants to go; so in the same way the ego is in the habit of transforming the id's will into action as if it were its own" (p. 25). And here is Selzer, a half-century later, implicitly summoning Freud's simile to a more surgical locale, where the primitive life of instinct settles on the scalpel while the presence of a struggling ego is relegated to the surgeon's hand: "The unguarded knife is like the unbridled war-horse that not only carries its helpless rider to his death, but tramples all beneath its hooves. The hand of the surgeon must tame this savage thing. He is a rider reining to capture a pace" (1976, p. 100).

Selzer is unique among contemporary surgeons in probing the complicated relationship between the surgeon and his knife, thereby problematizing the relationship between surgeon and surgical act that his nineteenth-century forebears took for granted. In pondering the elements of merger, disjunction, instinct, control, and creation that congeal in the scalpel, he takes us far indeed from the image of the surgeon that underwrote Freud's surgical metaphor:

> So close is the joining of knife and surgeon that they are like the Centaur—the knife, below, all equine energy, the surgeon, above, with his delicate art. One holds the knife back as much as advances it to purpose. One is master of the scissors. One is partner, sometimes rival, to the knife. In a moment it is like the long red fingernail of the Dragon Lady. Thus does the surgeon curb in order to create, restraining the scalpel, governing it shrewdly, setting the action of the operation into a pattern, giving it form and purpose [1976, pp. 100–101].

With Selzer's vision of conflicted partnership between surgeon and scalpel, of a prerogative to penetrate hemmed in by restraint and shrewd governance, we are in touch with aspects of the surgical calling far removed from Freud's late nineteenth-century vision of the operative mentality. For psychoanalysts and others seeking medical anchorage for psychological methods of restoration and cure, for Freud's descendants no less than for Freud, medicosurgical metaphors will always be useful templates, perhaps even central templates, of curative intervention. The problem, I submit, has never been with medicosurgical analogies per se. Rather, it has always resided in the truncated vision of medicosurgical activity that underlies and informs such analogizing—and in the tendentious use of such analogizing by the supporters and detractors of classical psychoanalytic technique.

One may object that any such analogizing lends a specious concreteness to mind matters and is hence tendentious, even conceptually regressive, in its own way. Given the very nature of mind, it will be held, depth-psychological therapy has nothing to learn from the hard realities of surgery. But such a demurrer mistakenly conflates surgery with major operative surgery and thereby ignores the range of curative initiatives and therapeutic responsibilities that have fallen to surgeons throughout history. And it ignores the degree to which these initiatives and these responsibilities have frequently been imbricated with ontological puzzles about the relationship of mind and body, of self and other. The surgical point of view, comprehended historically, far transcends operative contingencies and the contributions of individual surgeons (Temkin, 1951).

Modern surgery, both in its therapeutic obligations and in its technical ministrations, opens to a wealth of metaphoric possibility that awaits appropriation by contemporary doctors of the mind. We have briefly considered Ferenczi's transmutation of Freud's surgical metaphor into an obstetrical metaphor, with analytic treatment figuring as a "midwifery of thought." This image, which fruitfully combines elements of passive receptiveness (the analyst as "onlooker at a natural proceeding . . .") and active intervention (" . . . but who must be at hand at the critical moment with the forceps in order to complete the act of parturition that is not progressing spontaneously") has yet to be pursued beyond Ferenczi's early writings of the 1920s. Yet the obstetrical metaphor approximates Selzer's vision of the modern surgical act, of operative restraint in the service of a creative therapeutic task, far more adequately than Freud's original metaphor did.

Nor does Ferenczi's transformation of Freud's medicosurgical method end with the suggestion that we construe the analyst's ministrations as an obstetrical act. It was Ferenczi, we recall, who broached the possibility of administering ether or chloroform to traumatized patients, thereby "anesthetiz[ing] the traumatic pain to such a degree that the circumstances related to the trauma would become accessible" (1932, p. 138). Is the anesthetic aspect of medicosurgical metaphors relevant to contemporary discussion of the adjunctive role of pharmacotherapy in psychoanalysis and psychotherapy (Roose, 1995)? Analogizing from the pain-deadening preconditions of surgical intervention to the pharmacological control of symptomatic distress in the interest of mobilizing the patient's introspective capacity may tend to a certain reliance on pharmacotherapy in psychoanalytic-type treatments of the future. But the analogy invites caution as well. Major anesthesia has always entailed risk, and these risks, too, invite metaphoric extrapolation to the realm of talking therapy. Chloroform anesthesia, to follow up on Ferenczi's suggestion, rendered patients insensible to pain at the risk of respiratory failure and cardiovascular accident, as evidenced by the fascinating history of chloroform death from the mid-nineteenth to the mid-twentieth century (Lawrence, 1992b). Can we say something *analogous* about a reliance (or overreliance) on pharmacotherapy for those patients convinced of the usefulness of a psychotherapeutic task framed within a psychological theory of therapeutic action?

The surgical history of the past half century provides many other possibilities of metaphoric enlargement and transformation. Here are but three examples. Sir Berkeley Moynihan, the eminent British surgeon whose major contributions to abdominal surgery span the first four decades of the century, observed that "every surgical operation is an experiment in bacteriology" (quoted in Moore, 1995, p. 74). Moynihan's intent, of course, was to underscore the risk inherent in penetrating the skin barrier that protects large animals—human beings included—from an inhospitable microbiological world. Therapeutic consideration of the sequelae of *invasive* interpretation—long debated in terms of issues of psychological readiness, holding environments, therapeutic "containing" functions, and, of course, matters of tact and timing—may be usefully deepened by this aspect of medicosurgical discourse.

And then there is the example of Francis Moore, one of the preeminent surgical researchers of the past half century, who deemed "the dangerous inaccuracy, inadequacy, and often disastrous ineffectiveness of supportive care for patients who had sustained severe injuries, burns, or major operations" among the most pressing *surgical* problems of the 1930s and 40s. Consideration of supportive aftercare as a *component* of psychotherapeutic management—including psychoanalytic treatment—follows metaphorically from what Moore, in his pioneering clinical research, delineated as the biology of convalescence (1995, pp. 116ff.). More fundamentally still, various notions of psychological self-righting, including the therapeutic mobilization of psychological growth processes, may be metaphorically enriched by consideration of the sequelae of Moore's research, the field of study known as metabolism in convalescence.

Finally, the debt of modern surgery to twentieth-century immunology has long been a matter of record. Rooted in Leo Loeb's and Alexis Carrell's biological study of the behavior of autotransplants and homotransplants[7] in various tissues and organs in the 1920s and 30s, the field gained impetus from Thomas Gibson's and Sir Peter Medawar's systematic study of resistance to tissue homografts among British burn victims during World War II. Understanding how foreignness is recognized at the cellular level, including the manner in which "individuality differentials" persist even in successful grafts and

---

[7] Autotransplants are grafts utilizing the patient's own tissue; homotransplants are grafts from one individual to another of the same species.

transplants, is among the triumphs of immunogenetics. Of special moment to surgery, in turn, has been immunological study of ways in which cellular "recognition" of foreignness can be attenuated in order to prevent rejection of tissue grafts and organ transplants. The existence of certain "privileged" tissues or transplant sites, of a "privileged time" for transplantation, of chemical agents that depress the immunological responsiveness of tissue and organ recipients, and of "specific immunological tolerance"[8] have all been woven into surgical consciousness over the past half century (Woodruff, 1977, pp. 42–68; Moore, 1995, 166–171). Do these conceptual tools offer nothing to therapists and analysts? Or may they perhaps contribute to an understanding of psychological notions of self and other, and especially of the ground and operation of internalization—a kind of homotransplant in the realm of psychic structure—as an aspect of psychological growth and therapeutic remediation?

The very salience of such a question derives from the shaping impact of metaphoric preferences on notions of care-giving self and care-receiving other. Medicosurgical analogizing, I submit, lends special force to the therapeutic obligations of "doctors of the mind," whose epistemological scruples may fly in the face of their patients' culturally shaped expectations of authoritative assistance from a professional healer. It is the medicosurgical tradition that, since the seventeenth century, has embodied the belief that life and good health are values (Temkin, 1946, pp. 98–100). Psychoanalysts and others who minister to suffering minds assume helping responsibilities that

---

[8] Another product of the research of Medawar and his colleagues during the 1940s, "specific immunological tolerance" or "actively acquired immune tolerance" followed from the clinical finding that animals grafted near birth would accept additional grafts from the same donor animal for the rest of its life. That is, the graft recipient "became tolerant of that other animal's proteins and tissues, apparently mistaking them for 'self'" (Moore, 1995, p. 170). Woodruff (1977, p. 52) defines the condition more technically "as a state of reduced or absent reactivity to one particular antigen (or group of antigens) in consequence of previous exposure to the same, or a closely related, antigen." Can this insight illuminate, however metaphorically, psychological processes of identification, incorporation, and internalization with respect to different "objects" offered to "subjects" in different contexts and at different stages in the life cycle?

are part and parcel of this tradition. To claim that patients present with minds that are "ill," with bona fide "mental illness," is of course to make a metaphorical leap at the outset. But the leap pays off, if only as an ethical rider to an increasingly "postmodern" psychotherapeutic contract, with its insistence on the mutual construction of meanings by therapist and patient, each freighted with the full burden of his or her subjectivity. Ontological ambiguity about what "it" is that ails mind and spirit—and how it gains expression in dialogue with another person—should never be allowed to mask the reality that "mental" patients suffer, and that they come to "doctors" for real help, even for "cure." The "it" that stretches into the realm of metaphor and symbol in one direction remains grounded in the pain of organismic dysfunction in the other[9]— even if it defies our understanding to say just where one realm ends and the other begins.

It follows, then, that the demise of *Freud's* surgical metaphor hardly betokens the irrelevance of medicosurgical analogizing in the psychotherapeutic domain. As long as therapists and analysts lay claim to the identity of professional healers committed to a healing endeavor, they will have much to learn from medicosurgical templates of healing activity. This is not to suggest that psychotherapists will profit from the wholesale appropriation of such templates in their model making. On the contrary, it is the very conceptual elasticity of such templates, their metaphorical richness, that is their strength. Medicosurgical analogizing, I believe, provides analysts and therapists with the opportunity not only to reap the harvest of twentieth-century medicosurgical science, but also to demarcate more fully what is distinctive about their particular genre of therapeutic endeavor. Almost a century after Freud introduced his surgical metaphor, the question that remains is not whether doctors of the mind are surgeons, but rather what type of surgeon they choose to be.

---

[9] Recent writing on the role of bodily experience in the psychotherapeutic process is a heartening sign of renewed attentiveness to the organismic "ground" of psychological suffering. See, for example, the essays collected in Lewis Aron and Frances Sommer Anderson, *Relational Perspectives on the Body* (1998).

References

Collections of published Freud correspondence with textual abbreviations

Freud Letters (FL): Freud, Ernst L., editor (1960). *Letters of Sigmund Freud.* Translated by Tania & James Stern. New York: Basic Books.

Freud-Abraham Letters (FAL): Abraham, Hilda C. & Freud, Ernst L., editors (1965). *A Psychoanalytic Dialogue: The Letters of Sigmund Freud and Karl Abraham.* Translated by Bernard Marsh & Hilda C. Abraham. New York: Basic Books.

Freud-Andreas-Salomé Letters (FAnSL). Pfeifer, Ernst, editor (1966). *Sigmund Freud and Lou Andreas-Salomé: Letters.* Translated by William and Elaine Robson-Scott. New York: Harcourt Brace Jovanovich.

Freud-Ferenczi Correspondence, vol. 1 (FFC, 1): Falzeder, Ernst, Brabant, Evan, & Giampieri-Deutsch, Patrizia, editors (1992). *The Correspondence of Sigmund Freud and Sándor Ferenczi, volume 1, 1908–1914.* Translated by Peter T. Hoffer. Cambridge: Harvard University Press.

Freud-Ferenczi Correspondence, vol. 2 (FFC, 2): Falzeder, Ernest & Brabant, Eva, editors, with the collaboration of Giampieri-Deutsch, Patrizia (1996). *The Correspondence of Sigmund Freud and Sándor Ferenczi, volume 2, 1914–1919.* Cambridge: Harvard University Press.

Freud-Fliess Letters (FFlL): Masson, Jeffrey Moussaieff, translator and editor (1985). *The Complete Letters of Sigmund Freud to Wilhelm Fliess, 1887–1904.* Cambridge: Harvard University Press.

Freud-Groddeck Letters (FGL): Schacht, Lore, editor (1977). Translated by Gertrud Mander. *The Meaning of Illness: Selected Psychoanalytic Writings by Georg Groddeck, Including His*

229

Correspondence with Sigmund Freud. New York: International Universities Press.

Freud-Jones Correspondence (FJC): Paskauskas, R. Andrew, editor (1993). *The Complete Correspondence of Sigmund Freud and Ernest Jones, 1908–1939.* Cambridge: Harvard University Press.

Freud-Jung Letters (FJL): McGuire, William, editor (1974). Translated by Ralph Manheim & R. F. C. Hull. Princeton, NJ: Princeton University Press.

Freud-Pfister Letters (FPL): Meng, Heinrich & Freud, Ernst L., editors (1963). *Psycho-Analysis and Faith: The Letters of Sigmund Freud and Oskar Pfister.* Translated by Eric Mosbacher. London: Hogarth Press.

Freud-Silberstein Letters (FSL): Boehlich, Walter, editor (1990). *The Letters of Sigmund Freud to Eduard Silberstein, 1871–1881.* Translated by Arnold J. Pomerans. Cambridge: Harvard University Press.

References

Abraham, Hilda C. (1974). Karl Abraham: An Unfinished Biography. *Int. Rev. Psychoanal,* 1:17–72.

Abraham, Karl (1921). Psychoanalysis and the War Neuroses. In: *Clinical Papers and Essays on Psychoanalysis,* edited by H. C. Abraham. Translated by H. C. Abraham & D. R. Ellison. New York: Brunner/Mazel, 1955, pp. 59–67.

Abraham, Karl (1925). Psychoanalysis and Gynecology. In: *Clinical Papers and Essays on Psychoanalysis,* edited by H. C. Abraham. Translated by H. C. Abraham & D. R. Ellison. New York: Brunner/Mazel, 1955, pp. 91–97.

Alexander, Franz (1927). Discussion on Lay Analysis. *Int. J. Psycho-Anal.,* 8:224–230.

Alexander, Franz (1936). Addenda to "The Medical Value of Psychoanalysis." *Psychoanal. Quart.,* 5:548–559.

Alexander, Franz (1950). *Psychosomatic Medicine: Its Principles and Applications.* New York: Norton.

Anzieu, Didier (1975). *Freud's Self-Analysis.* Translated by Peter Graham. Madison, CT: International Universities Press, 1986.

Aron, Lewis (1996). *A Meeting of Minds: Mutuality in Psychoanalysis.* Hillsdale, NJ: The Analytic Press.

Aron, Lewis & Anderson, Frances Sommer, eds. (1998). *Relational Perspectives on the Body.* Hillsdale, NJ: The Analytic Press.

Aron, Lewis & Harris, Adrienne. (1993). Sándor Ferenczi: Discovery and Rediscovery. In: *The Legacy of Sándor Ferenczi.* Edited by

Lewis Aron & Adrienne Harris. Hillsdale, NJ: The Analytic Press, pp. 1–35.

Aziz, Shahid R. (1995). The Oral Surgical Operations of Grover Cleveland: A Presidential Cover-Up. *J. Oral Maxillofac. Surg.*, 53:1088–1090.

Babington, Anthony (1997). *Shell-Shock: A History of the Changing Attitudes to War Neurosis.* London: Leo Cooper.

Ballenger, John Jacob (1969). *Diseases of the Nose, Throat, and Ear*, 11ᵗʰ edition. Philadelphia: Lea & Febiger.

Barron, James W. & Hoffer, Axel (1994). Historical Events Reinforcing Freud's Emphasis on "Holding Down the Countertransference." *Psychoanal. Quart.*, 63:536–540.

Bazelon, David L. (1974). The Perils of Wizardry. *Amer. J. Psychiat.*, 131:1317–1322.

Becker, Hortense Koller (1963). Carl Koller and Cocaine. In: *Cocaine Papers by Sigmund Freud*. Edited by Robert Byck. New York: New American Library, 1974, pp. 261–319.

Benjamin, Jessica (1997). Psychoanalysis as a Vocation. *Psychoanal. Dial.*, 7:781–802.

Bernays, Anna (1940). My Brother Sigmund Freud. *Amer. Mercury*, 51:203.

Bernfeld, Siegfried (1951). Sigmund Freud, M.D., 1882-1885. *Int. J. Psycho-Anal.*, 32:204–217.

Bernfeld, Siegfried (1953). Freud's Studies on Cocaine. In: *Cocaine Papers by Sigmund Freud*. Edited by Robert Byck. New York: New American Library, 1974, pp. 321–352.

Billroth, Theodor (1876). *The Medical Sciences in the German Universities: A Study in the History of Civilization*. Translated from the German. New York: Macmillan, 1924.

Billroth, Theodor (1910). *Briefe*. Hanover & Leipzig: Hahnsche Buchhandlung.

Bini, Lucio (1938). Experimental Researches on Epileptic Attacks Induced by the Electric Current. *Amer. J. Psychiat.*, 94 (suppl):172–174.

Blum, Harold (1996). The Irma Dream, Self-Analysis, and Self-Supervision. *J. Amer. Psychoanal. Assn.*, 44:511–532.

Bollorino, Francesco, Valdre, Rossella, & Gianneli, Maria Vittoria (1995). Ugo Cerletti and the Discovery of Electroshock. *Psychiatry On-Line*, issue 5, paper 1.

Bonner, Thomas Neville (1963). *American Doctors and German Universities: A Chapter in International Intellectual Relations, 1870–1914.* Lincoln: University of Nebraska Press.

Bonner, Thomas Neville (1995). *Becoming a Physician: Medical Education in Great Britain, France, Germany, and the United States, 1750–1945*. New York: Oxford University Press.

Brenner, Charles (1976). *Psychoanalytic Technique and Psychic Conflict*. New York: International Universities Press.

Breuer, Josef & Freud, Sigmund (1895). Studies on Hysteria. *Standard Edition*, 2. London: Hogarth Press, 1955.

Brill, A. A. (1921). *Fundamental Conceptions of Psychoanalysis*. New York: University Press of America, 1985.

Brody, Eugene B. (1958). Superego, Introjected Mother, and Energy Distribution in Schizophrenia: Contribution from the Study of Anterior Lobotomy. *J. Amer. Psychoanal. Assn.*, 6:481–501.

Brody, Eugene B. & Rosvold, H. Enger (1952). Influence of Prefrontal Lobotomy on Social Interaction in a Monkey Group. *Psychosom. Med.*, 14:406-415.

Brome, Vincent (1983). *Ernest Jones: A Biography*. New York: Norton.

Brooks, John J., Enterline, Horatio T. & Aponte, Gonazlo E. (1980). The Final Diagnosis of President Cleveland's Lesion. *Transactions and Studies of the College of Physicians of Philadelphia*, 2:1–25.

Carson, Ben (1990). *Gifted Hands: The Ben Carson Story*. Grand Rapids, MI: Zondervan.

Cerletti, Ugo & Bini, Lucio (1938). L'Elettroshock. *Arch. Gen. Neurol. Psichiat. Psicoanal.*, 19:266.

Clarke, Edwin & Jacyna, L. S. (1987). *Nineteenth-Century Origins of Neuroscientific Concepts*. Berkeley: University of California Press.

Conley, Frances, K. (1998). *Walking Out on the Boys*. New York: Farrar, Straus & Giroux.

Connaughton, Dennis (1991). *Warren Cole, M.D. and the Ascent of Scientific Surgery*. Chicago: Warren and Clara Cole Foundation.

Coriat, Isador H. (1917). *What is Psychoanalysis?* New York: Arno Press, 1973.

Corning, James Leonard (1885). Spinal Anaesthesia and Local Medication of the Cord. In: *Milestones in Anesthesia: Readings in the Development of Surgical Anesthesia, 1665–1940*. Edited by Frank Cole. Lincoln: University of Nebraska Press, 1965, pp. 154–159.

Crile, George W. (1897). A New Method of Applying Cocaine for Producing Surgical Anesthesia, with the Report of a Case. In: *Milestones in Anesthesia: Readings in the Development of Surgical Anesthesia, 1665–1940*. Edited by Frank Cole. Lincoln: University of Nebraska Press, 1965, pp. 160–163.

Crile, George W. (1903). *Blood Pressure in Surgery: An Experimental and Clinical Research*. Philadelphia: Lippincott.
Dally, Ann (1991). *Women Under the Knife: A History of Surgery*. New York: Routledge.
Davenport, Horace W. (1987). *Doctor Dock: Teaching and Learning Medicine at the Turn of the Century*. New Brunswick, NJ: Rutgers University Press.
Deutsch, Felix (1956). Reflections on Freud's One Hundredth Birthday. *Psychosom. Med.*, 4:279–283.
Diethelm, Oskar (1939). An Historical View of Somatic Treatment in Psychiatry. *Amer. J. Psychiat.*, 95:1165–1179.
Dubois, Paul (1905). *The Psychic Treatment of Nervous Disorders*. Translated and edited by Smith Ely Jelliffe & William A. White. New York & London: Funk & Wagnalls.
Duden, Barbara (1991). *The Woman Beneath the Skin: A Doctor's Patients in Eighteenth-Century Germany*. Cambridge: Harvard University Press.
Eissler, K. R. (1986). *Freud as an Expert Witness: The Discussion of War Neuroses Between Freud and Wagner-Jauregg*. Translated by Christine Trollope. Madison, CT: International Universities Press.
Ellis, Harold (1996). *Operations That Made History*. London: Greenwich Medical Media.
Ellman, Steven J. (1991). *Freud's Technique Papers: A Contemporary Perspective*. Northvale, NJ: Aronson.
English, Peter C. (1980). *Shock, Physiological Surgery, and George Washington Crile: Medical Innovation in the Progressive Era*. Westport, CT: Greenwood.
Erickson, Isabel & Ramsey, Mary (1938). Nursing Care in Shock Therapy. *Bull. Menn. Clin.*, 2:155–160.
Erikson, Erik (1954). The Dream Specimen of Psychoanalysis. *J. Amer. Psychoanal. Assn.*, 2:5–55.
Faulker, Howard J. & Pruitt, Virginia D., eds. (1988). *The Selected Correspondence of Karl A. Menninger, 1919–1945*. New Haven, CT: Yale University Press.
Fenichel, Otto (1935). Concerning the Theory of Psychoanalytic Technique. In: *Collected Papers, First Series*. Edited by Hanna Fenichel & David Rapaport. New York: Norton, 1953, pp. 332–348.
Fenichel, Otto (1936). *Problems of Psychoanalytic Technique*. Translated by David Brunswick. New York: Psychoanalytic Quarterly, 1941.
Ferenczi, Sándor (1917). Two Types of War Neuroses. In: *Further Contributions to the Theory and Technique of Psychoanalysis*,

compiled by John Rickman. Translated by Jane Isabel Suttie. New York: Basic Books, 1952, pp. 124–141.

Ferenczi, Sándor (1919a). On the Technique of Psychoanalysis. In: *Further Contributions to the Theory and Technique of Psychoanalysis*, compiled by John Rickman. Translated by Jane Isabel Suttie. New York: Basic Books, 1952, pp. 177–189.

Ferenczi, Sándor (1919b). Technical Difficulties in the Analysis of a Case of Hysteria. In: *Further Contributions to the Theory and Technique of Psychoanalysis*, compiled by John Rickman. Translated by Jane Isabel Suttie. New York: Basic Books, 1952, pp. 189–197.

Ferenczi, Sándor (1921). The Further Development of an Active Therapy in Psychoanalysis. In: *Further Contributions to the Theory and Technique of Psychoanalysis*, compiled by John Rickman. Translated by Jane Isabel Suttie. New York: Basic Books, 1952, pp. 198–217.

Ferenczi, Sándor (1925). Contraindications to the 'Active' Psychoanalytical Technique. In: *Further Contributions to the Theory and Technique of Psychoanalysis*, compiled by John Rickman. Translated by Jane Isabel Suttie. New York: Basic Books, 1952, pp. 217–230.

Ferenczi, Sándor (1932). *Clinical Diary*. Edited by Judith Dupont. Translated by Michael Balint & Nicola Zarday Jackson. Cambridge: Harvard University Press, 1988.

Ferenczi, Sándor, Abraham, Karl, Simmel, Ernst & Jones, Ernest (1921). *Psychoanalysis and the War Neuroses*, with an introduction by Prof. Sigm. Freud. London: International Psychoanalytical Press.

Ferenczi, Sándor & Rank, Otto (1923). *The Development of Psychoanalysis*. Translated by Caroline Newton. New York: Dover, 1924.

Fink, Max (1984). Meduna and the Origins of Convulsive Therapy. *Amer. J. Psychiat.*, 141:1034–1041.

Flescher, Joachim (1950). The "Discharging Function" of Electric Shock and the Anxiety Problem. *Psychoanal. Rev.*, 37:277–280.

Fluhmann, C. Frederic (1955). The Rise and Fall of Suspension Operations for Uterine Retrodisplacement. *Bull. Johns Hopkins Hosp.*, 96:59–70.

Fortune, Christopher (1996). Mutual Analysis: A Logical Outcome of Sándor Ferenczi's Experiments in Psychoanalysis. In: *Ferenczi's Turn in Psychoanalysis*. Edited by Peter L. Rudnytsky et al. New York: New York University Press, pp. 170–186.

Frank, Jan (1950). Some Aspects of Lobotomy (Prefrontal Leucotomy) Under Psychoanalytic Scrutiny. *Psychiatry*, 13:35–42.

Freeman, Walter & Watts, James W. (1942). *Psychosurgery: Intelligence, Emotion and Social Behavior Following Prefrontal Lobotomy for Mental Disorders.* Springfield, IL: Thomas.

Freud, Sigmund (1887). Craving for and Fear of Cocaine. In: *Cocaine Papers by Sigmund Freud.* Edited by Robert Byck. New York: New American Library, 1974, pp. 169–176.

Freud, Sigmund (1895). Project for a Scientific Psychology. In: *The Origins of Psychoanalysis. Letters to Wilhelm Fliess, Drafts and Notes: 1887–1902.* Edited by M. Bonaparte, A. Freud, & E. Kris. Translated by E. Mosbacher & J. Strachey. New York: Basic Books, 1954, pp. 347–445.

Freud, Sigmund (1900). The Interpretation of Dreams. *Standard Edition*, 4 & 5. London: Hogarth Press, 1953.

Freud, Sigmund (1909). Five Lectures on Psychoanalysis. *Standard Edition*, 11:1–56. London: Hogarth Press, 1957.

Freud, Sigmund (1910). The Future Prospects of Psychoanalytic Therapy. *Standard Edition*, 11:139–151. London: Hogarth Press, 1957.

Freud, Sigmund (1912). Recommendations to Physicians Practicing Psychoanalysis. *Standard Edition*, 12:109–120. London: Hogarth Press, 1958.

Freud, Sigmund (1913). On Beginning the Treatment (Further Recommendations on the Technique of Psychoanalysis). *Standard Edition*, 12:121–144. London: Hogarth Press, 1958.

Freud, Sigmund (1915). Observations on Transference-Love (Further Recommendations on the Technique of Psychoanalysis). *Standard Edition*, 12:157–173. London: Hogarth Press, 1958.

Freud, Sigmund (1917). Introductory Lectures on Psychoanalysis (Part III). *Standard Edition*, 16. London: Hogarth Press, 1963.

Freud, Sigmund (1919a). Lines of Advance in Psychoanalytic Therapy. *Standard Edition*, 17:157–168. London: Hogarth Press, 1955.

Freud, Sigmund (1919b). Introduction to *Psychoanalysis and the War Neuroses. Standard Edition*, 17:205-210. London: Hogarth Press, 1955.

Freud, Sigmund (1920a). Beyond the Pleasure Principle. *Standard Edition*, 18:1–64. London: Hogarth Press, 1955.

Freud, Sigmund (1920b). The Psychogenesis of a Case of Homosexuality in a Woman. *Standard Edition*, 18:145–172. London: Hogarth Press, 1955.

Freud, Sigmund (1920d). Memorandum on the Electrical Treatment of War Neurotics. *Standard Edition*, 17:211–215. London: Hogarth Press, 1955.

Freud, Sigmund (1920c). Dr. Anton von Freund. *Standard Edition*, 18:267-268. London: Hogarth Press, 1955.

Freud, Sigmund (1921). Group Psychology and the Analysis of the Ego. *Standard Edition*, 18:65–143. London: Hogarth Press, 1955.

Freud, Sigmund (1923). The Ego and the Id. *Standard Edition*, 19:1–66. London: Hogarth Press, 1961.

Freud, Sigmund (1924). A Short Account of Psychoanalysis. *Standard Edition*, 19:189–209. London: Hogarth Press, 1961.

Freud, Sigmund (1925a). The Resistances to Psychoanalysis. *Standard Edition*, 19:211–222. London: Hogarth Press, 1961.

Freud, Sigmund (1925b). An Autobiographical Study. *Standard Edition*, 19:1–70. London: Hogarth Press, 1959.

Freud Sigmund (1926a). The Question of Lay Analysis. *Standard Edition*, 19:177–250. London: Hogarth Press, 1959.

Freud, Sigmund (1926b). Inhibitions, Symptoms and Anxiety. *Standard Edition*, 20:75–175. London: Hogarth Press, 1959.

Freud, Sigmund (1927a). Postscript to "The Question of Lay Analysis." *Standard Edition*, 20:251–258. London: Hogarth Press, 1959.

Freud, Sigmund (1933). New Introductory Lectures on Psychoanalysis. *Standard Edition*, 22:5–182. London: Hogarth Press, 1964.

Freud, Sigmund (1937a). Analysis Terminable and Interminable. *Standard Edition*, 23:209–253. London: Hogarth Press, 1964.

Freud, Sigmund (1937b). Constructions in Analysis. *Standard Edition*, 23:255–269. London: Hogarth Press, 1964.

Freud, Sigmund (1938). An Outline of Psychoanalysis. *Standard Edition*, 23:144–207. London: Hogarth Press, 1964.

Friedman, Lawrence (1988). *The Anatomy of Psychotherapy*. Hillsdale, NJ: The Analytic Press.

Friedman, Lawrence J. (1990). *Menninger: The Family and the Clinic*. New York: Knopf.

Frosch, John & Impastato, David (1948). The Effects of Shock Treatment on the Ego. *Psychoanal. Quart.*, 17:226–239.

Gabbard, Glen O. & Lester, Eva P. (1995). *Boundaries and Boundary Violations in Psychoanalysis*. New York: Basic Books.

Galdston, Iago (1952). Convalescence. In: *When Doctors Are Patients*. Edited by Max Pinner & Benjamin F. Miller. New York: Norton, pp. 342–348.

Gay, Peter (1988). *Freud: A Life for Our Time.* New York: Norton.

Gilbert, Martin (1994). *The First World War: A Complete History.* New York: Holt.

Glauber, I. Peter (1953). A Deterrent in the Study and Practice of Medicine. *Psychoanal. Quart.,* 22:381–412.

Glover, Edward (1927). Discussion on Lay Analysis. *Int. J. Psychoanal.* 8:212–220.

Glover, Edward (1955). *The Technique of Psycho-Analysis.* New York: International Universities Press, 1967.

Glueck, Bernard (1937). The Effect of the Hypoglycemic Therapy on the Psychotic Process. *Amer. J. Psychiat.,* 94:171–173.

Greenberg, Jay (1991). *Oedipus and Beyond: A Clinical Theory.* Cambridge: Harvard University Press.

Greenson, Ralph, R. (1967). *The Technique and Practice of Psychoanalysis.* New York: International Universities Press.

Grinstein, Alexander (1980). *Sigmund Freud's Dreams.* New York: International Universities Press.

Grob, Gerald N. (1983). *Mental Illness and American Society, 1875–1940.* Princeton: Princeton University Press.

Grob, Gerald N., ed. (1985). *The Inner World of American Psychiatry, 1890–1940: Selected Correspondence.* New Brunswick, NJ: Rutgers University Press.

Grotjahn, Martin (1938). Psychiatric Observations of Schizophrenic Patients During Metrazol Treatment. *Bull. Menn. Clin.,* 2:142–150.

Grotjahn, Martin (1952). A Psychoanalyst Passes a Small Stone with Big Troubles. In: *When Doctors Are Patients.* Edited by Max Pinner & Benjamin F. Miller. New York: Norton, pp. 89–95.

Hale, Nathan (1995). *The Rise and Crisis of Psychoanalysis in the United States: Freud and the Americans, 1917–1985.* New York: Oxford University Press.

Hall, R. J. (1884). Hydrochlorate of Cocaine. In: *Milestones in Anesthesia: Readings in the Development of Surgical Anesthesia, 1665–1940.* Edited by Frank Cole. Lincoln: University of Nebraska Press, 1965, pp. 149–153.

Haller, John S. (1981). Hypodermic Medication: Early History. *NY State J. Med.,* 81:1671–1679.

Hamilton, Victoria (1996). *The Analyst's Preconscious.* Hillsdale, NJ: The Analytic Press.

Harmat, Paul (1988). *Freud, Ferenczi und die ungarische Psychoanalyse.* Tübingen: Diskord.

Harvey, A. McGehee (1981). *Science at the Bedside: Clinical Research in American Medicine, 1905–1945.* Baltimore: Johns Hopkins University Press.

Haythornthwaite, Philip J. (1992). *The World War One Sourcebook*. New York: Cassell.

Hertzler, Arthur E. (1938). *The Horse and Buggy Doctor*. New York: Harper.

Hirschmüller, Albrecht (1978). *The Life and Work of Josef Breuer: Physiology and Psychoanalysis*. New York: New York University Press.

Hoang, Hoat M. & O'Leary, J. Patrick (1997). President Grover Cleveland's Secret Operation. *Amer. Surg.*, 63:758–759.

Hoffman, Irwin Z. (1998). *Ritual and Spontaneity in the Psychoanalytic Process: A Dialectical-Constructivist View*. Hillsdale, NJ: The Analytic Press.

Horney, Karen (1927). Discussion on Lay Analysis. *Int. J. Psycho-Anal.*, 8:255–259.

Howard-Jones, Norman (1971). The Origins of Hypodermic Medication. *Sci. Amer.*, 224:96–102.

Jacyna, Stephen (1992). Physiological Principles in the Surgical Writings of John Hunter. In: *Medical Theory, Surgical Practice: Studies in the History of Surgery*. Edited by Christopher Lawrence. London & New York: Routledge, pp. 135–152.

Jelliffe, S. E. (1938). Some Observations on Obsessive Tendencies Following Interruption of the Frontal Association Pathways. *J. Nerv. Ment. Dis.*, 88:232–233.

Johnson, Loren B. T. (1928). The Psychiatrist Looks at Medicine. *Psychoanal. Rev.*, 15:247–260.

Johnston, William (1972). *The Austrian Mind: An Intellectual and Social History*. Berkeley: University of California Press.

Jones, Ernest (1918). War Shock and Freud's Theory of the Neuroses. In: *Psychoanalysis and the War Neuroses*. Edited by Sándor Ferenczi et al. London: International Psychoanalytical Press, 1921, pp. 44–59.

Jones, Ernest (1920). Review of *Psychical Surgery: A Brief Synopsis of the Analytical Method in the Treatment of Mental and Psychical Disturbances*, by Joseph Ralph. *Int. J. Psycho-Anal.*, 1:487.

Jones, Ernest (1926). Memoir of Karl Abraham. In: *Karl Abraham, Selected Papers on Psychoanalysis*. London: Hogarth Press, pp. 13–45.

Jones, Ernest (1927). Discussion on Lay Analysis. *Int. J. Psycho-Anal.*, 8:174–198.

Jones, Ernest (1930). Psychoanalysis and Psychiatry. In: *Papers on Psychoanalysis*. Boston: Beacon, 1961, pp. 365–378.

Jones, Ernest (1934). Psychoanalysis and Modern Medicine. In: *Papers on Psychoanalysis*. Boston: Beacon, 1961, pp. 341–350.

Jones, Ernest (1938). The Unconscious Mind and Medical Practice. In: *Papers on Psychoanalysis*. Boston: Beacon, 1961, pp. 351–364.

Jones, Ernest (1953). *The Life and Work of Sigmund Freud, vol. 1*. New York: Basic Books.

Jones, Ernest (1955). *The Life and Work of Sigmund Freud, vol. 2*. New York: Basic Books.

Jones, Ernest (1957). *The Life and Work of Sigmund Freud, vol. 3*. New York: Basic Books.

Jones, Ernest (1959). *Free Associations: Memories of a Psychoanalyst*. New York: Basic Books.

Kalinowsky, Lothar B. & Hoch, Paul H. (1946). *Shock Treatments and Other Somatic Procedures in Psychiatry*. New York: Grune & Stratton.

Keen, William W. (1917). The Surgical Operations on President Cleveland in 1893. *The Saturday Evening Post*, September 22, 1917, pp. 24–25, 53, 55.

Kerr, John (1993). *A Most Dangerous Method: The Story of Jung, Freud, and Sabina Spielrein*. New York: Knopf.

Keynes, Geoffrey (1952). Introduction to *The Apologie and Treatise of Ambroise Paré*. New York: Dover, 1968.

Koller, Carl (1884). On the Use of Cocaine for Producing Anaesthesia on the Eye. In: *Milestones in Anesthesia: Readings in the Development of Surgical Anesthesia, 1665–1940*. Edited by Frank Cole. Lincoln: University of Nebraska Press, 1965, pp. 141–148.

Koller, Carl (1928). Personal Reminiscences of the First Use of Cocaine as a Local Anesthetic in Eye Surgery. Read at the Sixth Annual Congress of the Anesthetists of the United States and Canada in Joint Meeting with the *International Anesthesia Research Society*, 7(1), January–February, 1928.

Kornblith, Alice B., Zlotolow, Ian M., Gooen, Jane, Huryn, Joseph M., Lerner, Todd, Strong, Elliot W., Shah, Jatin P., Spiro, Ronald H., & Holland, Jimmie C. (1996). Quality of Life of Maxillectomy Patients Using an Obturator Prosthesis. *Head & Neck*, 18:323–334.

Krüll, Marianne (1979). *Freud and His Father*. Translated by Arnold J. Pomerans. New York: Norton, 1986.

Kubie, Lawrence S. (1936). *Practical Aspects of Psychoanalysis: A Handbook for Prospective Patients and Their Advisors*. New York: Norton.

Lakoff, George & Johnson, Mark (1980). *Metaphors We Live By*. Chicago: University of Chicago Press.

Lawrence, Christopher (1992a). Democratic, Divine and Heroic: The History and Historiography of Surgery. In: *Medical Theory, Surgical Practice: Studies in the History of Surgery*. Edited by Christopher Lawrence. London & New York: Routledge, pp. 1–47.

Lawrence, Christopher (1992b). Experiment and Experience in Anaesthesia: Alfred Goodman Levy and Chloroform Death, 1910–1960. In: *Medical Theory, Surgical Practice: Studies in the History of Surgery*. Edited by Christopher Lawrence. London & New York: Routledge, pp. 263–293.

Lawrence, Ghislaine (1992). The Ambiguous Artifact: Surgical Instruments and the Surgical Past. In: *Medical Theory, Surgical Practice: Studies in the History of Surgery*. Edited by Christopher Lawrence. London & New York: Routledge, pp. 295–314.

Leed, Eric J. (1979). *No Man's Land: Combat and Identity in World War I*. Cambridge: Cambridge University Press.

Lesky, Erna (1976). *The Vienna Medical School of the 19ᵗʰ Century*. Translated by L. Williams and I. S. Levij. Baltimore: Johns Hopkins University Press.

Lichtenberg, Joseph D. (1994). How Libido Theory Shaped Technique. *J. Amer. Psychoanal. Assn.*, 42:727–739.

Lohser, Beate & Newton, Peter M. (1996). *Unorthodox Freud: The View from the Couch*. New York: Guilford.

Luce, Edward A. (1983). The Ordeal of Sigmund Freud: A Postscript. *Clinics Plastic Surg.*, 10:715–716.

Magee, Maggie & Miller, Diana C. (1997). *Lesbian Lives: Psychoanalytic Narratives Old and New*. Hillsdale, NJ: The Analytic Press.

Majno, Guido (1975). *The Healing Hand: Man and Wound in the Ancient World*. Cambridge: Harvard University Press.

Masson, Jeffrey Moussaieff (1984). *The Assault on Truth: Freud's Suppression of the Seduction Theory*. New York: Farrar, Straus & Giroux

Meade, Richard H. (1968). *An Introduction to the History of General Surgery*. Philadelphia: Saunders.

Menninger, Karl A. (1930). *The Human Mind*. New York: Knopf.

Menninger, Karl A. (1934). Polysurgery and Polysurgical Addiction. *Psychoanal. Quart.*, 3:173–199.

Menninger, Karl A. (1936). Psychiatry and Medicine. *Bull. Menn. Clin.*, 1:1–9.

Menninger, Karl A. (1938). The Cinderella of Medicine. *Bull. Menn. Clin.*, 2:180–187.

Menninger, Karl A. (1957a). Psychological Factors in the Choice of Medicine as a Profession. *Bull. Menn. Clin.*, 21:51–58.

Menninger, Karl A. (1957b). Psychological Factors in the Choice of Medicine as a Profession (continued). *Bull. Menn. Clin.*, 21:99–106.

Menninger, Karl A. (1958). *Theory of Psychoanalytic Technique.* New York: Science Editions, 1961.

Menninger, William C. (1938). The Results with Metrazol as an Adjunct Therapy in Schizophrenia and Depressions. *Bull. Menn. Clin.*, 2:129–141.

Menninger, William C. (1940). An Evaluation of Metrazol Treatment. *Bull. Menn. Clin.*, 4:95–104.

Menninger, William C. (1953). Psychiatry and the Practice of Medicine. *Bull. Menn. Clin.*, 17:170–179.

Millet, John A. P. & Mosse, Eric P. (1944). On Certain Psychological Aspects of Electroshock Therapy. *Psychosom. Med.*, 6:226–236.

Mills, Charles K. (1919). Introduction to E. E. Southard, *Shell-Shock and Other Neuropsychiatric Problems, Presented in Five Hundred and Eighty-nine Case Histories from the War Literature, 1914–1918.* New York: Arno Press, 1973, pp. v–xviii.

Mitchell, Stephen A. (1993). *Hope and Dread in Psychoanalysis.* New York: Basic Books.

Mitchell, Stephen A. (1997). *Influence and Autonomy in Psychoanalysis.* Hillsdale, NJ: The Analytic Press.

Molnar, Michael, trans. & annot. (1992). *The Diary of Sigmund Freud, 1929–1939: A Record of the Final Decade.* New York: Scribner.

Moore, Francis D. (1995). *A Miracle and A Privilege: Recounting A Half Century of Surgical Advance.* Washington, DC: Joseph Henry Press.

Morgan, Elizabeth (1980). *The Making of a Woman Surgeon.* New York: Putnam.

Morris, Robert T. (1935). *Fifty Years a Surgeon.* New York: E. P. Dutton.

Morrison, William Wallace (1948). *Diseases of the Ear, Nose, and Throat.* New York: Appleton-Century-Crofts.

Moscucci, Ornella (1990). *The Science of Woman: Gynaecology and Gender in England, 1800–1929.* Cambridge: Cambridge University Press.

Moxon, Cavendish (1928). The Bearing of Rank's Discovery on Medicine. *Psychoanal. Rev.*, 15:294–299.

Muhl, Anita M. (1929). Problems in General Medicine from the Emotional Standpoint. *Psychoanal. Rev.*, 16:390–396.

Mühlleitner, Elke (1992). *Biographisches Lexikon der Psychoanalyse: Die Mitglieder der Psychologischen Mittwoch-Gesellschaft und der Wiener Psychoanalytischen Vereinigung 1902-1938.* Tübingen: Diskord.

Müller-Braunschweig, Carl (1927). Discussion on Lay Analysis. *Int. J. Psycho-Anal.*, 8:231-238.

Mumford, James Gregory (1908). *Surgical Memoirs.* New York: Moffat, Yard.

Myerson, Abraham (1939). The Attitude of Neurologists, Psychiatrists, and Psychologists Towards Psychoanalysis. *Amer. J. Psychiat.*, 96:623-641.

Nolen, William A. (1970). *The Making of a Surgeon.* New York: Random House.

Nolen, William A. (1980). *A Surgeon's Book of Hope.* New York: Coward, McCann & Geoghegan.

Nuland, Sherwin B. (1988). *Doctors: The Biography of Medicine.* New York: Knopf.

Nunberg, Hermann (1927). Discussion on Lay Analysis. *Int. J. Psycho-Anal.*, 8:247-248.

Oberndorf, C. P. (1927). Discussion on Lay Analysis. *Int. J. Psycho-Anal.*, 8:201-207.

Olch, Peter D. (1975). William S. Halsted and Local Anesthesia: Contributions and Complications. *Anesthesiology*, 42:479-486.

Park, Katharine (1985). *Doctors and Medicine in Early Renaissance Florence.* Princeton: Princeton University Press.

Pernick, Martin S. (1985). *A Calculus of Suffering: Pain, Professionalism, and Anesthesia in Nineteenth-Century America.* New York: Columbia University Press.

Phillips, Adam (1988). *Winnicott.* Cambridge: Harvard University Press.

Pichler, Hans & Trauner, R. W. (1948). *Mund und Kieferchirurgie.* Berlin: Urban & Schwarzenberg.

Pinner, Max & Miller, Benjamin F., eds. (1952). *When Doctors Are Patients.* New York: Norton.

Racker, Heinrich (1958). Classical and Present Techniques in Psychoanalysis. In: *Transference and Countertransference.* New York: International Universities Press, 1968, pp. 23-70.

Ragen, Therese & Aron, Lewis (1993). Abandoned Workings: Ferenczi's Mutual Analysis. In: *The Legacy of Sándor Ferenczi.* Edited by Lewis Aron & Adrienne Harris. Hillsdale, NJ: The Analytic Press, pp. 217-226.

Rainer, J. Kenyon (1987). *First Do No Harm: Reflections on Becoming a Brain Surgeon.* New York: Villard.

Ralph, Joseph (1920). *Psychical Surgery: A Brief Synopsis of the Analytical Method in the Treatment of Mental and Psychical Disturbances.* Los Angeles: Ralph.

Reich, Wilhelm (1927). Discussion on Lay Analysis. *Int. J. Psycho-Anal.,* 8:252–255.

Reik, Theodor (1927). Discussion on Lay Analysis. *Int. J. Psycho-Anal.,* 8:241–244.

Rey, Roselyne (1993). *The History of Pain.* Translated by L. E. Wallace, J. A. Cadden, & S. W. Cadden. Cambridge, MA: Harvard University Press, 1995.

Rioch, David McK. (1985). Recollections of Harry Stack Sullivan and of the Development of His Interpersonal Psychiatry. *Psychiatry,* 48:141–158.

Roazen, Paul (1975). *Freud and His Followers.* New York: Knopf.

Robinson, Victor (1931). *The Story of Medicine.* New York: New Home Library.

Rodman, F. Robert, ed. (1987). *The Spontaneous Gesture: Selected Letters of D. W. Winnicott.* Cambridge, MA: Harvard University Press.

Romano, John (1990). Reminiscences: 1938 and Since. *Amer. J. Psychiat.,* 147:785–792.

Romm, Sharon (1983a). *The Unwelcome Intruder: Freud's Struggle with Cancer.* New York: Praeger.

Romm, Sharon (1983b). The Oral Cancer of Sigmund Freud. *Clinics Plastic Surg.,* 10:709–714.

Romm, Sharon & Luce, Edward A. (1984). Hans Pichler: Oral Surgeon to Sigmund Freud. *Oral Surg.,* 57:31–32.

Roose, Steven P. (1995). Does Anxiety Obstruct or Motivate Treatment? When to Talk, When to Prescribe, and When to Do Both. In: *Anxiety as Symptom and Signal.* Edited by Steven P. Roose & Robert A. Glick. Hillsdale, NJ: The Analytic Press, pp. 155–169.

Rosen, George (1975). Nostalgia: A 'Forgotten' Psychological Disorder. *Psychol. Med.,* 5:340–354.

Rothstein, William G. (1972). *American Physicians in the Nineteenth Century: From Sects to Science.* Baltimore: Johns Hopkins University Press.

Roudinesco, Elisabeth (1993). *Jacques Lacan.* Translated by Barbara Bray. New York: Columbia University Press, 1997.

Sabbatini, Renato M. E. (1997/1998). The History of Shock Therapy in Psychiatry. *Brain & Mind* (on-line), issue 4.

Sacks, Oliver (1984). *A Leg to Stand On.* New York: Harper & Row.

Schafer, Roy (1983). *The Analytic Attitude.* New York: Basic Books.

Schilder, Paul (1937). The Psychotherapeutic Approach to Medicine. *Psychoanal. Rev.*, 24:264–275.

Schilder, Paul (1939). Notes on the Psychology of Metrazol Treatment of Schizophrenia. *J. Nerv. Ment. Dis.*, 89:133.

Schmideberg, Melitta (1930). The Role of Psychotic Mechanisms in Cultural Development. *Int. J. Psycho-Anal.*, 11:387–415.

Schmitz, Robert L., Boring, Christeta, & Cupic, Milorad M. (1993). Murphy's Practice in General. In: *The Remarkable Surgical Practice of John Benjamin Murphy*. Edited by Robert L. Schmitz & Timothy T. Oh. Urbana: University of Illinois Press, pp. 22–36.

Schmitz, Robert L. & Oh, Timothy T. (1993). Murphy's Life. In: *The Remarkable Surgical Practice of John Benjamin Murphy*. Edited by Robert L. Schmitz & Timothy T. Oh. Urbana: University of Illinois Press, pp. 1–21.

Schüller, A. (1919). Zur Behandlung der Kriegsneurosen. *Wiener Mediz. Wchschr.*, 69:974–980.

Schur, Max (1966). Some Additional "Day Residues" of "The Specimen Dream of Psychoanalysis." In: *Psychoanalysis – A General Psychology: Essays in Honor of Heinz Hartmann*. Edited by Rudolph M. Loewenstein et al. New York: International Universities Press, pp. 45–85.

Schur, Max (1972). *Freud: Living and Dying*. New York: International Universities Press.

Selzer, Richard (1976). *Mortal Lessons: Notes on the Art of Surgery*. New York: Simon & Schuster.

Selzer, Richard (1979). *Confessions of a Knife*. New York: Simon & Schuster.

Selzer, Richard (1986). *Taking the World in for Repairs*. New York: Penguin, 1987.

Shainberg, Lawrence (1979). *Brain Surgeon: An Intimate View of His World*. Philadelphia: Lippincott.

Shapiro, Theodore (1984). On Neutrality. *J. Amer. Psychoanal. Assn.*, 32:269–282.

Shorter, Edward (1985). *Bedside Manners: The Troubled History of Doctors and Patients*. New York: Simon & Schuster.

Shorter, Edward (1992). *From Paralysis to Fatigue: A History of Psychosomatic Illness in the Modern Era*. New York: Free Press.

Silbermann, Isidor (1940). The Psychical Experiences During the Shocks in Shock Therapy. *Int. J. Psycho-Anal.*, 21:179–200.

Simmel, Ernst (1918). *Kriegs-Neurosen und "Psychisches Trauma": Ihre gegenseitigen Beziehungen dargestellt auf Grund psycho-analytischer, hypnotischer Studien*. München: Otto Nemnich.

Simmel, Ernst (1921). Contribution [no title] to S. Ferenczi, et al., *Psychoanalysis and the War Neuroses*. London: International Psychoanalytical Press, pp. 30–43.

Simmel, Ernst (1926). The 'Doctor-Game,' Illness and the Profession of Medicine. *Int. J. Psycho-Anal.*, 7:470–483.

Simmel, Ernst (1927a). Discussion on Lay Analysis. *Int. J. Psycho-Anal.*, 8:259–273.

Simmel, Ernst (1927b). Psychoanalytic Treatment in a Sanitarium. *Int. J. Psycho-Anal.*, 8:70–89.

Simmel, Ernst (1944). War Neurosis. In: *Psychoanalysis Today*. Edited by Sándor Lorand. New York: International Universities Press, pp. 227–248.

Siraisi, Nancy G. (1990). *Medieval and Early Renaissance Medicine: An Introduction to Knowledge and Practice*. Chicago: University of Chicago Press.

Southard, E. E. (1919). *Shell-Shock and other Neuropsychiatric Problems, Presented in Five Hundred and Eighty-Nine Case Histories from the War Literature, 1914–1918*. New York: Arno Press, 1973.

Starzl, Thomas E. (1992). *The Puzzle People: Memoirs of a Transplant Surgeon*. Pittsburgh: University of Pittsburgh Press.

Stern, Donnel B. (1997). *Unformulated Experience: From Dissociation to Imagination in Psychoanalysis*. Hillsdale, NJ: The Analytic Press.

Stewart, Byron (1942). Present Status of Shock Therapy in Neuropsychiatry with Special Reference to Prevention of Complications. *Bull. Menn. Clin.*, 6:15–27.

Stolorow, Robert D. & Atwood, George E. (1992). *Contexts of Being: The Intersubjective Foundations of Psychological Life*. Hillsdale, NJ: The Analytic Press.

Stone, Leo (1961). *The Psychoanalytic Situation: An Examination of Its Development and Essential Nature*. New York: International Universities Press.

Strauss, Ronald P. (1989). Psychosocial Responses to Oral and Maxillofacial Surgery for Head and Neck Cancer. *J. Oral Maxillofacial Surg.*, 47:343–348.

Sullivan, Harry S. (1943). Editorial. *Psychiatry*, 6 May 1943, pp. 227–230.

Sulloway, Frank K. (1979). *Freud, Biologist of the Mind: Beyond the Psychoanalytic Legend*. New York: Basic Books.

Swales, Peter J. (1982). Freud, Fliess, and Fratricide: The Role of Fliess in Freud's Conception of Paranoia. Privately printed.

Swales, Peter J. (1983). Freud, Cocaine, and Sexual Chemistry: The Role of of Cocaine in Freud's Conception of the Libido. Privately printed.

Swales, Peter J. (1986). Freud, His Teacher, and the Birth of Psychoanalysis. In: *Freud: Appraisals and Reappraisals—Contributions to Freud Studies, vol. 1*. Edited by Paul E. Stepansky. Hillsdale, NJ: The Analytic Press, pp. 3–82.

Swales, Peter J. (1997). Freud, Filthy Lucre, and Undue Influence. *Rev. Existen. Psychol. Psychiat.*, 23:115–141.

Temkin, Owsei (1946). An Essay on the Usefulness of Medical History for Medicine. In: *The Double Face of Janus and Other Essays in the History of Medicine*. Baltimore: Johns Hopkins University Press, 1977, pp. 68–100,

Temkin, Owsei (1951). The Role of Surgery in the Rise of Modern Medical Thought. In: *The Double Face of Janus and Other Essays in the History of Medicine*. Baltimore: Johns Hopkins University Press, 1977, pp. 487–496.

Thompson, M. Guy (1994). *The Truth About Freud's Technique: The Encounter with the Real*. New York: New York University Press.

Thorwald, Jürgen (1956). *The Century of the Surgeon*. Translated by Richard & Clara Winston. New York: Pantheon, 1957.

Thorwald, Jürgen (1957). *The Triumph of Surgery*. Translated by Richard & Clara Winston. New York: Pantheon, 1960.

Timmes, Edward, ed. (1995). *Freud and the Child Woman: The Memoirs of Fritz Wittels*. New Haven: Yale University Press.

Tourney, Garfield (1969). History of Biological Psychiatry in America. *Amer. J. Psychiat.*, 126:29–42.

Toussaint, Rose-Marie (1998). *Never Question the Miracle: A Surgeon's Story*. New York: Ballantine.

Trotter, Wilfred (1916). *Instincts of the Herd in Peace and War*, 2nd ed. London: Unwin, 1919.

Valenstein, Elliot S. (1973). *Brain Control: A Critical Examination of Brain Stimulation and Psychosurgery*. New York: Wiley.

Valenstein, Elliot S. (1986). *Great and Desperate Cures: The Rise and Decline of Psychosurgery and Other Radical Treatments for Mental Illness*. New York: Basic Books.

Wallerstein, Robert (1998). *Lay Analysis: Life Inside the Controversy*. Hillsdale, NJ: The Analytic Press.

Wangensteen, Owen H. & Wangensteen, Sarah D. (1998). *The Rise of Surgery: From Empiric Craft to Scientific Discipline*. Minneapolis: University of Minnesota Press.

Wertham, Fredric (1952). A Psychosomatic Study of Myself. In: *When Doctors Are Patients*. Edited by Max Pinner & Benjamin F. Miller. New York: Norton, pp. 102–118.

Wilds, John & Harkey, Ira (1990). *Alton Ochsner: Surgeon of the South*. Baton Rouge: Louisiana State University Press.

Wilson, A. Cyril (1943). An Individual Point of View on Shock Therapy. *Int. J. Psycho-Anal.*, 24:59–61.

Winnicott, D. W. (1944). Kinds of Psychological Effect of Shock Therapy. In: *Psycho-Analytic Explorations*. Edited by Clare Winnicott, Ray Shepherd, & Madeleine Davis. Cambridge, MA: Harvard University Press, 1989, pp. 529–533.

Winnicott, D. W. (1947). Physical Therapy of Mental Disorder. In: *Psycho-Analytic Explorations*. Edited by Clare Winnicott, Ray Shepherd, & Madeleine Davis. Cambridge, MA.: Harvard University Press, 1989, pp. 534–541.

Winnicott, D. W. (1949). Leucotomy. In: *Psycho-Analytic Explorations*. Edited by Clare Winnicott, Ray Shepherd, & Madeleine Davis. Cambridge, MA.: Harvard University Press, 1989, pp. 543–547.

Winnicott, D. W. (1951). Notes on the General Implications of Leucotomy. In: *Psycho-Analytic Explorations*. Edited by Clare Winnicott, Ray Shepherd, & Madeleine Davis. Cambridge, MA.: Harvard University Press, 1989, pp. 548–552.

Woodruff, Michael (1977). *On Science and Surgery*. Edinburgh: Edinburgh University Press.

Youngson, A. J. (1979), *The Scientific Revolution in Victorian Medicine*. New York: Holmes & Meier.

Index

⚮

Horney, Karen, 168
Horsley, Sir Victor, 119
"Hospital diseases" (sepsis),
   28, 28n
Hug-Hellmuth, Hermine,
   154
Hunter, John, 25–26, 26n
Hypnosis, 18; *see also*
   Cathartic method
   and treatment of war
     neuroses, 102n, 103,
     112–113
Hypodermic syringe
   development of, 42n
   Freud's technique with, 46–
     47, 62

I

Immunology, surgery and,
   225–226
Impastato, David, 194n, 206n
*Inhibitions, Symptoms, and
   Anxiety* (Freud), 161–
   162, 170
Interpretation of Dreams, The
   (Freud), 60–66
Iodoform, 55, 55n
   gauze, 56–57, 123; use of
     in Freud's surgery, 133

J

Jablonsky, A., 190
Jackson, Hughlings, 37
Jelliffe, Smith Ely, 194, 202
Jokl, Katharine, 121, 148
Jones, Ernest
   assessment of Abraham,
     114, 176; on Abraham's
     death, 152, 153
   assessment of Simmel,
     103–104, 111n

on Freud's surgery;
   ambulatory, 126;
   resections, 136
and Loe Kann, 68–69, 117
as physician, 176
on role of medical
   knowledge in
   psychoanalysis, 163–
   164
medical problems of, 148–
   149, 148n
and Morfydd Owen, 117–
   121
retreat from medicosurgical
   models, 176–179, 182
sexual impulsiveness of, 21
surgical training of, 119
on war neuroses, 106n
and Wilfred Trotter, 119–
   120
Jones, Herbert, 117

K

Kalinowsky, Lothar, 192
Kann, Loe, 21, 68–69, 78,
   120n, 176
Kauders, Walter, 108–109
Kazanjian, Varaztad, 146n
Keen, William W., 122n, 123
Killian, Gustav, 82
Klein, Melanie, 154
Kocher, Theodor, 36, 38, 86,
   213
Koller, Carl, *xi*, 42–43, 46, 63
   surgery on Jakob Freud, 48
Königstein, Leopold, 46
   surgery on Jakob Freud, 48,
   64
Krafft-Ebing, Richard von,
   52n
Kris, Ernst, 154
Kubie, Lawrence, 7n